IMMANUEL KANT

FOR PRESIDENT MENGLER

– THANK YOU FOR YOUR KIND WORDS IN MY TENURE LETTER!

– COLIN Mllan

6.21.16

# IMMANUEL KANT

## The Very Idea of a Critique of Pure Reason

J. Colin McQuillan

Northwestern University Press
Evanston, Illinois

Northwestern University Press
www.nupress.northwestern.edu

Printed in the United States of America

10  9  8  7  6  5  4  3  2  1

**Library of Congress Cataloging-in-Publication Data**

Names: McQuillan, J. Colin, author.
Title: Immanuel Kant : the very idea of a Critique of pure reason / J. Colin McQuillan.
Description: Evanston, Illinois : Northwestern University Press, 2016. | "This book began as a doctoral dissertation in philosophy at Emory University." | Includes bibliographical references and index.
Identifiers: LCCN 2016017436 | ISBN 9780810132481 (pbk. : alk. paper) | ISBN 9780810132450 (cloth : alk. paper) | ISBN 9780810132498 (e-book)
Subjects: LCSH: Kant, Immanuel, 1724–1804. Kritik der reinen Vernunft. | Criticism (Philosophy) | Knowledge, Theory of. | Reason.
Classification: LCC B2779 .M38 2016 | DDC 121—dc23 LC record available at https://lccn.loc.gov/2016017436

# Contents

# Acknowledgments

This book began as a doctoral dissertation in philosophy at Emory University. I am very thankful for the guidance and support of my dissertation director, Rudolf Makkreel. I owe special thanks to Ursula Goldenbaum for the many hours she spent with me in directed studies. Rudi and Ursula taught me much of what I know, though they should not be blamed for any mistakes I have made.

The research that led to this book began in Germany, where I enjoyed the *Gastfreundschaft* of Jürgen Stolzenberg, Robert Schnepf, and Uli and Bella Ruth Reichard at the Martin-Luther-Universität Halle-Wittenberg. My friends in Berlin helped make the months I spent in that city some of the most productive and enjoyable I have ever experienced. When I returned to the United States, I benefited from the advice of Karl Ameriks, David Carr, and David Pacini, who also served on my dissertation committee. The recommendations of Karin de Boer, Andrew Cutrofello, Verena Erlenbusch, Joseph Tanke, and the reviewers for Northwestern University Press have also been extremely helpful. My editor, Henry Carrigan, was very patient as I revised and then rewrote the manuscript.

I probably would not have written this book or studied philosophy without the encouragement of my parents, James and Eileen McQuillan. I am also grateful to have friends like Christina Nickel-Somers, Nate Holdren and Angelica Mortenson, Tzuchien Tho and Amy Anderson-Tho, Joseph Tanke and Molly Slota, Andrew Ryder, Christopher Edelman and Amelia Morten Edelman, Alexander Cooper, Matthew and Jamie McAndrew, Smaranda Aldea and James Ives, and many others. Thanks are also due to my fellow graduate students at Emory University, my former colleagues at the Emory Writing Center and the University of Tennessee Knoxville, and my colleagues at St. Mary's University.

# Introduction

This book is a study of the background, development, exposition, and justification of Kant's *Critique of Pure Reason*. It differs from other books on the same subject by focusing on Kant's conception of critique, rather than his arguments for the transcendental ideality of space and time, his deduction of the pure concepts of the understanding, or the objections he raises against traditional metaphysics in the "Transcendental Dialectic." The latter have been studied in exhaustive detail, but up to this point there has not been a single work that explains why Kant called the *Critique of Pure Reason* a critique. I regard this as a serious oversight in an otherwise exemplary body of scholarship.

I realize this claim will be met with surprise, if not suspicion. However, the research I conducted for this book confirmed that there are very few works that even try to explain why Kant called the *Critique of Pure Reason* a critique, fewer still that answer the question directly, and none that are well-documented enough to be trusted.[1] Most commentaries, introductions, and guides have something to say about what a critique of pure reason is, but the majority of these works offer only a few casual remarks before moving on. Few provide any evidence for their claims and almost all of them fail to provide documentation. The rare works that offer more extensive commentary often substitute a summary of the contents of the first *Critique* for an explanation of what a critique of pure reason is. They also tend to repeat familiar but erroneous claims about Kant's critique—that it is meant to overcome dogmatism and skepticism, that it is a critique of metaphysics, that it is intended to provide a foundation for the natural sciences, and so on—that are easily refuted by a close reading of the text.[2] In the end, there are very few commentaries, introductions, and guides that are helpful for understanding Kant's conception of critique.

Books and articles that try to extend Kant's conception of critique to other fields are also unhelpful. These works almost always assume the validity of a certain account of Kant's critique, often the same kinds of accounts that are to be found in commentaries, introductions, and guides. Then they use that account to say something about some other subject, usually aesthetics or politics. Although some of these works make excellent contributions to the fields to which they are applied, they add little to our understanding of Kant's critique. Less successful applications also raise questions about the use we make of concepts we do not understand. I do not mean to suggest that we should not appropriate concepts from one field and apply them to another; however, I do think we ought to know something about the concepts we employ. Even when the philosophers who coined those concepts are dead and gone, there is still good reason to respect the use they make of terms, the nature of their claims, and the structure of their arguments. Doing otherwise risks misunderstanding and misrepresentation, which ought to have no place in academic scholarship. I am aware that some philosophers and literary theorists think misunderstanding is unavoidable and misrepresentation is justifiable when it helps to advance one's own position; yet I remain committed to the view that even the least understanding is preferable to the most profound misunderstanding. And I have never understood why anyone thinks a good argument needs the support of a bad interpretation.[3]

While I do not claim to have understood everything about Kant's critique, I have tried to represent its development, definition, and justification as accurately as possible. Unlike most accounts of Kant's intellectual development and the evolution of the critical philosophy, which divide the pre-critical period into an elaborate series of stages that requires Kant to radically change his views every few years, I believe Kant's pre-critical works and his critical philosophy are largely continuous.[4] Although there are significant differences between the methods Kant employs before and after the publication of the *Critique of Pure Reason* in 1781, these differences do not concern the aims of his philosophy. Both the pre-critical works and the critical philosophy are meant to make metaphysics a science.[5] Their differences are best explained by a feature of the critical philosophy that is so obvious that it is often overlooked: Kant's critical philosophy begins with a critique of pure reason, while his pre-critical philosophy does not. It is Kant's conception of a critique and his insistence that philosophy must begin with a critique of pure reason that distinguishes his critical philosophy from his pre-critical philosophy, not just the arguments of the "Transcendental Aesthetic," the "Deduction of the Pure Concepts of the Understanding," and the "Transcendental Dialectic." Kant was insistent about this point, because he was convinced that his critique had allowed him to achieve what he set out to accomplish in his pre-critical philosophy: a revolutionary transformation of the method of metaphysics that would set metaphysics on the sure path of science.

Although Moses Mendelssohn called him the "all-crushing Kant" in the "Preliminary Remarks" to his *Morning Hours* (1786), Kant did not think he had transformed metaphysics by criticizing dogmatism and skepticism, rationalism or empiricism, or any other movement in the history of philosophy. His critique is not defined by its opposition to the views he espoused during his pre-critical period or the uncritical philosophies of his predecessors and contemporaries. Rather, the critique Kant began to formulate in the early 1770s was meant to survey "all the cognitions after which reason might strive **independently of all experience**" and use that cognition to demonstrate "the possibility or impossibility of a metaphysics in general."[6] Kant was so committed to the methodological significance of this demonstration that he applied his conception of critique more or less systematically to the philosophy of nature and morals throughout the 1780s and 1790s. This is quite an achievement, given the vacillations and reversals of the pre-critical period. During the 1760s and early 1770s, Kant often announced the publication of works that he claimed were "the culmination of my whole system," only to abandon them and begin again.[7] The fact that this process did not continue after 1781 suggests that Kant's conception of critique played a much greater role in the development of his critical philosophy than the scholarly literature would lead readers to believe.

This interpretation of Kant's critique is supported by close readings of programmatic passages from the *Critique of Pure Reason* and other works; however, it requires that we overcome some of the prejudices many of us hold about the nature of critique and the aims of criticism. In order to begin this process, I survey the different senses in which the word "critique" was used during the Enlightenment in chapter 1. Kant called the Enlightenment "the genuine age of criticism" for a reason; critique and its cognates were extremely popular terms in in the eighteenth century. They were so popular and so widely used that some scholars have denied that it is possible to determine what they mean exactly; yet it is possible see what Kant's critique has in common with other conceptions of critique and where it differs, by placing his terminology in its historical context and considering the background against which he defined his critical philosophy.

Having considered the historical context in which Kant formulated his critique in chapter 1, I begin to reconstruct the problem he intended his critique to solve in chapter 2. This problem can be traced back to Kant's pre-critical attempts to determine the proper method of metaphysics, which began in the 1750s with the *New Elucidation of the First Principles of Metaphysical Cognition* (1755), but intensified after the success of his *Inquiry Concerning the Distinctness of the Principles of Natural Theology and Morality* (1764) in the Prussian Royal Academy's prize-essay contest in 1763. While some scholars claim that Kant experienced a crisis during the 1760s and came to doubt the possibility and even the desirability of metaphysics, closer examination of works from this period reveals that Kant was making plans for an ambitious, systematic treatise on the proper method of metaphysics. He faced a number of difficulties as he tried to complete this treatise, but he never denied that metaphysics was possible or desirable.

Kant's plans for a new and improved metaphysics continued to evolve in the early 1770s. In a famous letter from 1772, he told Marcus Herz that he had finally discovered "the key to the whole secret of metaphysics."[8] In chapter 3, I explore the reasons why Kant called the work unlocking that secret a "critique" of pure reason. I also consider the reasons why his discovery led him to abandon the view of metaphysics he defended in his inaugural dissertation in 1770 and planned to extend in *The Bounds of Sensibility and Reason* in 1771–72. These works attempted to found metaphysics on the distinction between sensible and intellectual cognition, but Kant soon realized that this distinction could not explain the relation between intellectual cognition and its objects. It is the critique that Kant proposed—and not just the book bearing that title—that serves as the foundation for his critical philosophy, because it is the critique of pure reason that explains how the pure concepts of the understanding can relate to objects.

Turning from the development of Kant's critical philosophy to the *Critique of Pure Reason* itself, I consider in chapter 4 the definitions of a critique of pure reason that Kant presents in the "Preface" and "Introduction" to the first (A) and second (B) editions of the first *Critique*. The comparison of these definitions shows what Kant intended his critique to achieve. As a court of justice, the critique of pure reason would secure reason's rightful claims and dismiss its groundless pretensions. As a critique of the faculty of reason, it would survey "all the cognitions after which reason might strive independently of experience" and decide "the possibility or impossibility of metaphysics in general."[9] And because it also transforms "the accepted procedure of metaphysics," the critique of pure reason also makes the possibility of a scientific metaphysics a reality.[10] As we will see, Kant thought his attempt "succeeds as well as we could wish" and "promises to metaphysics the secure course of a science in its first part, where it concerns itself with concepts *a priori* to which the corresponding objects appropriate to them can be given in experience."[11]

Finally, in chapter 5, I explore the justifications Kant offers for his critique in response to negative reviews and objections from empiricist and rationalist critics. In the *Prolegomena to Any Future Metaphysics* (1783), he argues that his critique is necessary because it demonstrates the possibility of metaphysics and shows how metaphysics can become actual as a science. In the "Preface" to the second (B) edition of the *Critique of Pure Reason* (1787), he promotes the utility of his critique for practical philosophy, theoretical philosophy, and the enlightenment of the public. He defended the originality of his critique in response to Eberhard's claim that Leibniz's philosophy "contains just as much of a critique of reason as the more recent one" and anticipates "everything that is true in the latter, but still more besides."[12] The last justification Kant offers for his critique concerns its historical necessity. Building on a claim he makes in the "History of Pure Reason" with which he concludes the first *Critique*, Kant argues that "the critical path" is the only one that is still open to philosophy; the only one that will allow metaphysics to make progress as a science; and the only one that will settle the disputes that have made metaphysics a battlefield. Even if his critique failed to secure the "treaty of perpetual peace in philosophy" that Kant promised, his arguments for the originality, utility, and necessity of a critique of pure reason are still worth noting.

While I think these chapters make important contributions to Kant scholarship, I do not expect them to be the last word on Kant's critique or its relation to his critical philosophy. On the contrary, I hope they inspire new debates about some of the most basic features of the critical philosophy, more informed discussions about why they are critical, and continued research on the ways Kant thought his critique would set metaphysics on the sure path of science. Given widespread doubts about the value of Kant's theoretical philosophy and general skepticism about metaphysics, I think these developments are both necessary and worthwhile.

# A Note on Texts and Translations

I have treated the *Akademie Ausgabe* of *Kant's Gesammelte Schriften* (Berlin: Georg Reimer, later Walter de Gruyer, 1900– ) and *The Cambridge Edition of the Works of Immanuel Kant* (Cambridge: Cambridge University Press, 1992– ) as standard editions of Kant's works. I have left some titles in German, but all quotations have been translated into English. While I have generally quoted from existing translations, I have sometimes found it necessary to alter the translation of the passages I have quoted. I have indicated where, how, and why my translations differ from the published versions in the endnotes. In places where I wish to emphasize or elaborate upon a specific lexical or grammatical point, I have also provided commentary in the endnotes.

Complete bibliographical information for a work cited is included in the first endnote referring to that work and also in the bibliography. Subsequent references use shortened forms of titles—*Inquiry* for *Inquiry Concerning the Distinctness of the Principles of Natural Theology and Morality*, *On a Discovery* for *On a Discovery Whereby Any New Critique of Pure Reason Is to Be Made Superfluous by an Older One*, and so on—followed by the page number. References to the volume and page number of the corresponding passages in the *Akademie* edition are included in parentheses at the end of each reference to Kant's works. Information about where to find a particular work in the Cambridge edition can be found in the bibliography. References to correspondence (*Briefwechsel*), notes (*Reflexionen*), and lectures (*Vorlesungen*) not included in the Cambridge edition refer only to the *Akademie* edition unless otherwise noted.

IMMANUEL KANT

# 1

# The Genuine Age of Criticism

In an important article called "Critique and Related Terms Prior to Kant," Giorgio Tonelli notes that "the boundless secondary literature about Kant does not offer a single account of the history of the term *critique* prior to its appearance in his works."[1] Tonelli made this claim shortly before his death in 1978, but things have not changed significantly since then. The numerous commentaries, introductions, guides, and companions to Kant and the *Critique of Pure Reason* that have appeared in recent years have little to offer those who want to know why Kant called his first *Critique* a critique.[2]

Tonelli is willing to excuse some of the neglect with which scholarly literature has treated Kant's conception of critique, because critique was such a fashionable term during the eighteenth century.[3] Kant called this period "the genuine age of criticism" because the Enlightenment subjected everything, even the holiness of the church and the majesty of the state, to criticism.[4] The breadth of Enlightenment criticism inevitably led "critique" and its cognates to lose their specificity, making it very difficult to determine what a philosopher like Kant might mean when he uses them.[5]

Still, we should not assume that Kant used terms like "critique" in an ambiguous or indeterminate way. Tonelli claims that Kant used critique "not just casually, as obvious fashionable terms of his time, but also, and, I think, primarily, in a hitherto unsuspected meaningful way."[6] In "Critique and Related Terms," he surveys the specific meanings associated with critique and its cognates in disciplines like medicine, biblical hermeneutics, philology, literary criticism, aesthetics, and logic in order to determine what that meaningful way might be.[7] I have serious doubts about the conclusion Tonelli draws at the end of his article, where he claims that Kant derived his conception of critique from an obscure tradition in early modern logic. However, I think he is right to place Kant's conception of critique in its historical context.

By following Tonelli's example and considering the different senses in which critique was used during the eighteenth century, I hope to shed new light on a term that is central to Kant's critical philosophy. I begin with an overview of the historical development of criticism during the eighteenth century, emphasizing the way critique and its cognates were used in philology, literary criticism, aesthetics, and logic during that period. While I think there are important differences between Kant's conception of critique and the way the term was used in all of these disciplines, those differences can be used to identify the features that distinguish Kant's conception of critique. They will also help to correct a number of misconceptions about the critical philosophy that have found their way into accounts of Kant's intellectual development and the history of modern philosophy.

## Philological Critique

Critique and its cognates derive from the Greek verb κρίνω.[8] Originally, the word seems to have belonged to medicine, where it referred to the determination of the "crisis" or "turning point" of an illness. However, a number of classical authors also use κρίνω in a more general sense, meaning "to judge" or "to decide."[9] In several plays by Aristophanes, the word is used in a substantive form—κριτής—to refer to the judge in a poetic contest.[10] This conception of the critic can also be found in the title of a work called *Reply to Critics, Addressed to Diodorus,* which Diogenes Laertius includes in a list of works by the Stoic philosopher Chrysippus.[11] Diogenes classifies *Reply to Critics* as a work on logic dealing with ethical concepts, but the title is listed in a series of works devoted to poetry and oratory, so it is likely that it was a defense of Chrysippus's views on those subjects. A fragment from Stobaeus, which says the Stoics regarded the sage as "the only good poet and orator and dialectician and critic," confirms the relationship between poetry, oratory, and critique in antiquity.[12]

This relationship declined in Medieval Latin, but it was revived during the Renaissance, when humanist scholars began to question the authenticity of the texts that had been handed down to them from antiquity.[13] Soon the humanists were raiding the libraries of monasteries, collecting manuscripts, and producing new editions of classical texts. While they are far from critical by modern standards, these editions were based on the best manuscripts available to the humanists, who immersed themselves in studies of the linguistic and historical sources from which they derived. The desire to establish what a text says in the original language and understand what authors from different historical periods might have meant represents a critical perspective that Renaissance philology did much to advance.

In the seventeenth century, humanists began to worry that philosophers had "knocked the good books from the hands of the young" with their new science.[14] Yet the philological conception of critique did not change with the scientific revolution. Even Francis Bacon, who denounced "antiquities and citations of authors and authorities; also disputes, controversies, and dissenting opinions—in a word, philology" in his *New Organon* (1620), still used the word critique in the same way as his humanist predecessors.[15]

This much is clear from a passage in *Of the Dignity and Advancement of Learning* (1605) where he discusses the three aspects of critique.[16] According to Bacon, the first aspect of critique pertains to "the true correction and amended edition of approved authors, whereby both themselves receive justice and their students light," while the second refers to "the interpretation and explication of authors—commentaries, scholia, annotations, collections of beauties, and the like."[17] Finally, he says, it is appropriate for a critic to insert "some brief judgment concerning the authors edited, and comparison of them with other writers on the same subjects; that students may by such censure be both advised what books to read and better prepared when they come to read them."[18] Bacon may have had humanists like Julius Caesar Scaliger in mind when he emphasizes this third aspect of critique, calling it "the critic's chair" and claiming that those who judge stand "above the stature of critics."[19] Scaliger was an accomplished humanist, experienced in the correction and interpretation of texts, but he was famous for his comparison of Homer and Virgil in his *Poetices* (1561/1581), where the force of his criticisms of Homer shocked many readers.[20]

Critique remained a philological concept during the second half of the seventeenth century, especially in the historical-critical biblical scholarship of Isaac La Peyrère, Richard Simon, and Spinoza. In the "Preface" to his *Critical History of the Text of the New Testament* (1678), Simon argues that a critical study of Greek and Latin manuscripts of the New Testament is necessary to correct "the defects of those who compile the different readings out of the manuscripts, without distinguishing the good from the bad."[21] He is aware that his work will be controversial, because it suggests that our understanding of scripture depends on mundane facts about texts and their transmission. Yet he points out that the same task had been undertaken by Saint Jerome, his followers, and even some of the women in his circle. "Not content to read the Scripture in the Vulgar Tongue," Simon says, these women "diligently enquired after the correctest copies, Learning those very Tongues in which they were writ."[22] Following their example, his critique examines the different manuscripts of the New Testament to try to discover what it really says.[23] Simon is also eager to show that those who practice the art of criticism do not intend to destroy the authority of scripture, despite the scandalous implications of Spinoza's studies of the Hebrew Bible in his *Theological-Political Treatise* (1670).[24]

Pierre Bayle employs a similar conception of critique at the end of the seventeenth century in his *Historical and Critical Dictionary* (1697). In his entry on the Pyrrho, Bayle argues that "the stories of Antigonus Carystius to the effect that Pyrrho did not prefer one thing to another and that neither a chariot nor a precipice could ever make him take a step forward or backward and that his friends who followed him around often saved his life" are to be regarded as "bad jokes or impostures."[25] Recognizing the illegitimacy of this testimony allows Bayle to paint what he considers to be a more accurate portrait of the ancient skeptic than is to be found in other sources. Another important example is Bayle's entry on Spinoza, which is meant to correct Louis Moreri, who accused Spinoza of advocating "atheism, libertinage, and the freedom of all religions" in his historical dictionary.[26] Bayle refers to the accounts of peasants who had met the philosopher and testified that he was "sociable, affable, honest, obliging, and of a well-ordered morality," despite his alleged atheism.[27] What distinguishes Bayle's accounts of the lives of Pyrrho and Spinoza is their claim to authenticity; Bayle rejects unreliable testimony about Pyrrho and presents credible evidence about Spinoza's character. His dictionary is critical in the philological sense, because it contains accurate accounts of the lives and opinions of historical figures, based on reliable sources.[28] It is not critical because it documents the errors of Bayle's predecessors and exposes the ignorance of his contemporaries.

Tonelli claims the philological conception of critique declined during the eighteenth century, but there is evidence that it survived well into the nineteenth century. Tonelli himself lists several works by German polyhistors, published in the first half of the eighteenth century, that use the term this way.[29] There are also a number of sources from the late eighteenth century and even the nineteenth century where critique is used in its philological sense.[30] Kant refers to this conception of critique in one of his *Reflexionen* on Meier's *Vernunftlehre* (1752), where he uses the "critique of the Latin language" as an example of ignorance and intellectual poverty, because it only constitutes "a very small object of scholarly cognition."[31] Kant may have had the same conception of critique in mind when he denies that he is engaged in a "critique of books and systems" in the *Critique of Pure Reason*.[32] In any case, he did not seem to have thought very much of philological critique. In a number of passages in his logic lectures, Kant recognizes that philology requires a great deal of learning; yet he denies that it can "extend our understanding by one degree."[33] In other places, references to philology appear in dangerously close proximity to discussions of pedantry.[34]

## Literary Criticism

Literary criticism began to distinguish itself from philology during the famous "Quarrel of the Ancients and the Moderns" in the French Academy at the end of the seventeenth century. The defenders of the ancients, Nicolas Boileau and Jean Racine, thought the arts had achieved an unsurpassed perfection in the classical world, so they struggled to preserve the connection between philology and criticism. During the phase of the dispute known as the "Homer Quarrel," they argued forcefully that knowledge of ancient Greek was essential to appreciate the beauty of the poetry in the *Iliad* and the *Odyssey*.[35] Moderns like Charles Perrault tended to dismiss their appeals to dead languages as only so much pedantry. They maintained that Homer would have to suffer the judgment of critics, if the *Iliad* was found to be clumsy, vulgar, and ridiculous, even if it had been the model for epic poetry in antiquity.[36]

The British were engaged in their own "Battle of the Books" at about the same time as the "Quarrel" in the French Academy. Curiously, the positions associated with the ancients and the moderns in France were reversed in Britain. William Wotton, one of the British moderns, promoted Richard Bentley's philology as the best way to recover ancient texts and classical wisdom.[37] At one point in his *Reflections upon Ancient and Modern Learning* (1694), Wotton even suggests that philology provides the moderns with a distinct advantage over the ancients, because it allows them to understand the ancients better than they understood themselves.[38] Ancients like William Temple and his secretary Jonathan Swift thought this was nonsense. Temple earnestly sought to show that modern critics had abandoned the wit, sense, and genius of the ancients to trouble the world with "vain niceties and captious Cavils, about Words and Syllables, in the Judgment of Stile; about Hours and Days, in the Account of ancient Actions or Times; about antiquated Names of Persons or Places, with many such worthy trifles; and all this, to find some Occasion of censuring and defaming such Writers as are, or have been, most esteemed in the World."[39] Swift was less delicate than his employer; he savagely mocked Bentley, Wotton, and the other critics who focused on "the faults and blemishes, and oversights, and mistakes of other writers" in *A Tale of a Tub* and its appendix *The Battle of the Books* (1710).[40]

John Dryden takes aim at the same critics in his *Author's Apology for Heroic Poetry and Poetic License* (1677). He argues that "criticism, as it was first instituted by Aristotle, meant a standard of judging well."[41] This definition is noteworthy, not only because it is one of the first passages in which the English word "criticism" appears in a discussion of literature, but also because it does not include the correction and interpretation of literary works.[42] Dryden's critic is solely concerned with the quality of the works he judges. His primary task is "to observe those excellencies that should delight a reasonable reader," though he might also point out certain "lapses of the pen" when doing so will help improve an author's work. Lest the critic be mistaken for a fault-finder and error-monger, however, Dryden notes that it is "malicious and unmanly" to focus on the worst lines in a poem. "They wholly mistake the nature of criticism," he argues, "who think its business is principally to find fault."[43]

Dryden's conception of criticism was carried into the eighteenth century by such luminaries as Joseph Addison and Alexander Pope. Addison, the editor of the *Spectator* (1711–12), repeats Dryden's claim that a critic should "discover the concealed beauties of a writer and communicate to the world such things as are worth their observation" in an essay on the qualities a "just critic" ought to possess.[44] He even goes so far as to suggest that a preoccupation with faults and errors is the mark of a false critic, who has "neither Taste nor Learning."[45] Pope worried about the danger these critics posed to poetry in *An Essay on Criticism* (1711), where he inveighs against "the bookful blockhead with loads of learned lumber in his head" and laments that critics are eager to judge "where Angels fear to tread."[46] Still, Pope holds out hope for critics who are "blest with a Taste exact, yet unconfin'd; a Knowledge both of Books and Humankind; gen'rous Converse; a Sound exempt from Pride; and Love to Praise, with Reason on his Side."[47]

In his *Dictionary of the English Language* (1755), Samuel Johnson defines "critick" as "a man skilled in the art of judging literature; a man able to distinguish the faults and beauties of writing."[48] This definition reflects the growing tendency to associate criticism with literary criticism, but Johnson also rejects one of the central claims made by his predecessors Dryden and Addison. Johnson denies that a critic must highlight the best features of a literary work in an article from *The Rambler* (1750–52), where he says "the duty of criticism is neither to depreciate, nor dignify by partial representations, but hold out the light of reason, whatever it may discover; and to promulgate the determinations of truth, whatever she shall dictate."[49] By avoiding selective praise and blame and holding critical judgment to a more objective standard, Johnson thinks critics can avoid the charges of bias and prejudice that are often leveled against them, giving their judgment that much more authority.

In Germany, the development of literary criticism began in earnest in the middle of the eighteenth century. Like their predecessors in France and Britain, the German critics had to position themselves with respect to the ancients and the moderns. However, they also had to respond to French and British criticism, which had emerged earlier and in relation to more developed national literatures. Some of the early German critics thought German literature should follow the French model; they sought to establish a set of rules that could be used to distinguish perfect works of art from those that were less perfect. Often these rules were derived from Aristotle, reflecting a preference for the ancients over the moderns. Others rejected French classicism and the limitations it imposed on literature. Inspired by the emotional intensity of Shakespeare and Milton, they promoted the sentimentalism of the British literary tradition. In many cases, German critics went further than their British counterparts in defending the rights of genius to violate the formal rules of art. In a series of debates, lasting well into the nineteenth century, both parties sought to determine the course that German literature would follow.

The conception of criticism that Gotthold Ephraim Lessing, Moses Mendelssohn, and Friedrich Nicolai develop in their *Letters Concerning the Newest Literature* (1759–60) represents a considerable advance over the positions defended by the German neoclassicists and the sentimentalists. Lessing, Mendelssohn, and Nicolai differ from the neoclassicists by privileging the practice of criticism over the formation of general rules. This allows Lessing to rank Shakespeare above Corneille in the famous seventeenth letter of the *Litteraturbriefe*, yet it does not lead him to deny the relevance of reason and rules for the arts, as many of the sentimentalists had done.[50] If an artist is really a genius, then Lessing thinks he will carry "the proof of all rules within himself."[51] He will make the best use of the means available to him and exploit the medium in which he is working in better ways than lesser artists. By treating his work as a model and an example, we can discover what techniques are best for achieving different artistic effects, what makes an audience feel compassion when they are spectators to a tragedy, and so forth. We can also ask a genius his opinion, because his knowledge of the art in which he excels makes him the best judge of the works of others. "Not every critic is a genius," Lessing says in his *Hamburg Dramaturgy* (1767–69), "but every genius is a born critic."[52]

By engaging with particular works of art and finding ways to account for their effects, Lessing, Mendelssohn, and Nicolai thought gifted critics could improve the quality of German literature. Nicolai, in particular, stresses that "precise and sound criticism is the only means of achieving and determining good taste."[53] Kant does not seem to have shared this view. There are no sustained discussions of literary criticism in any of his works, though a few passages in *Observations on the Feeling of the Beautiful and Sublime* (1764) prove that he was aware of the debates about Homer and Milton, as well as the debates about the principles of tragedy that were still exercising the judgment of German critics.[54] The scattered remarks on poetry and literature in his notes, lectures, and correspondence do not show any serious engagement with literary criticism. And Kant does not even mention literary criticism in the section of the *Critique of the Power of Judgment* (1790) devoted to the fine arts. He does, however, seem to deny the value of literary criticism in an earlier section of the third *Critique*, where he tries to show that an objective principle of taste is impossible. Drawing a contrast between his own "transcendental critique" and the practice of criticism "as an art," Kant asserts that criticism "merely seeks to apply the physiological (here psychological) and hence empirical rules, according to which taste actually proceeds to the judging of its objects (without reflecting on its possibility), and criticizes the products of fine art, just as the former criticizes the faculty of judging them itself."[55] The critique of taste that Kant undertakes in the first part of the *Critique of the Power of Judgment* is, apparently, far removed from the empirical psychological criticism of art and literature as it was practiced during the eighteenth century.

## The Critique of Taste

It should not be surprising that debates in literary criticism eventually gave rise to general reflections about the standards of critical judgment. During the eighteenth century, these reflections often took the form of a "critique of taste," in which philosophers sought to define the standards of critical judgment in general terms, without reference to any particular work of art or literature. This critique was often used to justify literary criticism and lend its judgments weight and authority; however, its aims are really quite different. Literary criticism tries to determine the strengths and weaknesses of a particular work, while the critique of taste tries to determine whether critical judgment appeals to the right standards and invokes the proper principles.

The separation of literary criticism and the critique of taste can be seen in the work of philosophers like Francis Hutcheson. Hutcheson was a philosopher without literary ambitions, who never made any serious contributions to literary criticism. Yet his interest in the passions and their significance for moral philosophy led him to compose *An Inquiry into the Original of Our Ideas of Beauty and Virtue* (1725), which contains a treatise on beauty, order, harmony, and design. Hutcheson argues that we perceive these qualities through a special, internal sense that he calls "fine genius" or "taste."[56] At the end of the treatise, after distinguishing absolute and relative beauty, and noting the role that custom, education, and example play in the cultivation of taste, Hutcheson presents a moral and theological defense of the special sense he had postulated. He contends that God's goodness makes it morally necessary that "the internal Sense of Men should be constituted as it is at present, so as to make Uniformity amidst Variety the Occasion of Pleasure."[57] Without this sense, Hutcheson thinks humanity would be at a loss to explain the design in nature, which is a sign of God's presence in creation. And if that sense were not a source of pleasure, Hutcheson thinks we would not appreciate the goodness of God and his creation.

Hutcheson's treatise made a strong impression on David Hume, who went on to make his own contributions to the critique of taste. When he announced the publication of *A Treatise of Human Nature* (1739–40), Hume included criticism among the "four sciences which comprehend almost everything, which it can any way import us to be acquainted with, or which can tend either to the improvement or ornament of the human mind."[58] As a result, he gave criticism a prominent place alongside logic, morals, and politics in the new science of man he proposed in the *Treatise*.[59] The subject was so important to Hume that he planned to devote the fourth volume of the *Treatise* to criticism, though poor sales of the earlier volumes led him to abandon his plans. Still, he continued to reflect on the nature of criticism, eventually publishing an essay called "Of the Standard of Taste" (1757).

In his essay, Hume searches for a rule that will reconcile all the sentiments of humanity.[60] He considers a number of different possibilities, but ultimately concludes that the judgment of those with good taste can be considered the standard of taste. Of course, Hume recognizes that those with good taste often disagree in their critical judgments; yet he denies that this threatens the authority of their judgment or their ability to reconcile the sentiments of those with less refined taste. "Whether any particular person be endowed with good sense and a delicate imagination, free from prejudice, may often be the subject of dispute, and be liable to great discussion and enquiry," Hume argues, "but that such a character is valuable and estimable will be agreed in by all mankind."[61] The deference we show to the judgment of those with good taste is, in other words, sufficient proof that their judgment constitutes the standard of taste, even if we disagree about which critics have the best taste.

In the Introduction "On Taste" that he added to the second edition of *A Philosophical Enquiry into the Origins of Our Ideas of the Sublime and Beautiful* (1759), Edmund Burke presents a very different account of the standard of taste. Like Hume, Burke is interested in the principles that govern human sentiments.[62] Yet he pursues these principles through a study of "that faculty, or those faculties of the mind which are affected with, or which form a judgment of the works of imagination and the elegant arts," exploring the physiological and psychological causes of the feelings of pleasure and pain we derive from the qualities of different kinds of objects.[63] Burke concludes that some things are naturally more pleasing to the senses, imagination, and judgment of human beings than others, so he devotes long passages of his *Enquiry* to explaining why we find small, smooth, and sweet things more pleasing than other kinds of objects.[64] He acknowledges that some might raise objections to his conclusions, but Burke thinks their disagreement can only be the result of a defect in their judgment.[65] Human nature requires that the principles of good taste must be uniform in all creatures who share the same basic faculties.

Special attention should also be paid to Henry Home, Lord Kames, since his *Elements of Criticism* (1762) is sometimes said to be the source of Kant's conception of critique.[66] Home is not very well known today, but he was famous for his writings on law, politics, and history during the eighteenth century. *Elements of Criticism* is his contribution to the critique of taste. Home claims that no attempt has ever been made "to reduce the science of criticism to any regular form."[67] His own efforts to make criticism a regular science begin with an account of sensibility, in which he pays special attention to the relationship between perception and emotion. He then proceeds to distinguish the objects that are naturally agreeable and naturally disagreeable to human sensibility, focusing on qualities like beauty, grandeur, novelty, grace, and wit. By noting their effects on human nature, Home thinks he will be able to determine the principles of the fine arts, which will provide a rational foundation for critical judgment.[68] When we are finally in possession of those principles, Home thinks that "the fine arts, like morals, [will] become a rational science; and, like morals, may be cultivated to a high degree of refinement."[69]

Kant was familiar with the works of Hutcheson, Hume, Burke, and Home, but that does not mean he derived the conception of critique that he employed in the *Critique of Pure Reason* from their critique of taste.[70] It is important to remember that when Kant discusses the critique of taste during the pre-critical period, he is almost always highlighting the difference between the merely empirical standards of taste and the rational principles of sciences like logic and metaphysics. This is apparent in Kant's logic lectures, where he frequently draws a contrast between aesthetics and logic when he wants to explain why logic is a science. Kant argues that logic is a science because it is based on rational principles that are established independently of experience. Aesthetics cannot be a science because it "derives its rules *a posteriori*" and "only makes more universal, through comparison, the empirical laws according to which we cognize the more perfect (beautiful) and the more imperfect."[71] Because they are empirical and comparative, the rules established by a critique of taste do not possess the universality and necessity of scientific principles, which means they cannot "determine judgment sufficiently" or "hand down a decisive judgment concerning taste."[72] Comments like these are found in a number of Kant's notes and lectures from the 1760s to the early 1780s, suggesting that he thought there were profound differences between the empirical critique of taste and the methods employed by rational sciences like logic and metaphysics.

The unflattering portrait of the critique of taste that Kant paints in his lectures also distances him from the rationalist tradition in aesthetics that emerged in Germany during the eighteenth century. The beginnings of this tradition can be traced back to Johann Christoph Gottsched, whose *Attempt at a Critical Poetics for the Germans* (*Versuch einer critischen Dichtkunst vor die Deutschen*, 1730) is often maligned for its neoclassical view of tragedy and its rejection of Milton and Shakespeare. Still, the reasons Gottsched called his book a "critical" poetics merit some attention. Gottsched defends his title in the "Preface" to the first edition of his work, where he notes that "it will not please many, that I have called my poetics a *critical* poetics; partly because they misunderstand everything critical; partly because they do not trust that I have sufficient capacity to bring a work of this kind to completion."[73] He thinks those who raise the first kind of objection can easily be shown that critique is not a philological search for errors in the manuscripts of works written by ancient authors, but a noble art that judges things according to their own proper rules.[74] In response to those who object that he is not qualified to publish a critical poetics, Gottsched gives an account of his education, his experience, and the evolution of his work. More important than these biographical details, however, is a claim he makes in later editions of the "Preface" about how the rules of an art are to be determined. Gottsched differs from many of his contemporaries because he thinks these rules are derived from reason and philosophy, rather than sensibility or taste. Without a solid foundation in philosophy, Gottsched does not think a critic can hope to understand individual works of art, much less the rules of art in general.[75]

Georg Friedrich Meier and Alexander Baumgarten made similar efforts to found aesthetics on philosophy, but they rejected Gottsched's conception of critique, as well as his taste and judgment. In one of his polemics against "the literary dictator of Germany," Meier argues that Gottsched's *Critical Poetics* is actually a threat to the good taste of the German people, because it is inconsistent and incomplete, and actually misleads readers about the differences between good and bad poems.[76] A year later, in the first volume of his *Foundations of All Beautiful Sciences*

(*Anfangsgründe aller schönen Wissenschaften,* 1748–50), Meier tried to lay an alternative foundation for aesthetics, based on Baumgarten's lectures. Meier argues that aesthetics is the science of a particular kind of cognition, beautiful cognition, which is derived from the lower cognitive faculty of sensibility.[77] Baumgarten takes a similar approach in the *Aesthetica* (1750/1758), but argues explicitly against the claim that aesthetics can be equated with or reduced to critique. Critique is for Baumgarten only one part of the general, theoretical science of aesthetics.[78] That science is not founded on philosophical insight into the rules governing art, but an account of the perfection of sensible cognition, which Baumgarten calls beauty.[79]

Kant's hostility to the aesthetic rationalism of Meier and Baumgarten is evident in the passages from the lectures on logic cited above. Kant praises Home for recognizing that aesthetics is an empirical critique of taste, in order to disparage Baumgarten's attempts to make aesthetics a rational science like logic.[80] Similar criticisms of Baumgarten are to be found in a footnote to the "Transcendental Aesthetic" of the *Critique of Pure Reason*, where Kant says the Germans call the critique of taste "aesthetics" because of Baumgarten's failed attempt to bring "the critical estimation of the beautiful under principles of reason, and elevating its rules to a science."[81] He apparently held the view that the critique of taste was merely empirical until 1787, when he wrote to Karl Leonhard Reinhold, claiming to have discovered the a priori principles for a critique of taste, based on an analysis of the faculties of the human mind and the feelings of pleasure and displeasure.[82] Nothing like these a priori principles are to be found in Kant's pre-critical works, notes, or lectures suggesting that the discovery of the a priori principles of aesthetic judgment marks the beginning of Kant's critical aesthetics, which is still a critique of taste, but which is also very different from the empirical critique of taste Kant endorses during the pre-critical period.

## Critical Logic

At the end of his article "Critique and Related Terms Prior to Kant: A Historical Survey," Tonelli argues that the use of "critique" and its cognates in logic constitutes "the most specific and interesting evolution of the terms Critique, etc." in the eighteenth century.[83] He concludes that the logical conception of critique is essential for understanding Kant, because the decision to call the *Critique of Pure Reason* a critique "not only reflected the prestige of a term very fashionable in that time," but also indicates that it is "a work primarily on Logic."[84] These claims are likely to surprise Kant scholars and historians of modern philosophy, many of whom are unfamiliar with logical conceptions of critique and remain unaware of a tradition Tonelli considers very influential.

Tonelli tries to demonstrate his claims by surveying the ways "critique" and its cognates were used in logic in the eighteenth century. The first work he considers, Fortunato da Brescia's *Intellectual Philosophy* (*Philosophia Mentis*, 1741), treats critique as a second part of logic that was neglected by the Scholastics, because it is concerned with something other than strictly logical perfection.[85] Da Brescia thinks critique contributes a great deal to the operation of the intellect and the practice of judgment, so he insists on including it in his logic. When he finally discusses the rules of this art, in the second part of his treatise, da Brescia says critique is "the art of judging facts belonging to history, as well as great works, their different readings, their meaning, their style, and their authors."[86] He then provides a set of rules for judging the correctness of propositions in general; things we know through the senses; matters of religious doctrine; things established by human reason; genuine and spurious works; and contingent future events.[87] Tonelli takes this to mean that all of these subjects belong to critique, which is itself a part of logic.

The second work Tonelli discusses identifies logic and critique, instead of making critique a part of logic. In his *Elements of the Logical-Critical Art* (*Elementorem artis logicocriticae*, 1745), Antonio Genovisi says he calls logic an *ars logicocriticam* because it is "the art that extends, forms, and guides reason and judgment in the pursuit of wisdom."[88] He objects to the separation of logic and critique in Scholasticism, because he thinks "we acquire wisdom either through our own reasoning and experiments, or through the opinions and authority of others."[89] Works on logic that exclude critique are imperfect, because they do not recognize this fact and do not tell us how to judge the authority and opinions of others.[90] When Genovisi returns to this subject in book 4 of the *Elements*, he proposes a number of principles that govern the use of the senses; the correct use of observation and experimental evidence; the authority of human authors; divine authority; how to recognize the word of God; the interpretation of sacred scripture; the recognition and correction of mistakes and corruptions in books; how to distinguish genuine works from forgeries; and the art of hermeneutics.[91] Other authors might have considered these subjects part of philology during the eighteenth century, but Tonelli is convinced that their inclusion in Genovisi's *Elements* constitutes a specifically logical conception of critique.

Similar conceptions of critique are found in works by Catholic philosophers in Germany from the same period. *Critical Logic* (*Logica Critica*,

1760) by the Franciscan eclectic Hermann Osterrieder is a good example. Like Da Brescia, Osterrieder objects to the emphasis the Scholastics placed on formal logic, especially syllogistic and dialectic. He argues that the theoretical focus of this logic needs to be supplemented with an applied or practical logic, which will serve as a rule for judgment. And he identifies this practical logic with critique when he says that it deals with "the most important and most general rules of the art of criticism," as well as "the judgment of historical events, works of genius, the correctness of various readings, their meaning, style, and authors."[92] Later, he says critique is "that art with whose help and rules we distinguish between true and false with respect to literature."[93] Osterrieder's discussion of the rules of that art is actually very similar to Da Brescia's *Intellectual Philosophy* and Genovisi's *Elements*. He examines the uses of divine and human authority; the value of evidence from the senses, experience, and scientific experiments; the use of hypotheses; and the art of hermeneutics, which helps us distinguish genuine works from forgeries, understand an author's intended meaning, and interpret sacred scripture.[94] Tonelli does not think this similarity is accidental. He is convinced that the works that incorporate these subjects into logic form a coherent tradition, which regards logic as an *ars critica*.[95]

Tonelli thinks he can discern the influence of this tradition in Baumgarten's *Lecture on Logic* (*Acroasis Logica*, 1761) and his posthumous *Delineation of the Encyclopedia of Philosophy* (*Sciagraphia encylcopaedia philosophia*, 1768). He explains the division of the *Acroasis Logica* into general and special logic with reference to the distinction between theoretical and practical logic in the *ars critica* tradition and also claims that Baumgarten includes chapters on the critique of invention and the critique of scripture under the influence of the Catholic thinkers.[96] He draws similar conclusions from a passage in the *Sciagraphia*, where Baumgarten says critique is part of practical logic.[97] This definition supplements the one Baumgarten includes in his *Metaphysics* (1739), which defines critique as "the art of judgment" and "the science of the rules for distinct judgment of perfection or imperfection."[98] This definition could be included in logic, but Baumgarten only applies it to aesthetic critique, which he defines as "the art of cultivating taste" and "the art of sensible judgment and presenting such judgment."[99] The *Sciagraphia* makes it clear that there is a logical critique as well as an aesthetic critique and that both of them have an important role to play in judgment. While aesthetic critique cultivates sensible judgment and good taste, logical critique allows us to judge the perfections and imperfections of our own cognition, the cognition of others, and oral and written propositions.

Kant read Baumgarten and used his *Metaphysics* in his lectures, so Tonelli declares "it can be assumed that if Kant selected the title of *Cri-

*tique* for his major work, this not only reflected the prestige of a term very fashionable in that time, and the general meaning of that term in philosophy; but, in accordance with the spirit of his enterprise, he selected it as a qualification of his work as a work on Logic, and in particular on a Logic centered on verification and correction."[100] Unfortunately, Tonelli does not provide a single citation supporting his claim that Kant derived his conception of critique from Baumgarten or the *ars critica* tradition. This should not be surprising, since Baumgarten is the only figure Tonelli associates with the *ars critica* tradition that Kant seems to have been familiar with. There are no references to any of the other figures or works Tonelli mentions anywhere in Kant's works, correspondence, notes, or lectures.[101]

While I think this is strong evidence against Tonelli's conclusion, there are a few references to logic as an *ars critica* and *logica critica* in some of Kant's notes and lectures that could be used to support his claims.[102] In the *Blomberg Logic*, for example, Kant says "the logic that is an organon can prescribe rules to a learnedness that is already present, and then it is called *logica critica*, or it can prescribe rules through which one can achieve learnedness, and then it is called *logica dogmatica*."[103] While Kant goes on to say "all logics are not dogmatic but critical," he still denies that logic is a critique only a few pages later, where he concludes that "logic is not merely a critique," because "it is an actual doctrine that can be proved."[104] The context makes it clear that Kant denies logic is a critique because he wants to emphasize that it is a science and distance it from aesthetics. If logic were a critique, then it would only be able to make a posteriori comparisons and generalizations like the ones found in aesthetics. It would not be able to demonstrate anything a priori, because critique lacks the a priori principles that are necessary for science. Similar arguments can be found in the *Philippi Logic*, the *Vienna Logic,* the *Pölitz Logic*, the *Dohna-Wundlacken Logic*, and *Jäsche Logic*, raising serious doubts about any attempt to trace Kant's conception of critique back to logic.[105]

## Kant's Critique

Surveys of eighteenth-century philology, literary criticism, aesthetics, and logic may not adequately explain the origin of Kant's conception of critique. There is little evidence that Kant derived his conception of critique from any of these sources. And there is considerable evidence that he was either unconcerned with or openly hostile to the conceptions of critique employed in these disciplines. Still, there are a number of things we can learn by examining the different ways critique and its cognates were used during "the genuine age of criticism."

These examinations are perhaps most helpful in refuting a common prejudice about the nature and function of criticism. While it is not unusual to think critique is primarily concerned with faults and errors, there is a more positive history of critique in the eighteenth century that needs to be considered. An argument could be made that positive conceptions of critique actually play a far more influential role in early modern philology, literary criticism, aesthetics, and logic than any of the conceptions associated with fault-finding and error-mongering. Such an argument would find considerable historical support in the survey contained in this chapter.

To understand what I mean by positive history and positive conceptions of critique, consider the aims of early modern philology. One could see philological critique as a process of identifying errors and corruptions in texts and scholarship. Yet the identification of error was not an end in itself. It was a means philologists used to reach an authentic understanding of ancient texts, their authors, and the historical context in which they were written. Philologists employed other means as well, including the collection, collation, and comparison of manuscripts; the publication of new editions with scholarly notes, commentary, indexes, and appendixes; and vigorous international debates about the interpretation of classical texts.[106] It hardly seems fair to reduce their efforts to understand the language, literature, and history of antiquity to the identification of error and corruption.

Similar things could be said about literary criticism. It is easy to find complaints about the ignorance and pettiness of literary critics in the broadsheets and pamphlets of the eighteenth century. Yet poets like Alexander Pope looked to them for guidance, hoping critics would praise their best verses and suggest ways the rest might be improved.[107] Extending this model to national literature, Friedrich Nicolai recommended the sharpest criticism as the best way to improve German literature.[108] Johann Gottfried Herder regarded the criticism that Nicolai published in his *Litteraturbriefe* (1759–65) with some suspicion, but he appreciated its nonpartisan and reflective character. He also recognized that the best criticism could inspire genius and help writers overcome the obstacles that constrain their creativity.[109] Critics are not always the persecutors that literary martyrs make them out to be.

The critique of taste likewise did more than police the boundaries of good taste during the eighteenth century. Just as literary criticism tried to improve individual works and national literature, aesthetics promoted the appreciation of natural beauty and works of art. Kant thought this was especially important, because it is essential for the cultivation of human sociality. In the *Blomberg Logic* (early 1770s), he says "at the ground of everything that has to do with taste lies a sociability and through this taste elevates itself very much; he who only chooses that which pleases himself and no other has no taste at all."[110] Kant says something similar in the *Collins Anthropology* (c. 1772–73), where he argues that "taste is the *principium* through which human beings can enjoy a socially universal gratification . . . everything beautiful one loves and seeks only for society . . . that one now chooses from beauty, one does this from love for society, for one has a particular gratification when one possesses something that pleases others."[111] Such views were not uncommon in Kant's time.

Logical critique also did more than maintain the benevolent dictatorship of Enlightenment rationality. The works Tonelli includes in the *ars critica* tradition tried to overcome the formalism of Scholastic logic to make logic practical and useful. They saw critique as a way of applying logical rules to judgment, formulating reliable hermeneutical principles, and making proper use of divine and human authority. They thought doing so would improve human reason in much the same way that critical thinking classes help undergraduate students. That Kant tried to do much the same thing is clear from a passage in the announcement of his lectures for the winter semester of 1765–1766, where he says logic can be divided into the critique and rule of the healthy understanding and the critique and rule of real learning.[112] Only the latter can be identified with the science of logic, but Kant says the former should be placed at the beginning of philosophy and, indeed, all academic instruction, as a guide for the student "who wishes to migrate from the land of prejudice and error, and enter the realm of a more enlightened reason and the sciences."[113]

Clearly, one finds very positive ways of thinking about critique in philology, literary criticism, aesthetics, and logic in the eighteenth century. My view is that these positive conceptions of critique take precedence over the negative conceptions of critique associated with the identification of error in philology, complaints about works of inferior quality in literary criticism, the denunciation of bad taste in aesthetics, and the rejection of faulty reasoning in logic, because they better explain the aims and objectives of critique in those disciplines. The same model can be extended to Kant's *Critique of Pure Reason*. While Kant often employs negative conceptions of critique, especially in his attack on the dialectical illusions of traditional metaphysics in the "Transcendental Dialectic," they do not reflect the primary aims and objectives of his critical philosophy.[114] Mistaking them for the defining features of Kant's critique would be disastrous, because it would misrepresent the context in which he developed his critical philosophy and ignore the programmatic statements he makes about its aims in the first (A) and second (B) editions of the *Critique of Pure Reason* (1781/1787), the *Prolegomena to Any Future Metaphysics* (1783), and later works like *On a Discovery Whereby Any New Critique of Pure Reason Is to Be Made Superfluous by an Old One* (1790) and *What Real Progress Has Metaphysics Made in Germany Since the Time of Leibniz and Wolff?* (1793/1804).

# 2

# The Culmination of My Whole Project

Accounts of Kant's intellectual development often claim that his views on metaphysics underwent dramatic change during the 1760s.[1] During this period, they say, Kant recognized the futility of his pre-critical philosophy, abandoned his metaphysical commitments, and began an entirely new phase of his intellectual development. The *Remarks* (c. 1764–65) he wrote in his copy of *Observations on the Feeling of the Beautiful and Sublime* (1764) have led some scholars to conclude that Kant came to see metaphysics as "a science of the limits of human reason."[2] Others have suggested that Kant's growing disaffection for metaphysics ultimately led him to complete skepticism. They argue that Kant denied the possibility and even the desirability of metaphysics in works like *Dreams of a Spirit-Seer, Elucidated by Dreams of Metaphysics* (1766).[3]

The idea that Kant's views on metaphysics changed radically during the 1760s appeals to many scholars, because it provides a transition between the rationalist works of the pre-critical period and the critical philosophy that Kant began to formulate in the early 1770s. Unfortunately, the same idea makes it very difficult to explain some of the things Kant told his most important correspondents at the time. If Kant saw metaphysics as a science of the limits of human reason, why would he tell Johann Heinrich Lambert "all of my endeavors are directed mainly at the proper method of metaphysics and thereby also the proper method for philosophy as a whole" in a letter from the end of 1765?[4] And why would Kant tell Moses Mendelssohn he thinks "the true and lasting welfare of the human race depends on metaphysics" only a few months later?[5] Some scholars believe Kant was being disingenuous in his letters to Lambert and Mendelssohn, because he was flattered by the collaboration Lambert proposed earlier in their correspondence and because he was trying to placate Mendelssohn, who had criticized him for making light of metaphysics in a review of *Dreams of a Spirit-Seer*.[6] Yet it should be noted that Kant wrote his letter to Lambert after he had sent the manuscript of *Dreams of a Spirit-Seer* to his publisher.[7] And he continued to make claims like the one in his letter to Mendelssohn in published works, lectures, notes, and correspondence throughout his life.[8] Could it be that

Kant really was working on the project he described to Lambert? Did he sincerely believe what he told Mendelssohn? Is it possible that Kant remained committed to metaphysics during this turbulent decade?

I think all of these questions can be answered in the affirmative. Although Kant's attempts to place metaphysics on a new foundation can be traced back to his first work on the subject, *A New Elucidation of the First Principles of Metaphysical Cognition* (1755), I will begin with the question posed by the Prussian Royal Academy for its 1763 prize-essay competition. The answer Kant presented to the academy established his reputation and put him in contact with the most important philosophers in Germany. Soon, Kant was corresponding with those philosophers and they began reading his works, reviewing them in leading journals, and promoting his career. This is significant for the development of the critical philosophy, because the recognition Kant received encouraged him to take on new and more ambitious projects.

During the 1760s, Kant announced a series of publications in which he tried to capitalize on the success of his *Inquiry* and extend its claims about the ways metaphysics might be improved. Many of the works he announced were never completed, but they still have a great deal to tell us about the development of his views on metaphysics. Kant's letters to Lambert and Mendelssohn document the difficulties he faced as he tried to determine the proper method of metaphysics and set metaphysics on a new path. They also explain why Kant eventually abandoned a work he regarded as "the culmination of my whole project" just a few months before *Dreams of a Spirit-Seer* was published.[9] While many scholars take this as evidence that Kant's growing disaffection with metaphysics led him to deny the possibility and desirability of metaphysics, I will show that *Dreams of a Spirit-Seer* is actually a cautionary tale about how not to proceed in metaphysics.[10] Kant learned that lesson the hard way during the 1760s, before he began formulating his critical philosophy in the early 1770s.

## The Distinctness of Metaphysics

Kant's *Inquiry Concerning the Distinctness of the Principles of Natural Theology and Morality* (1764) is an answer to the question the Royal Prussian Academy of the Sciences posed for its prize-essay competition in 1763. The question had been written by the head of the academy's class of speculative philosophy, Johann Georg Sulzer, who asked "whether metaphysical truths in general, and the first principles of the *Theologiae naturalis* and morality in particular, admit of distinct proofs to the same degree as geometrical truths; and if they are not capable of such proofs, one wishes to know what the genuine nature of their certainty is, to what degree the said certainty can be brought, and whether this degree is sufficient for complete conviction."[11] After the academy approved Sulzer's question, the competition was officially announced in the magazine *Berlinische Nachrichten von Staats- und gelehrten Sachen* in June 1761.

Sulzer's question was inspired by the work of the former president of the academy, Pierre-Louis Moreau de Maupertuis. In his *Examen philosophique de la preuve de l'existence de Dieu employée dans l'Essai Cosmologie* (1756), Maupertuis had argued that only proofs in mathematics could be considered scientific, because they are solely concerned with numbers and quantities.[12] Proofs involving numbers and quantities are certain because they are exact. The same cannot be said of "the variety of sentiments that one observes in the subjects of morals, politics, natural law, metaphysics, and other subjects," which are so diverse that they rarely agree with one another.[13] Because they do not always agree, the truths philosophers claim to prove in metaphysical demonstrations are probable at best. Probable truths are uncertain, so Maupertuis concluded that metaphysical demonstrations could not be considered scientific.

Maupertuis's skepticism dominated the academy's prize-essay competitions in philosophy during the 1740s and 1750s. With the support of the Prussian king, Frederick II, Maupertuis used the academy's competitions to promote Lockean empiricism and Newtonian physico-theology, which were then popular in France.[14] He also sought to undermine the Leibnizian-Wolffian philosophy that persisted in German universities. As a result, the academy's 1747 question on monadology, its 1751 question on determinism, and its 1755 question on optimism became sources of public controversy, in which German philosophers struggled to defend the rationalism of Leibniz and Wolff from British empiricism and French materialism.[15] Because Maupertuis enjoyed the favor of the king, however, the German philosophers were at a considerable disadvantage. The submissions that won the 1747 and 1755 prize-essay competition attacked Wolff and dismissed Leibniz.[16]

It was fortunate for Kant that things had changed in the academy by 1763. Maupertuis had given up the presidency of the academy in 1756, leaving the mathematician Leonhard Euler to manage its affairs.[17] Euler was, to be sure, no more sympathetic to rationalist metaphysics than Maupertuis had been. He tormented the Wolffians in the 1740s and even helped to engineer their defeat in the 1747 prize-essay competition.[18] Unlike Maupertuis, however, Euler was not favored by the king. Euler's influence also declined after the Seven Years' War, when a commission led by Sulzer found that David Köhler, the academy's treasurer, had embezzled a considerable portion of the funds raised by the academy's monopoly on calendar sales in Prussia.[19] Euler opposed the commission's recommendations concerning the restructuring of the academy's finances, further tarnishing his reputation with the king. The scandal eventually led Euler to leave Berlin and return to St. Petersburg in 1766.[20]

The departure of Maupertuis and the decline of Euler's influence allowed the philosophers in the academy to reconsider the certainty of metaphysical proofs in their 1763 prize-essay competition. They proceeded in a way that was respectful of the former president of the academy and mindful of the preferences of the king, who shared Voltaire's distaste for German philosophy.[21] Still, the results of the competition prove that the academy had a very different view of metaphysics in 1763 than it did in 1747 or 1755. Mendelssohn eventually won the competition with his essay *On Evidence in Metaphysical Sciences*, but his victory over Kant's *Inquiry Concerning the Distinctness of the Principles of Natural Theology and Morality* was only secured by Sulzer's tie-breaking vote.[22] Neither of these essays could have won a prize-essay competition sponsored by the academy when Maupertuis was president, because both defend the certainty of metaphysical proofs.

Mendelssohn was aware that "many discerning minds of proven ability reject the first principles of metaphysics and believe that no science other than mathematics can be utterly convincing."[23] He was also aware that those discerning minds had dominated the academy that would judge his essay. Mendelssohn and Lessing had objected to the academy's campaign against rationalist metaphysics in their brilliant *Pope: A Metaphysician!* In that work, the authors even went so far as to suggest that the academy could not tell the difference between a real philosopher (Leibniz) and a poet wearing a beard (Pope).[24] Mendelssohn's tone is more restrained in *On Evidence*, but he is not afraid to tell a truth he thinks needs to be told. He insists that metaphysics possesses the same degree of certainty as mathematics. The two sciences differ only in the "perspicuity" (*Faßlichkeit*) of their proofs.[25]

A few words should be said about Mendelssohn's conception of perspicuity. Perspicuity is a kind of subjective certainty; we feel confident that perspicuous proofs are certain and accept their conclusions with ease. "To say that a truth is perspicuous," Mendelssohn argues, "is to say that anyone who has ever grasped the proof must immediately be fully convinced of the truth and so set at ease that he does not feel the slightest resistance to assuming it."[26] Still, it should not be assumed that proofs that lack perspicuity are dubious or uncertain. There are difficult proofs that strain our attention, confusing proofs that must be carefully analyzed, and even controversial proofs that generate vigorous debate that are nevertheless certain. The absence of perspicuous metaphysical proofs cannot be regarded as evidence against the certainty of metaphysical demonstrations.

Mendelssohn thinks metaphysical proofs lack perspicuity because philosophers do not possess the precise forms of notation that mathematics employs. Mendelssohn's view of mathematics is perhaps naive, because he maintains that a mathematical notation stands in a natural and essential relation to its referent.[27] The former expresses the latter clearly and distinctly in every case, allowing the mathematician to show that appearances "stand in a necessary connection with one another in such a way that one can infer from one of them the presence of another."[28] Things are quite different in metaphysics, because philosophical language does not stand in the same kind of relation to its referent. As a result, Mendelssohn says, "the slightest inattentiveness makes it possible for thought to lose sight of the subject matter, leaving behind merely empty signs; in which case even the most cogent philosopher must appear to be playing with words."[29] Verbal disputes are common in metaphysics, because philosophers cannot rely on the language they use to clearly and distinctly represent the truths they seek to demonstrate.[30]

Mendelssohn also thinks metaphysical proofs are less perspicuous than mathematical proofs because philosophers cannot assume their proofs are correct without first examining them. The perspicuity of mathematical demonstrations allows mathematicians to grasp their implications immediately, while philosophers must accept "the necessity of always returning to the first principles with every step forward that one takes in philosophy."[31] Mendelssohn is enthusiastic about this peculiarity of philosophical inquiry, because he thinks "one never makes this journey back to the beginning without enormous benefit, since philosophical concepts cast rays of light that reciprocally lend distinctness to one another and must be pursued."[32] Yet he recognizes that this constant return to first principles prevents metaphysics from making much progress as a science. Philosophers always busy themselves with things they think they have already proven, so they are only rarely able to demonstrate that "the object of his basic concepts, from which he infers his truths, is actually to be encountered, so that he can infer from those truths the actual existence of its consequences."[33]

Although he recognizes that metaphysical demonstrations lack perspicuity, Mendelssohn thinks they are essential to the progress of mathematics. Mathematics is a science of quantities, so it is unable to define terms like "magnitude" and "extension" without metaphysics.[34] Even relations like "more" and "less" remain obscure in mathematics, if metaphysicians are not able to determine their "inner characteristics."[35] As a science of qualities, metaphysics analyzes the constitution of concepts, clarifies their contents, and notes the characteristics that distinguish them from other things. Taken to their logical conclusion, Mendelssohn says, metaphysical investigations of the inner characteristics of things produce proofs that are no less certain than those of geometry.[36] Metaphysical proofs lack the perspicuity of mathematical proofs, because they must confront all of the challenges philosophers face when they reason with uncertain terms and constantly return to first principles. Yet there can be no question that they are certain, so long as we accept that philosophy is "knowledge of constitutions, based on reason."[37]

At this point, the differences between Mendelssohn's *On Evidence* and Kant's *Inquiry* become apparent. Mendelssohn tries to show that mathematics and metaphysics are both analytical sciences whose analyses of quantity and quality depend upon and reinforce one another, while Kant insists that mathematics and metaphysics employ radically different and mutually exclusive methods.[38] Kant's insistence is often interpreted as an attack on the Leibnizian-Wolffian philosophy that Mendelssohn defends in his essay.[39] It is not unusual to read that Kant wanted to dispense with the rationalism of Wolff's mathematical method and replace it with the empirical methods of the natural sciences.[40] Yet these accounts are profoundly misleading. They misrepresent Kant's criticism of the mathematical method by casting it as an attack on reason. They also present a prejudiced view of Kant's attitude toward metaphysics, obscuring a more fundamental difference between Mendelssohn's and Kant's views on the subject. This more fundamental difference is essential for understanding the course Kant's intellectual development would take during the 1760s, because it explains why Kant began work on *The Proper Method of Metaphysics* after his success in the academy's prize-essay competition.

To understand this more fundamental difference between Mendelssohn and Kant, consider their views on the status of metaphysics and its achievements. Mendelssohn treats metaphysics as an established science with a proven method and significant results. It only differs from mathematics in the perspicuity of its proofs. While Kant says something similar at the end of the "Third Reflection" of his *Inquiry*, the rest of the work suggests that metaphysics lacks "permanence and stability."[41] Kant also makes claims to this effect in the "First Reflection" of the *Inquiry*, where he acknowledges that metaphysics is "without doubt the most difficult of all the things into which man has insight," but also declares that "so far no metaphysics has ever been written."[42] Kant agrees with the academy that "there is good reason to ask about the path in which one proposes to search for metaphysical understanding in the first place," but that is because he does not think any of the paths laid out by his predecessors have reached their destination.[43] In order to make real progress in meta-physics, Kant thinks we will have to travel along a different route.

Because he does not think metaphysics is a science, Kant interprets the academy's question as a challenge. In the "Introduction" to the *Inquiry*, he writes "the question proposed for consideration is such that, if it is appropriately answered, higher philosophy must as a result acquire a determinate form."[44] In order to determine the form metaphysics should take, Kant focuses on its method. The kind of science metaphysics will be is determined by the method it employs. When the proper method of metaphysics has been established, Kant thinks "the endless instability of opinions and scholarly sects will be replaced by an immutable rule which will govern didactic method and unite reflective minds in a single effort."[45] And this will show metaphysics "the true degree of certainty to which it may aspire, as well as the path by which certainty may be attained."[46]

Kant emphasizes the difference between the methods of mathematics and metaphysics in the *Inquiry* in order to show which path will lead to certainty in metaphysics. Mathematics provides a useful contrast to the proper method of metaphysics, because Kant thinks philosophers appeal to the method of mathematics "in contexts where it cannot possibly be employed."[47] This is especially problematic in metaphysics, because mathematics makes use of a synthetic method, which begins with definitions established through "the *arbitrary combination* of concepts." [48] For example, a mathematician might define a circle as "a regular figure, in which all of the points on its circumference are equally far from the middle point."[49] This definition combines the concepts of regularity, circumference, equidistance, and a middle point, but the mathematician is perfectly free to include whatever concepts he or she likes. Ultimately, it is the construction of the figure corresponding to the definition, and not the clarification of the concepts that belong to it, that will demonstrate its truth. As long as the concepts included in the definition do not contradict one another, the mathematician will be able construct the figure that results from their combination.

Kant does not think philosophers can construct definitions from the arbitrary combination of concepts, because metaphysics must follow an analytic method. This means philosophers must take concepts as they are given. When concepts are given "confusedly or in an insufficiently determinate fashion," philosophers must clarify and distinguish their contents through analysis.[50] Analysis allows philosophers to determine what the characteristic marks of a concept are and whether they can be combined without contradiction.[51] A philosopher is only able to formulate definitions after the characteristic marks of a concept have been clarified and distinguished and their consistency has been established. This is achieved by "*separating out* that cognition which has been rendered distinct by means of analysis."[52] If all of the concepts included in a definition are clear and distinct, then the definition is adequate, complete, and determinate.[53] If not, then further analysis is required to clarify the concept and its definition.

Kant is confident that metaphysical analysis will eventually yield definitions that are as certain as mathematical proofs, but he notes a curious problem with some of its results in the *Inquiry*.[54] In many cases, Kant says, metaphysical analysis leads to unanalyzable concepts (*unauflösliche Begriffe*) and indemonstrable propositions (*unerweisliche Sätze*).[55] Among the "uncommonly many" unanalyzable concepts with which metaphysics must concern itself, he lists "the concept of *representation*, the concepts of *being next to each other* and *being after each other*."[56] He then includes "*space, time,* and the many different *feelings* of the human soul, such as the feeling of the s*ublime,* the *beautiful,* the *disgusting,* and so forth" as well as "pleasure and displeasure" and "desire and aversion" in a list of concepts which may only be partly analyzed.[57] Kant thinks these concepts and propositions can be explained if they are examined *in concreto,* but he denies they can be proven, asking "on what basis could such a proof be constructed, granted that these propositions constitute the first and simplest thoughts I can have of my object, when I first call it to mind?"[58]

Kant thinks these unanalyzable concepts are "actually necessary for both the distinctness of cognition and the possibility of valid inferences" because they provide a limit to analysis.[59] Without unanalyzable concepts, the process of clarifying and distinguishing the contents of concepts would be interminable. Philosophers would have to break the marks of every concept down into their marks, those marks would have to be reduced to their marks, and so on. Unanalyzable concepts serve as fundamental truths, putting a stop to the infinite regress of analysis. When metaphysical analysis reaches an unanalyzable concept, philosophers know they can proceed no further. They can start combining concepts and proposing definitions, without being afraid that they will compound the confusion with which they began, because their definitions are founded on fundamental truths. When these definitions stand at the beginning of metaphysical demonstrations "like the axioms of geometry," Kant thinks philosophers can be sure that what follows will be as clear, certain, and convincing as any mathematical proof. [60]

Mendelssohn and Kant may disagree about whether metaphysics had actually produced convincing proofs, but they both affirm that metaphysical demonstrations could be as certain as mathematical proofs in their answers to the academy's 1763 prize-essay question. They might also disagree about the method of mathematics; Mendelssohn thinks mathematics and metaphysics employ similar methods, while Kant thinks mathematics follows a synthetic method that is opposed to the analytical method of metaphysics. Yet they both regard metaphysics as an analytical science that is primarily concerned with the clarification of concepts. The fact that the academy approved of this answer, in both Mendelssohn's and Kant's submissions, suggests that they wished to encourage the conception of philosophy Mendelssohn and Kant defended against the anti-metaphysical bias of the academy under Maupertuis and Euler.

## The Proper Method of Metaphysics

When his *Inquiry* was published by the academy in a special volume with Mendelssohn's prize-winning essay *On Evidence* in 1764, Kant became a recognized and important figure in German philosophy.[61] He began corresponding with members of the academy and the enlightened philosophers in Berlin, especially Mendelssohn, Sulzer, and Lambert. These philosophers were the leading lights of the German intellectual world and they were beginning to see Kant as one of their own.

Mendelssohn published a series of reviews of Kant's works in the *Briefe, die neueste Litteratur betreffend*. Kant and his students Christian Jacob Krauss and Johann Gottfried Herder believed Mendelssohn to be the author of the reviews of *The False Subtlety of the Four Syllogistic Figures* (1762), *The Only Possible Argument in Support of a Demonstration of the Existence of God* (1763), and *Attempt to Introduce the Concept of Negative Magnitudes into Philosophy* (1763) that appeared in the *Litteraturbriefe* and even thanked him for introducing Kant to the public.[62] It is more likely that Mendelssohn commissioned the reviews from his friend Friedrich Gabriel Resewitz, but the editors of Mendelssohn's collected works suggest he might also have rewritten substantial portions of them.[63] In any case, the reviews helped establish Kant's reputation.[64] When one of Kant's colleagues in Königsberg objected to the review of *The Only Possible Argument*, the philosophers and theologians around Mendelssohn defended Kant, calling him "the subtlest philosophical brain, who had the gift to present the most abstract truths in the simplest way and to make them distinct for everyone."[65]

The reviews Mendelssohn published in the *Litteraturbriefe* served as a letter of recommendation to the philosophical public; yet Sulzer did more to promote Kant behind the scenes. He gave copies of Kant's works to a number of friends and visitors, several of whom later became important correspondents of the philosopher from Königsberg. Sulzer gave copies of Kant's *Universal Natural History and Theory of the Heavens* and *The Only Possible Argument* to Johann Caspar Lavater while he was visiting Berlin in 1763–64, inspiring the peculiar fascination with Kant that would emerge in Lavater's correspondence and travel journals in the 1770s.[66] Lavater eventually wrote to Kant in 1774, introducing himself as a friend of Herder, and asking Kant to do a favor for a family friend. Kant must have mentioned his work on the *Critique of Pure Reason* in his response to Lavater, because the first indisputable reference to the first *Critique* as the title of a forthcoming work is found in a letter Lavater wrote to Kant in 1774, where he says he is "eagerly awaiting your *Critique of Pure Reason*" and asks a strange series of questions about its contents.[67]

Sulzer also gave a copy of Kant's *The Only Possible Argument* to Johann Heinrich Lambert, who quickly became one of Kant's most important correspondents. Lambert wrote to Kant in 1765 when he saw that Kant had announced a work called *The Proper Method of Metaphysics* (*Die eigentliche Methode der Metaphysik*) in the catalog of the Leipzig book fair.[68] In his first letter, Lambert tells Kant that the announcement inspired him to write directly and in a way that omitted the "customary circumlocutions" and "artificial mannerisms" of formal correspondence.[69] The sense of urgency in Lambert's letter can be explained by the title of the work Kant announced as well as its subject matter. Lambert had written a work with a similar title for the academy's 1763 prize-essay competition (*Über die Methode die Metaphysik, Theologie, und Moral richtiger zu beweisen*, 1762), though he did not finish in time to submit it to the contest.[70] Between 1763 and 1765, he worked to extend his essay into an architectonic treatment of "the primary elements of philosophical and mathematical knowledge" (*Anlage zur Architectonic oder Theorie des Einfachen und des Ersten in der philosophischen und mathematischen Erkenntniss*, 1771), which he hoped to publish in the near future.[71]

In his first letter to Kant, Lambert claims that his new work had been ready for publication for a year when he saw the announcement of *The Proper Method of Metaphysics*.[72] Whether Lambert's remarks are those of a jealous rival or a potential collaborator is difficult to discern. If Lambert was upset that Kant would publish a treatise on the proper method of metaphysics before he was able to get his own into print, he never says so directly.[73] Instead, he inquires about the kind of method that Kant will recommend for metaphysics, asking "what could be more natural than my desire to see whether what I have done is in accord with the method you propose?"[74] Lambert says he expects they will in large part agree. He also says he has "no doubts about the correctness of the method" Kant would propose, although he thinks his own method might be more far-reaching than Kant's.

According to Lambert, "a complete system of metaphysics must include more than has previously been thought," taking into account "all that is *simple* and *primary* in *every* part of human cognition."[75] Elaborating on what he clearly takes to be a very radical claim, Lambert explains that he thinks a complete system of metaphysics must include "not only the *principia* which are grounds derived from the form, but also the *axiomata* which must be derived from the matter of knowledge and actually only appear in simple concepts, thinkable in themselves and without self-contradiction, and also the *postulata* which state the universal and necessary possibilities of composition and connection of simple concepts."[76] He must have been aware that Kant had made similar claims in the *Inquiry*, where Kant had argued that philosophy contains all of the formal and material principles of human reason.[77] He may not have emphasized the ways in which these principles would enlarge the scope of metaphysics, as Lambert did; yet Kant clearly thought the kind of analysis he recommended would allow metaphysics to catalog the fundamental truths that constitute "all that is *simple* and *primary* in *every* part of human cognition."[78]

If Lambert thought his *Architectonic* would differ from Kant's work with respect to the number of principles, axioms, and postulates it contained, he nevertheless recognized the more fundamental agreement of their respective undertakings. Lambert could assure Kant that he had no doubts concerning the correctness of the method Kant would propose in *The Proper Method of Metaphysics*, because the method Kant had defended in his *Inquiry* was, for all intents and purposes, the same one Lambert had developed in his sketches for *On the Method of More Correctly Proving Metaphysics, Theology, and Morality*.[79] Like Kant, Lambert advocated a thoroughly analytic approach to metaphysics. Kant and Lambert both sought to reduce metaphysical concepts to their fundamental principles, in order to more correctly determine how they might be combined.[80]

In his response to Lambert, Kant makes it clear that he has also noticed the agreement of their methods, telling him this made him more confident in his approach, because their agreement was "a logical confirmation that shows that our methods satisfy the touchstone of universal human reason."[81] Yet Kant did not forget his earlier failures. "After many capsizings, on which occasion I always looked for the source of my error or tried to get some insight into the nature of my blunder," he tells Lambert, "I have finally reached the point where I feel secure about the method that has to be followed if one wants to escape the cognitive fantasy that has us constantly expecting to reach a conclusion, yet just as constantly makes us retrace our steps, a fantasy from which the devastating disunity among supposed philosophers also arises; for we lack a common standard with which to procure agreement from them."[82] The failure of Kant's earlier experiments seems to play an important role in shaping his insight into the "cognitive fantasy" that has plagued metaphysics, as well as his insight into its "common standard." These failures taught him to ask "what it is I have to know in order to solve a particular problem" and "what degree of knowledge is possible for a given question."[83] Keeping these conditions in mind made Kant's judgment "more limited but also more definite and secure than is customary in philosophy," allowing him to write a work like *The Proper Method of Metaphysics.*[84]

It is not entirely clear what Kant intended to include in the work he described to Lambert, but some scholars think Kant included an outline of *The Proper Method of Metaphysics* in the announcement of his lectures for the winter semester of 1766.[85] The *Announcement* was written and published in October 1765, only a month before Kant received his first letter from Lambert. It contains a description of the courses he would offer in the coming semester and a short account of the method his lectures on metaphysics would follow. Eckart Förster has argued that this account serves as a summary of Kant's views on the proper method of metaphysics at a time when he was struggling to write a book on the subject. Förster supports this interpretation with reference to the beginning of the *Announcement*, where Kant reminds students that he "sought to show in a short and hastily composed work that this science (metaphysics) has, in spite of the great efforts of scholars, remained imperfect and uncertain because the method peculiar to it has been misunderstood."[86] Kant attributes this misunderstanding to the confusion of the methods of mathematics and metaphysics. Too many philosophers forget that the method of metaphysics "is not *synthetic,* as is that of mathematics, but *analytic.*"[87]

In his *Announcement,* Kant claims that his efforts to correct this misunderstanding had revealed "both the source of the errors which have been committed and the criterion of judgment by reference to which alone all those errors can be avoided, if they can be avoided at all."[88] In an obvious reference to *The Proper Method of Metaphysics,* Kant also says he hopes to present a complete account of his findings in the near future.[89] In the meantime, he says he will "induce A.G. Baumgarten, the author of the text book on which this course will be based—and that book has been chosen chiefly for the richness of its contents and the precision of its method—to follow the same path."[90]

Förster seizes on these remarks, arguing that Kant's modification of Baumgarten must correspond to the method he planned to present in *The Proper Method of Metaphysics.*[91] On closer inspection, however, it seems less likely that Kant's plans for his lectures actually correspond to his idea of the proper method of metaphysics. In the *Announcement*, Kant says his course will begin with the study of empirical psychology, "the metaphysical science of *man* based on experience," before moving on to a discussion of "corporeal nature in general," drawn from "the chapters of the cosmology which treat of matter."[92] This constitutes a significant revision to the order of metaphysical topics in the Leibnizian-Wolffian tradition, which usually begin with ontology (*metaphysica generalis*) and then proceed to discuss cosmology, psychology, and theology (*metaphysica specialis*) in that order. Placing empirical psychology before cosmology is an especially remarkable change to the traditional order of presentation, because empirical psychology derives its knowledge of the soul, its faculties, and their cognition from experience.[93] This might suggest that Kant is trying to ground metaphysics in experience, but the reasons he gives for reorganizing the course in this manner emphasize the pedagogical benefits of beginning with empirical psychology. Kant even says that he has placed empirical psychology at the beginning of the course because it is the most beneficial subject for students who will not continue to study philosophy, which hardly suggests that empirical psychology and corporeal nature have any kind of methodological priority over the other parts of philosophy. The fact that Kant affords empirical psychology a certain pedagogical priority in the *Announcement* does not mean that he thought it was the foundation for metaphysics as such. Even if he did, there is no evidence of this in the *Announcement*, which does not mention the proper method of metaphysics after the introductory comments in the description of the metaphysics course. Consequently, the work provides less insight into Kant's views on the proper method of metaphysics than Förster suggests.

Kant's reasons for abandoning his plans for *The Proper Method of Metaphysics* are, unfortunately, much clearer than its contents. The problem, Kant says, is that "I noticed in my work that, though I had plenty of examples of erroneous judgments to illustrate my theses concerning mistaken procedures, I did not have the examples to show *in concreto* what the proper procedure should be."[94] In order to provide himself with more positive examples of the proper method of metaphysics, Kant told Lambert he had resolved to "publish a few little essays, the contents of which I have already worked out. The first of these will be the *Metaphysical Foundations of Natural Philosophy*, and the *Metaphysical Foundations of Practical Philosophy*. With the publication of these essays the main work will not have to be burdened excessively with detailed and yet inadequate examples."[95] Having these examples before him in his essays, Kant could refer to them, elaborate the method they followed, and explain why that method was correct.

The fact that Kant never published his essays or the work they were intended to promote is indicative of the problems he began to face in his search for the proper method of metaphysics. These problems were nothing new for Kant. They were the same difficulties that led him to reflect on his earlier failures and continue experimenting with different approaches to philosophical problems. The only difference is that his work now had a more clearly methodological focus and greater ambition. Like Lambert, Kant intended to give an extensive and systematic account of the proper method of metaphysics, which would build on the remarks of his *Inquiry*. The next work he published, however, would be chastened by the erroneous judgments and mistaken procedures he had encountered in his struggles with *The Proper Method of Metaphysics*. That work was *Dreams of a Spirit-Seer, Elucidated by the Dreams of Metaphysics* (1766).

## The Methods Now in Vogue

Kant published *Dreams of a Spirit-Seer* anonymously, but Mendelssohn identified him as the author in a short review published in the *Allgemeine deutsche Bibliothek* in 1767. In the review, Mendelssohn notes that "the joking profundity with which this work is written leaves the reader in doubt whether Mr. Kant wants to make metaphysics laughable or spirit-seeing plausible."[96] He must have expressed similar concerns in a letter to Kant shortly after receiving the book, because Kant wrote to assure him that he still held metaphysics in the highest esteem on April 8, 1766.[97]

Today, few scholars doubt that Kant was laughing at metaphysics in *Dreams of a Spirit-Seer*. Most think Kant's satire of fantastical visionaries like Emmanuel Swedenborg is really an attack on the rationalist metaphysics of Wolff and Mendelssohn.[98] Others see it as a work of self-criticism, disavowing the speculative excesses of Kant's own pre-critical philosophy.[99] Some even think it is evidence that Kant embraced radical Pyrrhonian skepticism during this time.[100] Despite their differences, the defenders of these claims all agree that *Dreams of a Spirit-Seer* represents the height of Kant's growing disaffection with metaphysics during the 1760s.[101] As a result, they see his letter to Mendelssohn as a disingenuous attempt to satisfy a philosopher who was too dogmatic to appreciate Kant's critique of metaphysics.[102]

While these views represent the overwhelming scholarly consensus about *Dreams of a Spirit-Seer*, I think it is likely that Kant meant everything he said in his letter to Mendelssohn. Only a month before the first copies of *Dreams of a Spirit-Seer* appeared in print, Kant told Lambert that he was working on a book he called "the culmination of my whole project."[103]

That book was not *Dreams of a Spirit-Seer,* but *The Proper Method of Metaphysics,* a work in which Kant planned to extend the claims of his *Inquiry* and capitalize on his success in the Prussian Royal Academy's prize-essay competition in 1763. If his growing disaffection with metaphysics led him to doubt the possibility and even the desirability of metaphysics, it is hardly likely that Kant would announce the publication of a systematic treatise on the subject at the same time!

Evidence that Kant was no more disaffected with metaphysics after the publication of *Dreams of a Spirit-Seer* than he was when he was working on *The Proper Method of Metaphysics* can be found in the letter to Mendelssohn, where Kant expresses the same hopes and frustrations he described in his correspondence with Lambert. While he admits to feeling "a certain hatred . . . toward the inflated arrogance of whole volumes full of what are passed off nowadays as insights," Kant tells Mendelssohn that they could reform and renew metaphysics, if only they could "draw up the plans for this heretofore haphazardly constructed discipline with a master's hand."[104] Kant thinks he will have something to contribute to these plans, because he has "reached some important insights in this discipline since I last published anything on questions of this sort, insights that will establish the proper procedure of metaphysics."[105] "To the extent that my other distractions permit," Kant writes, "I am gradually preparing to submit these ideas to public scrutiny, but principally to yours; for I flatter myself that if you could be persuaded to collaborate with me (and I include in this your noticing my errors) the development of the science might be significantly advanced."[106]

These remarks suggest that Kant's views on the possibility and desirability of metaphysics did not change in the four months between his letter to Lambert and his letter to Mendelssohn. Despite the miscarriage of his plans for *The Proper Method of Metaphysics* and the publication of *Dreams of a Spirit-Seer,* Kant was still trying to find the path that metaphysics should follow. He still intended to publish a systematic treatise on the subject, because he still thought "the true and lasting welfare of the human race depends on metaphysics."[107] Kant was aware that this claim would appear ludicrous to anyone but Mendelssohn—and it is perhaps even more so for contemporary philosophers—but I think it is an accurate statement of his views on metaphysics. Similar statements can be found in the first (A) and second (B) editions of the *Critique of Pure Reason,* as well as the *Prolegomena* (1783), *On a Discovery* (1790), and the unfinished essay on the progress of metaphysics (1793), proving that Kant never regarded "metaphysics itself, objectively considered" as something "trivial or dispensable."[108]

Scholars can be forgiven for being suspicious of Kant's attitude toward metaphysics, given the joking profundity of *Dreams of a Spirit-Seer*. In his letter to Mendelssohn, Kant explains the reasons for his tone. Unsure how a book on Swedenborg would be received, Kant says "it seemed to me wisest to forestall other people's mockery by first of all mocking myself."[109] More important are his reasons for turning his mockery on metaphysics. Kant is serious and emphatic when he tells Mendelssohn "that the path that has been selected is completely wrong, that the methods now in vogue must infinitely increase the amount of folly and error in the world, and that even the total extermination of all these chimerical insights would be less harmful than the dream science itself, with its confounded contagion."[110] These remarks recall passages in the *Inquiry*, where Kant says "so far no metaphysics has ever been written," as well as the correspondence with Lambert, where Kant advocates "the *euthanasia* of erroneous philosophy."[111] These comments all show considerable disdain for the state of metaphysics in Kant's time, but they do not contradict the claim that "the true and lasting welfare of the human race depends on metaphysics."[112] Nor did they prevent Kant from trying to set metaphysics on the right path. But they do help us understand why Kant thought his work on *The Proper Method of Metaphysics* was so important.

*Dreams of a Spirit-Seer* is a decidedly less ambitious work than *The Proper Method of Metaphysics* was meant to be. In his letter to Mendelssohn, Kant says *Dreams of a Spirit-Seer* was meant to serve the negative purpose of a *katharticon*.[113] By purging philosophy of the folly and error that characterized contemporary metaphysics, it would achieve what Kant called "the *euthanasia* of erroneous philosophy" in his letter to Lambert.[114] While Kant told Lambert that it would be inappropriate for erroneous philosophy to be "carried to the grave ceremoniously, with serious but dishonest hairsplitting," he argues that it is necessary to intervene in his letter to Mendelssohn.[115] Instead of letting nature take its course and leaving erroneous philosophy to destroy itself through trifling and chatter, Kant tries to dispatch erroneous philosophy in *Dreams of a Spirit-Seer*, so that real philosophers like Mendelssohn and himself could develop an *organon* that would provide metaphysics with a solid foundation.[116]

Kant's reasons for taking Swedenborg's visions of the spirit-world as an example of the erroneous judgments and mistaken procedures of contemporary metaphysics remain somewhat obscure. He could have attacked the folly and error of contemporary metaphysics more directly, without digressions about Swedish mystics. He could have also exposed the vacuity of one of the other pseudo-sciences that populated the intellectual landscape of the Enlightenment. Yet Kant chose to comment on Swedenborg's visions and expose the absurdities of tales he was already inclined to regard with suspicion.[117] These decisions have added to the

confusion surrounding *Dreams of a Spirit-Seer* and they have had perni-
cious effects on our understanding of Kant's intellectual development;
yet they do not obscure Kant's intentions entirely. A close reading of the
first part of *Dreams of a Spirit-Seer* and careful attention to its structure are
sufficient to determine the extent of Kant's critique of the methods of
metaphysics in his time.

The first, "dogmatic" part of *Dreams of a Spirit-Seer* is intended to
demonstrate why Swedenborg's visions are absurd. Instead of addressing them directly or evaluating the testimony given in their defense, as
he had tried to do in his letter to Charlotte von Knobloch in 1762–63,
Kant presents a genetic account of Swedenborg's visions. He states the
basic, metaphysical problem to which they pertain, the nature of "spirit"
(*Geist*), and then explains how we arrive at a concept of spirit. It is meth-
odologically important that Kant begins by acknowledging that he does
not know what spirit is. There is no evidence in experience that might
tell us what spirit is, so Kant has to consider the way the term is used in
ordinary language. He says he has "frequently used the word or heard
others use it," so he assumes "that something or other must be understood by the term, irrespective of whether this something be a figment of
the imagination or something real."[118] He then proceeds to "unfold the
concealed sense of the concept," though he adds a footnote explaining
why the method he is employing is fundamentally flawed.[119] The footnote
explains that a term is not necessarily meaningful simply because it is
used in a particular way, so the analysis of such terms does not automati-
cally lead to truth. If we are not careful, analysis of these terms might allow surreptitious concepts like spirit to pass from ordinary language into
metaphysics, paving the way for fantastical visionaries like Swedenborg,
who appropriate terms found in popular tales and scholarly theories for
their own purposes.[120]

Because there is no evidence in experience for surreptitious concepts like spirit, Kant thinks they can only be established by obscure inferences.[121] Obscure inferences may be derived from the imagination or
the confusions of ordinary language, but they always take something from
experience and transform it into a different kind of concept, without realizing that this transformation has taken place.[122] Nor do they test the validity of the inference, to make sure that the concept they produce really
follows from the experience.[123] Such inferences are dangerous, because
they "propagate themselves by attaching themselves to other concepts,
without there being any awareness of the experience itself on which they
were originally based or on the inference which formed the concept of
the basis of that experience," leading to greater and greater confusion.[124]
This claim is the key to understanding *Dreams of a Spirit-Seer*, because it

explains the mistaken procedure that gives rise to erroneous judgments, which are in turn made into entire systems of "occult philosophy."

The first two chapters of *Dreams of a Spirit-Seer* imitate the way surreptitious concepts lead to erroneous judgments and tangle themselves into the metaphysical knots of occult philosophy. When he defines spirit as unextended, immaterial, rational being, Kant does so as an example of the way some philosophers make obscure inferences from surreptitious concepts. He then draws conclusions from that definition, even though the only evidence for its truth comes from the way the word is used in ordinary language. This confirms that there is something wrong with the procedure Kant is employing. He admits as much when he says that he cannot prove that spirit exists or that its concept has been understood through his analysis. The definition of spirit that Kant presents is, consequently, impossible either to prove or disprove. He says there is "no hope either of our ever being able to establish their possibility by means of rational argument."[125]

Given the hatred Kant says he feels for this approach to metaphysics, it is no surprise that he would extend his criticism of the surreptitious concepts and obscure inferences of occult philosophy to contemporary metaphysics. Kant satirically characterizes metaphysicians like Wolff and Crusius as "waking dreamers" who "build castles in the sky in their various imaginary worlds, each happily inhabiting his own world to the exclusion of others" at the beginning of the third chapter of *Dreams of a Spirit-Seer.*[126] And while it is almost certainly this passage that led Mendelssohn to call Kant's motives and his attitude toward metaphysics into question in his review, Kant actually distinguishes the waking dreams of metaphysics from the fantastical visions of the spirit-seers in the third and fourth chapters.

Even if there are certain affinities between metaphysics and spirit-seeing, Kant argues that they "differ not merely in degree but in kind."[127] He calls metaphysicians waking dreamers because they speculate about matters like spirit, leading to folly and error of the kind described in the second chapter of *Dreams of a Spirit-Seer.* When metaphysicians draw conclusions on the basis of concepts derived from nothing more than ordinary language, they present theories that are no clearer than the obscure inferences with which they constructed their systems. These theories fail to provide a specific criterion that could be used to judge the validity of metaphysical claims. But metaphysicians could still "awaken completely . . . if they should eventually open their eyes to a view which does not exclude agreement with the understanding of other human beings."[128] This distinguishes them from spirit-seers, who are indifferent to the illusions and parallaxes that result from their visions. They do not care that their visions are nothing more than figments of their imagination or extrapolations from ordinary language. Kant attributes this attitude to a disturbance in the balance of spirit-seers' nerves, but his prescription is probably more important than his diagnosis. At the end of the third chapter, he condemns spirit-seers as "candidates for the asylum."[129]

In order to spare themselves the fate of the spirit-seers, Kant thinks metaphysicians must avoid the methods described in the first two chapters of *Dreams of a Spirit-Seer*. He begins to lay out an alternative procedure for them to follow in chapter 4. The first step is to purify their judgment and "eradicate every blind attachment which may have insinuated itself into my soul in a surreptitious manner."[130] *Dreams of a Spirit-Seer* can be seen as an experiment in just this kind of purification. By considering the visions of spirit-seers and the possibility that "there is some truth to their validity," Kant makes sure he does not dismiss them out of prejudice.[131] Having established that his suspicions are legitimate, he suggests that philosophers compare their judgments with the judgments of others. Kant emphasizes this step when he says he "formerly used to regard human understanding in general merely from the point of view of my own understanding."[132] "Now, he says, "I put myself in the position of someone else's reason, which is independent of myself and external to me, and regard my judgments, along with their most secret causes, from the point of view of other people. The comparison of the two observations yields, it is true, pronounced parallaxes, but it is also the only method for preventing optical deception, and the only means of placing concepts in the true positions which they occupy relatively to the cognitive faculty of human nature."[133] By taking account of different perspectives and acknowledging their significance, Kant thinks philosophers will be able to establish a standard measure for their judgment. This will make it possible for them "to arrive at a unanimous result by comparing different weighings."[134] Such a unanimous result would finally allow metaphysics to assume a determinate form, set aside the controversies of the schools, and unite reflective minds in the single effort that Kant described in his *Inquiry*.[135]

All of this should make it very clear that Kant is trying to distinguish the proper method of metaphysics from the delusions of visionaries like Swedenborg in *Dreams of a Spirit-Seer*. The way he does this is largely negative. He reveals the mistaken procedures that make metaphysics seem like spirit-seeing; he rejects the erroneous judgments metaphysicians make about things they do not understand; and he ridicules metaphysicians who build castles in the sky. Yet he also offers constructive criticism, which Kant would not have done, if he thought metaphysics was impossible or undesirable. The fact that he thinks metaphysics can wake up from its dreams, approach its work in a more balanced way, and finally become the "companion of wisdom" that it should be proves that Kant was, in the end, not as disaffected with metaphysics as most scholars believe.[136]

## A Science of the Limits of Human Reason?

There is a passage near the end of part II of *Dreams of a Spirit-Seer* that is often cited by those who think the work represents the height of Kant's disaffection with metaphysics.[137] In this passage, Kant calls metaphysics "a science of the limits of human reason."[138] He says something similar in the remarks he wrote in his copy of *Observations on the Feeling of the Beautiful and the Sublime* (1764–65).[139] For some scholars, these comments prove that Kant's attitude toward metaphysics had undergone a dramatic change during the 1760s.[140]

Those who cite these passages from the *Remarks* and *Dreams of a Spirit-Seer* rarely describe the context in which they appear. Kant's *Remarks* are difficult to contextualize, because it is not always clear whether they are intended as comments on the text or thoughts passing through Kant's mind that have nothing to do with the *Observations*.[141] The matter is more difficult still in the case of the remark claiming that metaphysics is a science of the limits of human reason, because the remark appears inside the back flyleaf (*Deckblatt Innenseite*) of the book, separated from any context that might explain the meaning of Kant's remark. Yet that does not mean Kant's reasons for calling metaphysics a science of the limits of human reason are entirely obscure.

The meaning of Kant's remark becomes much clearer when we consider the rest of the passage in which it appears. Kant writes, "One could say that metaphysics is a science of the limits of human reason . . . Doubt about metaphysics does not cancel out useful certainty, but only useless certainty . . . Metaphysics is useful in that it cancels out appearance, which can be harmful . . . In metaphysics, not to think of the opposite side is partiality, and not to say it is also a lie; in actions it is not otherwise."[142] Kant goes on for a few more lines, describing the dangers of "falling in love with appearance" and the madness of taking "appearance to be the thing in itself," but the meaning of the *Remark* should already be apparent.[143] Kant is pointing out the benefits of metaphysics, explaining how metaphysics helps us distinguish between appearance and reality, so that we do not mistake illusion for truth. He is not presenting a radically new definition of metaphysics when he calls it a science of the limits of human reason. He is merely describing one of its benefits.

The context of the passage in *Dreams of a Spirit-Seer* is similar. When he says metaphysics is the science of the limits of human reason in chapter 3 of part II, Kant is actually listing the benefits of metaphysics. The first is that metaphysics can "solve the problems thrown up by the enquiring mind, when it uses reason to spy after the more hidden properties of things."[144] Even if we are not always satisfied in our inquiries about the hidden properties of things, Kant says there is another benefit of metaphysics, which possesses a special importance for human reason.[145] According to Kant, this second benefit "consists both in knowing whether the task has been determined by reference to what one can know, and in knowing what relation the question has to the empirical concepts, upon which all our judgments must at all times be based."[146] In other words, metaphysics identifies the kinds of questions human reason can answer and under what conditions it can answer them. It reminds us that it is useless to try to answer questions that require "*data* which are to be found in a world other than the one in which we exist as a conscious being."[147] Recognizing that allows us to dismiss "the illusion and vain knowledge which inflates the understanding and fills up the narrow space which could otherwise be occupied by the teachings of wisdom and of useful instruction."[148] But none of that implies that metaphysics is impossible or undesirable. The claim that metaphysics is the science of the limits of human reason simply means that metaphysics tells us what we can and cannot know.

The repugnance and even hatred Kant told Mendelssohn he felt for the methods of contemporary metaphysics does not seem to have changed his view of metaphysics itself.[149] Kant may have blamed the miscarriage of *The Proper Method of Metaphysics* on the abundance of erroneous judgments that were available "to illustrate my theses concerning mistaken procedures."[150] And his inability to find "examples to show *in concreto* what the proper method should be" was no doubt frustrating for him.[151] Kant may also have vented his disappointment in a biting and sarcastic text, making fun of a Swedish spirit-seer and the kinds of philosophy that paved the way for his fanaticism. Yet there is no evidence that Kant doubted the possibility or desirability of metaphysics at any point during the pre-critical period.[152] Nor does it appear that the frustration of his earlier efforts deterred him in his search for the proper method of metaphysics. His inaugural dissertation *On the Form and Principles of the Sensible and the Intelligible World* (1770) and his correspondence with Marcus Herz in the early 1770s show that Kant's interest in the subject extended well beyond the 1760s. It would not be long before he found the method he would use to set metaphysics on the sure path of science—the critique of pure reason.

# 3

# The Key to the Whole Secret of Metaphysics

Kant relates some of the difficulties he encountered while "making plans for a work that might perhaps have the title *The Bounds of Sensibility and Reason*" in his February 21, 1772, letter to Marcus Herz.[1] In the course of his search for the nature and method of metaphysics, Kant explains, he found that he "still lacked something essential, something that in my long metaphysical studies I, as well as others, had failed to pay attention to and that, in fact, constitutes the key to the whole secret of hitherto still obscure metaphysics."[2] Kant then indicates that this "essential something" is to be found in the answer to the question "What is the ground of the relation of that in us which we call *representation* to the object?"[3]

The reason I have cited such a famous passage in such a well-known letter is not to offer a new interpretation of Kant's answer to the question concerning "the ground of the relation . . ." Nor do I wish to enter into the debate between those who see Kant's answer in light of his pre-critical philosophy and those who regard his account of the correspondence between intellectual representations and objects as a prefiguration of the "Deduction of the Pure Concepts of the Understanding" in the *Critique of Pure Reason*.[4] I will have things to say about these subjects later in the chapter, but I have cited Kant's letter to Herz for a different reason. The letter to Herz is the first text in which Kant refers to the critique that he would publish in 1781.[5] After describing his understanding of the question concerning "the ground of the relation . . ." and rejecting the answers proposed by other philosophers, Kant says he will soon publish a critique of pure reason that will explain the nature of theoretical and practical knowledge, along with the method and limits of metaphysics.[6]

It should be noted that Kant does not refer to the critique of pure reason as the title of a forthcoming work in his letter to Herz.[7] When Kant tells Herz that he is "now in a position to bring out a critique of pure reason," the phrase "a critique of pure reason" (*eine Critic der reinen Vernunft*) is not spaced (*gesperrt*) in the way that usually indicates a title in German typography.[8] The absence of spacing could be the result of an error in the transcription, typesetting, or printing of Kant's correspondence; unfortunately, Kant's letter seems to have been lost in the travails of German history, so there is no way to determine the correctness of the standard editions.[9] It is also possible that "critique of pure reason" was not intended as the title of a work Kant was preparing for publication. Lewis White Beck has noted that Kant "often used these words to refer to his whole philosophic project and program, even after the book called *Critique of Pure Reason* had been published," making the suggestion that Kant did not intend his reference to "a critique of pure reason" as a title more plausible.[10] However, in his 1772 letter to Herz, Kant announces his critique of pure reason immediately after explaining his answer to the question concerning "the ground of the relation . . ." And he raises this question immediately after explaining that his plans for *The Bounds of Sensibility and Reason* lacked something essential.[11] This suggests that the critique Kant announced at the end of his letter is something very different from the work he describes at the beginning of the letter.

In what follows, I hope to determine whether Kant's critique differs from the work he describes at the beginning of his letter to Herz and, if so, how they might differ. I will begin by reconstructing the context in which Kant formulated his plans for *The Bounds of Sensibility and Reason,* explaining how these plans emerged from the reception of Kant's inaugural dissertation *On the Form and Principles of the Sensible and the Intelligible World* (1770). After that, I will compare Kant's accounts of his plans for *The Bounds of Sensibility and Reason* in his correspondence with Herz in 1771 and 1772, in order to confirm that Kant intended *The Bounds of Sensibility and Reason* as both a restatement and an extension of the claims of his inaugural dissertation. In the final sections of this chapter, I will argue that *The Bounds of Sensibility and Reason* and the critique of pure reason that Kant describes in his 1772 letter to Herz are indeed very different projects. I will contend that Kant realized that the question concerning "the ground of the relation . . ." could never be answered by a work demarcating the boundary between sensible and intellectual cognition shortly before he wrote his letter to Herz in 1772. The fact that Kant found "the key to the whole secret of metaphysics, hitherto still hidden from itself" in a critique of pure reason at the same time is a matter of no small significance.[12]

## The Inaugural Dissertation

Kant began writing his inaugural dissertation *On the Form and Principles of the Sensible and the Intelligible World* when he was offered a chair in logic and metaphysics at the University of Königsberg in 1770. He had been offered similar positions in Erlangen in 1768 and Jena in 1769, but had chosen to wait for a position to become available in Königsberg.[13] Kant's chance came with the death of Christoph Langhansen on March 15, 1770.[14] The day after Langhansen's death, he wrote to the Prussian minister of culture and the king, recommending that Langhansen's chair in mathematics be offered to either Johann Buck, the man who had been promoted over Kant for Martin Knutzen's chair in 1758, or Carl August Christiani, who held a chair in moral philosophy in Königsberg. Kant did not hesitate to suggest that he be offered whichever chair became available as a result of these moves.[15]

The minister does not seem to have regarded Kant's letters as importune or opportunistic. At the beginning of his letter to the minister of culture—Carl Joseph Maximilian, Freiherr von Fürst und Kupfenberg—Kant thanks him for his concern he had shown regarding his fate.[16] It seems the minister had been looking out for Kant. In previous correspondence, he had probably assured Kant that he would not overlook the philosopher who had done so well in the academy's prize-essay competition in 1763. Nor would he leave a philosopher who was known throughout Germany without an appropriate position. Because of his reputation and his connections in Berlin, Kant was probably not surprised when Langhansen's chair was offered to Buck. Nor would he have been surprised when Frederick II offered him Buck's chair in logic and metaphysics.

Kant was officially installed as Professore Ordinario der Logic und Metaphysic in Königsberg on May 2, 1770. Because his chair had become available in such a peculiar manner, Kant did not have much time to prepare the inaugural dissertation required for his professorship. The work he submitted for disputation, *On the Form and Principles of the Sensible and the Intelligible World*, was defended on August 24, 1770, by Marcus Herz, a Jewish medical student who became one of Kant's most important correspondents in the 1770s.[17] The work must have been written almost as quickly as the *Inquiry*, but it was no less ambitious. At the beginning of the first section, Kant says his dissertation will explore the concept of "a whole which is not a part, that is to say, a *world*," as well as "the characteristic marks which belong to the distinct cognition of an object" and "the *two-fold genesis* of the concept out of the nature of the mind."[18] Armed with the concept of a world, an account of conditions of the distinct cognition of objects, and an understanding of their origins, Kant claims, we will be able to secure "a deeper insight into the method of metaphysics."[19]

Unfortunately, the outline Kant presents in the first section of his dissertation is not really an accurate guide to its contents. Kant does discuss the concept of a world, explaining its matter, form, and completeness. He claims the matter of a world consists of several substances, which are not modifications of a single substance. Its form is the set of reciprocal relationships that exist between substances and coordinates their inter-actions. The completeness of a world is the simultaneous positing of all the parts of the world that make it an absolute totality. Kant is particu-larly emphatic about this last aspect of the concept of a world, because he thinks it is impossible to understand how a world can be both infinite and whole unless one appreciates that the concept of a world presupposes its completeness. However, Kant's remarks on the concept of a world are less central to his dissertation than another problem, with which he seems to have been more deeply concerned: the distinction between sensible and intellectual cognition.

Kant begins to address the distinction between sensible and intellec-tual cognition at the end of the first section of his dissertation, when he claims that "neither the successive nor the simultaneous co-ordination of several things (since both co-ordinations depend on concepts of time) be-longs to a concept of a whole which derives from the understanding but only to the conditions of sensible intuition."[20] Apparently Kant thought our experience of time served as the empirical ground for concepts of succession and simultaneity. Yet he did not believe empirical concepts could provide an adequate account of the kind of relations that obtain between substances in a world. In order to distinguish a purely rational conception of succession and simultaneity from empirical concepts based on the experience of time, Kant proceeds to distinguish the form of the sensible world from the form of the intelligible world in sections 3 and 4 of his dissertation. There is, of course, much that could be said about the details of Kant's argument in these sections. In section 3, Kant claims that space and time are "the schemata and conditions of everything sensitive in human cognition."[21] And, in section 4, he argues that the form of the intelligible world is determined by the existence of a necessary being that creates, unifies, and harmonizes the plurality of substances in a world.[22] However, in the present context, the fact that Kant thinks one world is the object of sensible cognition, while the other is the object of intellectual cognition is what is most significant, because Kant uses the distinction between sensible and intellectual cognition to define the subject matter of metaphysics in a way that he had not in the *Inquiry* or in his correspon-dence with Lambert about *The Proper Method of Metaphysics*.

Because it is such an essential part of his plans for *The Bounds of Sensibility and Reason*, we should pay close attention to the way Kant in-troduces the distinction between sensible and intellectual cognition in the second section of his dissertation.[23] He begins by distinguishing the faculties of sensibility and the intellect. Kant calls sensibility "the recep-tivity of subject in virtue of which it is possible for the subject's own representative state to be affected in a definite way by the presence of some object," while intelligence is "the faculty of a subject in virtue of which it has the power to represent things which cannot by their own quality come before the senses of that subject."[24] It follows naturally from this distinction that sensible cognition is "cognition, insofar as it is subject to the laws of sensibility" and intellectual cognition is "subject to the laws of intelligence."[25] Sensible and intellectual cognition originate in different faculties—sensible cognition in sensibility, intellectual cognition in the intellect—so they are subject to different rules. We cannot sense things that have not affected us, but we can understand things we cannot sense. Intellectual cognition does not depend on sensible affection, so it must be a very different kind of cognition than sensible cognition.

Things become more complicated when Kant suggests that sensible and intellectual cognition have different objects, as well as different ways of cognizing objects. The difference between the objects of sensible and intellectual cognition is already implied in Kant's account of the difference between the faculties of sensibility and the intellect when he says the intellect represents things "which cannot by their own quality come before the senses of the subject."[26] This suggests that some objects cannot be perceived by the senses, because they cannot affect us and alter our representative state through our sensible faculty. Kant calls these objects *noumena*. He distinguishes them from objects of sensible cognition, which can alter our representative state through affection. These objects are called *phenomena*. Kant goes on to argue that the distinction between phenomena and noumena does not depend on the faculties of a subject that cognizes them, because the difference between them is "exempt from such subjective conditions" and "relates only to the object."[27]

The distinction between phenomena and noumena that Kant introduces in his dissertation presupposes an ontological distinction between two kinds of things. Some things (phenomena) are sensible (*sensibilia*), while others (noumena) are intelligible (*intelligibilia*). The matter is, however, even more complicated that that. Kant says, "representations which are thought sensitively are representations of things *as they appear*, while representations which are intellectual are representations of things *as they are*."[28] This claim goes well beyond the distinction between sensible things and intellectual things and the distinction between sensible and intellectual cognition, because it asserts that sensible and intellectual cognition represent sensible and intellectual things in different ways—as they appear or as they are in themselves.

To be sure, when Kant says "things which are thought sensitively are representations of things *as they appear*," he is making the rather obvious point that sensible cognition represents things as they appear to us.

Because sensible cognition arises when our representative state is modified by sensible affection, it is relative to the impression an object makes on us. Sometimes objects do not make a strong impression on us. Even when they do, they do not reflect every aspect of the object that affects us. Strong sensible impressions do not reveal the metaphysical essence of objects. They simply produce a greater modification of our representative state, making the representation of the object more vivid than it might otherwise be. Vivid representations might be interesting or exciting, but they do not necessarily correspond to the objects that affect us. Nor do we have good reason to suppose that vivid representations even resemble those objects. That makes it impossible for sensible cognition to go beyond appearances. Phenomena affect us sensibly, in ways that are determined by the disposition of our sensitive faculty, so sensible cognition is nothing more than cognition of the way phenomena appear to us.

Kant's claim that "representations which are intellectual are representations of things *as they are*" is not as easy to defend. Kant denies that intelligible objects—noumena, *intelligibilia*—are given to human understanding through intellectual intuition, since human beings do not possess such a faculty.[29] He also rejects the idea that human beings possess innate ideas of intelligible things.[30] Instead, Kant argues, our intellectual faculty acquires concepts of intelligible things by abstracting from the laws inherent to the mind.[31] In a parenthetical remark, he suggests we do this "by attending to [the mind's] actions on the occasion of an experience."[32] How exactly this is supposed to give us knowledge of intelligible things as they are is not entirely clear. Perhaps Kant thinks we can establish a set of necessary truths by reflecting on experience and determining what makes that experience possible. Or he might think the human mind can establish the existence of a necessary being purely intellectually, by considering the concept of such a being. His remarks on the real use of the understanding suggest he was more inclined toward the latter option. According to Kant, the real use of the understanding concerns concepts of things and relations that are "given by the very nature of the understanding," "contain no form of sensitive cognition," and "have been abstracted from no use of the senses."[33] In short, these concepts are purely intellectual, because they are produced by the mind through its own activity. Kant does not explain why they are supposed to represent intelligible objects as they are in themselves, but there can be little doubt that he thinks this is the essential difference between sensible and intellectual cognition.

Instead of dwelling on the problem of representing purely intellectual objects as they are in themselves, Kant focuses on what he thinks is a much more serious problem: the role the distinction between sensible and intellectual cognition plays in metaphysics. As we have seen, Kant thought sensible and intellectual cognition originate in different faculties, have different objects, and relate to their objects in different ways; however, he thought only intellectual cognition, noumena, and the relation between them were relevant to metaphysics. In order to explain why sensible cognition, phenomena, and their relation have no place in metaphysics, Kant repurposes his dissertation, calling it a specimen of a "propaedeutic science" that will teach "the distinction between sensible cognition and the cognition which derives from the understanding."[34]

Kant's propaedeutic science explains that metaphysics is "the philosophy which contains the first principles of the use of the pure understanding."[35] In order to understand this philosophy, Kant thinks we must separate the first principles of the use of the pure understanding from everything empirical. Empirical principles are derived from sensible cognition with the help of the logical use of the understanding. By comparing appearances and making generalizations about what is regular in experience, the logical use of the understanding allows sensible cognition to formulate general rules about the order and relation of phenomena. These rules are called empirical principles. In order to distinguish empirical principles from the first principles of the use of the pure understanding, however, we must turn from the logical use of the understanding to its real use. Only the real use of the understanding is relevant for metaphysics, because "empirical concepts do not, in virtue of being raised to greater universality, become intellectual in the *real* sense, nor do they pass beyond the species of sensitive cognition; no matter how high they ascend by abstracting, they always remain sensitive."[36] Because empirical concepts and principles are marked by their origin in sensibility, in other words, they can never be pure. And the first principles of the understanding must be entirely pure, without any connection to sensibility, sensible cognition, or phenomena, if metaphysics is to be the philosophy of those principles.

Of course, it might be objected that metaphysics does not need to restrict itself to the first principles of the use of the pure understanding. But that would miss the point of Kant's propaedeutic science, which defines the subject matter of metaphysics by distinguishing it from the subject matter of other sciences and other parts of philosophy. Kant employed a similar approach in his *Inquiry*, when he tried to define the proper method of metaphysics through its opposition to mathematics. The same opposition is found in Kant's dissertation, where mathematics becomes the science of sensible cognition.[37] In the end, however, it is not the distinction between metaphysics and mathematics that is essential for Kant's propaedeutic science. In his inaugural dissertation, the distinction between sensible and intellectual cognition provides the specific difference that Kant uses to define metaphysics. By excluding everything sensible from metaphysics, Kant hopes to determine what belongs to metaphysics and to no other science.

That the exclusion of sensible cognition and empirical principles from metaphysics is the ultimate goal of Kant's dissertation is clear from its concluding section. In part 5, Kant provides an outline of the method his propaedeutic science will follow as it teaches the distinction between sensible and intellectual cognition. He says that "every method employed by metaphysics, in dealing with what is sensitive and what belongs to the understanding, amounts, in particular, to this prescription: *great care must be taken lest the principles which are native to sensitive cognition transgress their limits and affect what belongs to the understanding.*"[38] Kant thinks this happens with some regularity, as indicated by his remarks about empirical conceptions of simultaneity and succession in part 1; however, he also thinks it can be prevented by rejecting subreptive axioms that conflate sensible and intellectual cognition.[39] The fallacies of these axioms can be avoided by recognizing that noumena are not subject to the same conditions as phenomena. While we must cognize the objects of sensible cognition as being in space and time, immaterial substances and their relations are not spatial or temporal.[40] Subjecting them to the conditions of sensible cognition is fallacious, so any axiom that suggests otherwise must be excluded from metaphysics. For similar reasons, we must reject formulations of the principle of noncontradiction that contain references to time. Neither time nor space plays any role in determining the possibility of an intelligible object—or any other aspect of its modality—so any axiom suggesting otherwise must be fallacious.[41] By excluding these axioms, rejecting subreptive fallacies, and eliminating everything sensible from metaphysics, Kant thinks his dissertation does philosophy a great service.[42]

## The Bounds of Sensibility and Reason

In 1770 Kant thought he had arrived at a position that he would never have to change.[43] In a letter to Johann Heinrich Lambert, Kant boasted that his inaugural dissertation contained "wholly certain and easy criteria" that could be used to examine "all sorts of metaphysical questions" and "decide with certainty . . . the extent to which these questions can or cannot be resolved."[44] He fully expected his dissertation to win Lambert's approval and the favor of the most important philosophers of his time. Unfortunately, Kant's attempt to "preserve metaphysics proper from any admixture of the sensible" and make "usefully explicit and evident without great strain" the significance of "something thought through a universal or a pure concept of the understanding" was not as well-received as he had hoped.[45]

When his dissertation was published, Kant asked Marcus Herz to deliver a copy to the Prussian minister of culture, Carl Joseph Maximilian, who had helped Kant secure his position in Königsberg. Herz also distributed copies of Kant's dissertation to Lambert, Sulzer, and Mendelssohn, the Berlin philosophers with whom Kant had been corresponding since the success of his *Inquiry* in the academy's prize-essay competition in 1763. Herz promoted Kant's work enthusiastically when he arrived in Berlin, but the response was not what Kant expected. Only Lambert seems to have devoted much time to Kant's dissertation, sending him a lengthy response in a letter from October 13, 1770.[46] Lambert agreed with Kant that "*human knowledge,* by virtue of being *knowledge* and by virtue of *having its own form,* is divided in accordance with the old *phenomenon* and *noumenon* distinction and, accordingly, arises out of two entirely different and, so to speak, *heterogenous* sources, so that what stems from the one source can never be derived from the other. Knowledge that comes from the senses thus is and remains sensible, just as knowledge that comes from the understanding remains peculiar to the understanding."[47] He nevertheless questioned "to what extent these two ways of knowing are so completely separated that they never come together."[48]

The other philosophers to whom Herz delivered copies of Kant's dissertation do not seem to have devoted much time to the work. Sulzer wrote to Kant on December 8, 1770, excusing himself from dealing with Kant's dissertation in greater depth, because he was too absorbed in his own work. However, Sulzer noted his general agreement with Kant's distinction between the sensible and the intellectual and promised to follow up when he had the time.[49] While Herz claimed that Mendelssohn told him he could not agree with the views expressed in Kant's dissertation because they did not agree with Baumgarten, Mendelssohn told Kant that his nervous infirmities made it impossible for him to make it through "a speculative work of this stature" in a letter from December 25, 1770.[50] As a result, Mendelssohn said, he was unable to address the central theses Kant had advanced in his dissertation and offered only a few comments about some incidental concerns.[51] Some of those comments raise serious questions about Kant's claims about the subjectivity of time, but they do not touch on the centerpiece of Kant's dissertation, the distinction between sensible and intellectual cognition.

Kant did not respond to the criticisms of his dissertation for many months after he received Lambert's, Sulzer's, and Mendelssohn's letters.

Nor did he respond to his critics directly. Kant begins his June 6, 1771, letter to Herz by saying he had been unable to respond to Herz's earlier correspondence, or to letters from Lambert and Mendelssohn, because "the kinds of letters with which these two scholars have honored me always lead me to a long series of investigations."[52] Kant tells Herz that "long experience has taught me that one cannot compel or precipitate insight by force in matters of the sort we are considering; rather, it takes quite a long time to gain insight, since one looks at one and the same concept intermittently, and regards its possibility in all its possible relations and contexts, and, furthermore, because one must above all awaken the skeptical spirit within, to examine one's conclusions against the strongest possible doubt and see whether they can stand the test."[53] Ultimately, these reflections led Kant to suspect that there was something missing from his dissertation. "The mere fact that men of such insight can remain unconvinced is," he says, "always a proof to me that my theories must at least lack clarity, self-evidence, or even something more essential."[54]

Although he claims it would take a long time and a great deal of effort to determine what his dissertation was missing, Kant tells Herz he is preparing a work called *The Bounds of Sensibility and Reason* only a few lines later.[55] Kant presents *The Bounds of Sensibility and Reason* as the product of the long investigations he was forced to undertake, because he had not convinced men of such insight as Lambert and Mendelssohn.[56] As he describes his plans to Herz, however, it becomes apparent that Kant did not plan to change anything substantial about the approach he employed in his inaugural dissertation. In his dissertation, he had used the distinction between sensible and intellectual cognition to exclude everything sensible from metaphysics, proving that metaphysics is "the philosophy which contains the first principles of the use of the pure understanding."[57] *The Bounds of Sensibility and Reason* is no different. Kant tells Herz that he will use the distinction between "that which depends on the subjective principles of the human mental powers (not only sensibility but also the understanding) and that which pertains directly to the facts" to explain "the foundational principles and laws that determine the sensible world, together with an outline of what is essential to the Doctrine of Taste, of Metaphysics, and of Moral Philosophy."[58] The fact that he planned to extend the approach he developed in his inaugural dissertation from metaphysics to moral philosophy and aesthetics also shows that Kant remained committed to the view of metaphysics he defended in his dissertation.

In his 1771 letter, Kant tells Herz that he has already "considered, weighed, and harmonized everything" he would need to write *The Bounds of Sensibility and Reason,* but he does not describe its contents or its structure until almost a year later.[59] At the beginning of his February 21, 1772, letter to Herz, Kant says he has "already made considerable progress in the effort to distinguish the sensible from the intellectual in the field of morals and the principles that spring therefrom."[60] Kant also says he has "outlined, to my tolerable satisfaction, the principles of feeling, taste, and power of judgment, with their effects—the pleasant, the beautiful, and the good."[61] He then describes his plans for *The Bounds of Sensibility and Reason* in some detail.

*The Bounds of Sensibility and Reason* was to be divided into two parts, one theoretical and one practical.[62] Each part would then be divided into two sections. The first (theoretical) part would be divided between "general phenomenology" and "metaphysics, but this only with regard to its nature and method."[63] The second (practical) part would deal with "the universal principles of feeling, taste, and sensuous desire" and "the basic principles of morality."[64] Some scholars, like Benno Erdmann, have argued that this outline is the starting point for Kant's critical philosophy, but it should be noted that the plan for *The Bounds of Sensibility and Reason* that Kant describes in his letter to Herz is very different than the structure of the *Critique of Pure Reason*.[65] The first *Critique* contains no phenomenology and does not distinguish phenomenology from metaphysics. Instead, the *Critique of Pure Reason* is divided into a "Transcendental Doctrine of Elements," containing a "Transcendental Aesthetic" and a "Transcendental Logic," and a "Transcendental Doctrine of Method," containing the "Discipline," "Canon," "Architectonic," and "History" of pure reason. None of these divisions correspond to anything Kant describes in the outline for *The Bounds of Sensibility and Reason* in his 1772 letter to Herz. Nor is there any evidence that Kant's plans for *The Bounds of Sensibility and Reason* gradually evolved into the outline of the *Critique of Pure Reason*. Giorgio Tonelli's studies of the development of Kant's plans for the *Critique of Pure Reason* prove that there was considerable variation and little continuity in the plans Kant describes in his notes and lectures from this period.[66]

In the end, the comparison of Kant's plans for *The Bounds of Sensibility and Reason* and the structure of the *Critique of Pure Reason* tells us very little about either work. Far more important are the tenses of the verbs Kant uses when he describes his plans for *The Bounds of Sensibility and Reason* in his 1772 letter to Herz. Careful attention to the language of his letter shows that Kant is speaking retrospectively when he tells Herz about the progress he had made on *The Bounds of Sensibility*. When Herz last visited Königsberg, Kant says he was "then making plans" (*nun machte ich mir den Plan*) for a work "that might perhaps have the title, *The Bounds of Sensibility and Reason*" (*welches etwa den Titel haben könte: Die Grentzen der Sinnlichkeit und der Vernunft*).[67] Kant reminds Herz of the debate they had about that work and then explains what had transpired after Herz's departure.[68] Kant says he "examined once more, in the intervals between my professional duties and my sorely needed relaxation, the project that we had debated, in order to adapt it to the whole of philosophy and other knowledge in order to understand its extent and limits."[69] In the course of these reflections, Kant noticed that he "still lacked something essential, something that in my long metaphysical studies I, as well as others, had failed to consider and which in fact constitutes the key to the whole secret of metaphysics, hitherto still hidden from itself."[70] The "key to the whole secret of metaphysics" is the answer to the question "What is the ground of the relation of that in us which we call *representation* to the object?"[71] It is only when he discusses the answer to this question that Kant shifts back to the present tense. And, when he does, he says "now I am in a position to bring out a critique of pure reason" (*ich itzo im Stande bin eine Critick der reinen Vernunft . . . vorzulegen*).

The retrospective character of the beginning of Kant's letter suggests that he had already abandoned his plans for *The Bounds of Sensibility and Reason* when he described its structure in his letter to Herz in 1772. Kant recounted his plans for *The Bounds of Sensibility and Reason*, not because they reflected the work he was doing at the time he was writing, but to provide background and context for the change that had taken place in his views after he had last spoken with Herz. The reasons for this change can be found in Kant's reference to a "debate" (*Disput*) that took place during Herz's visit to Königsberg. This reference is often overlooked in readings of Kant's letter, but the debate with Herz seems to have been instrumental in Kant's discovery of the question concerning "the ground of the relation . . ." And, unlike the objections from Lambert and Mendelssohn, Kant's debate with Herz seems to have made him reflect on the method he proposed in his inaugural dissertation and reconsider his plans to extend those methods in *The Bounds of Sensibility and Reason*. Instead of reformulating and extending the same ideas, Kant began to seriously question his view of metaphysics.[72]

Though his debate with Herz seems to have led Kant to abandon his plans for *The Bounds of Sensibility and Reason*, it is unlikely that Herz had serious reservations about Kant's dissertation or the project he had described in the letter from 1771.[73] After all, it was Herz who defended Kant's dissertation when Kant was appointed to his chair in Königsberg. He had also adopted the terms of Kant's dissertation in his *Observations on Speculative Philosophy* (1771), a work that is comparable in many ways to Kant's plans for *The Bounds of Sensibility and Reason*. Like Kant, Herz argues that the principles of metaphysics can be derived from the distinction between matters of fact and the "subjective principles of human mental powers."[74] He also follows Kant in his account of the difference between sensible and intellectual cognition, saying "what is sensible in our cognition is that by means of which our state behaves passively in the presence of external objects; what is intellectual [in our cognition] is the faculty to represent such things to which, due to their makeup, no access is permitted through the senses."[75] Finally, like Kant, Herz was committed to the idea that "representations which are thought sensitively are representations of things as they appear, while representations which are intellectual are representations of things as they are."[76]

Despite his commitment to the view of metaphysics Kant described in his dissertation, Herz was not afraid to raise some skeptical questions about the necessity of the agreement between intellectual representations and their objects. In his *Observations,* he asks how external things can be said to "agree" with our representations, when they exist "independently of all representation as well."[77] If our cognition is in every case a judgment, as Herz agrees it must be, then it is unclear how we can know the subject to which we attribute predicates in judgment, especially when that subject is supposed to remain "independent of our representations" in every case.[78] According to Herz, the grasp of this subject can only be intuitive, which would make Kant's claim that intellectual representations represent things "as they are" dependent on a faculty of intellectual intuition.[79] Kant had rejected the possibility of intellectual intuition in his inaugural dissertation, but he had not explained how intellectual cognition was to produce the concepts that corresponded to the necessary but independent existence of their objects.[80] Nor had he provided a guarantee that intellectual cognition would represent its objects in a way that could be considered valid.

The debate that took place in Königsberg must have convinced Kant that these were serious objections. His preoccupation with the question concerning "the ground of the relation . . ." suggests that he began to wonder how intellectual concepts could correspond to and validly represent intelligible objects that exist outside the mind. Kant's answer to that question led him to give up the view of metaphysics he had defended in his inaugural dissertation, as well as his plans for *The Bounds of Sensibility and Reason.* This had happened to Kant before, but there is an important difference between the miscarriage of Kant's plans for *The Proper Method of Metaphysics* and his abandoned plans for *The Bounds of Sensibility and Reason.* The difficulties he described in his correspondence with Lambert left Kant searching for some way to determine "what the proper procedure should be."[81] Shortly after his debate with Herz, however, Kant said he discovered "the key to the whole secret of metaphysics" in a critique of pure reason.[82] He never mentioned *The Bounds of Sensibility and Reason* again.

## The Ground of the Relation . . .

To understand why Kant rejected the view of metaphysics he defended in his inaugural dissertation and abandoned his plans for *The Bounds of Sensibility and Reason*, we must look more closely at his answer to the question concerning "the ground of the relation . . ." The answer Kant proposes in his 1772 letter to Herz is not fully developed, but it is clear that his focus had shifted from the "bounds" (*Grenzen*) of sensibility and reason to the "ground" (*Grund*) of the relation between representations and objects. This change is significant, because it shows that Kant no longer thinks metaphysics can be defined by the delimitation of its subject matter. And that may explain why he decided to present "the key to the whole secret of metaphysics" in a critique of pure reason, rather than carrying out his plans for *The Bounds of Sensibility and Reason*.

Kant's inaugural dissertation and his plans for *The Bounds of Sensibility and Reason* define the subject matter of metaphysics through the distinction between sensible and intellectual cognition. In his inaugural dissertation, Kant argues that a "propaedeutic science" that teaches the difference between sensible and intellectual cognition would prove that metaphysics is "the philosophy which contains the *first principles* of the use of the *pure understanding*."[83] A year later, in his account of his plans for *The Bounds of Sensibility and Reason*, Kant suggests that these distinctions are essential to philosophy and even "the most important ends of humanity in general," because they allow us "to distinguish with certainty and clarity that which depends on the subjective principles of human mental powers (not only sensibility but also the understanding) and that which pertains directly to the facts."[84] Kant told Herz he planned to "work out in some detail the foundational principles and laws that determine the sensible world" and present them alongside "an outline of what is essential to the Doctrine of Taste, of Metaphysics, and of Moral Philosophy," because he still thought metaphysics was defined by the distinction between sensible and intellectual cognition.[85] This approach is reflected in the emphasis he places on "bounds" in the title of *The Bounds of Sensibility and Reason*.

Rejecting the idea that the distinction between sensible and intellectual cognition provides metaphysics with an adequate foundation in 1772, Kant proposes that understanding the ground of the relation between representations and objects is the key to metaphysics. This approach differs from his earlier accounts of the bounds of sensibility and reason, because the grounds that Kant seeks are not boundaries that determine whether or not something belongs to metaphysics. The 1772 letter to Herz makes it clear that Kant no longer thinks intellectual cognition represents things as they are, simply because it is intellectual rather than sensible. If it represents things as they are in themselves, it is because the ground of the relation between "that in us that we call representation" and the objects to which they refer guarantees their validity. Thus, Kant contends that we must look to the ground of that relation to determine whether our representations correspond to their objects and whether that correspondence is valid. The conception of "objective validity" that Kant would later employ in the "Transcendental Deduction of the Pure Concepts of the Understanding" of the *Critique of Pure Reason* has its beginnings in this insight and the new approach to metaphysics that Kant associates with his critique in his letter to Herz.

While he concedes that "passive or sensuous representations have an understandable relationship to objects," Kant ultimately rejects the empiricist attempt to ground the relation between representations and objects in sensation. He does not consider the "understandable relationship" (*begreifliche Beziehung*) between representations and objects that is established by sensation to be a sufficient guarantee of the validity of that relationship.[86] It may be quite natural to think the objects that affect us in sensation are the cause of our representations, but there are good reasons to suspect that representations derived from sensation might not correspond to their objects. Attempts to make sensibility the ground of the relation between representations and objects risk making those representations invalid, because they try to derive cognition of objects from the mere appearance of those objects. If the appearance is unclear or illusory in any way, then it will not produce an objectively valid representation corresponding to the objects that affect us. The ground of valid representation is therefore irreducible to "the reception of representations through the senses" and cannot be "abstracted from sense perceptions."[87]

Rationalism is preferable to empiricism, for Kant, because "the principles that are derived from the nature of our soul have an understandable validity for all things insofar as those things are supposed to be objects of the senses."[88] Principles derived from the nature of our souls are intellectual cognitions, so it is no surprise that Kant thinks they have an "understandable validity" (*begreifliche Gültigkeit*). He says intellectual cognition represents things "*as they are*" rather than as "*as they appear*" in his inaugural dissertation, precisely because it is free from the confusion that accompanies sensible cognition, which threatens the validity of the relationship between sensible cognition and its objects.[89] Kant repeats this claim in the letter to Herz, emphasizing that intellectual cognition that represents things "*as they are*" must certainly be valid.[90] Unfortunately, rationalist accounts of the origin of these valid representations are not as easily comprehensible as empiricist attempts to trace the origin of representations back to sensibility, because they must show that representations that have their origin in something other than the objects they are supposed to represent can still represent those objects accurately and adequately. Kant is particularly concerned about this problem in his letter to Herz, because he had been content "to explain the nature of intellectual representations in a merely negative way, namely to state that they were not modifications of the soul brought about by the object," in his inaugural dissertation.[91] He now realizes that he had "silently passed over the further question of how a representation that refers to an object without being in any way affected by it can be possible."[92]

Kant does not think we have to choose between a plausible answer to the question concerning "the ground of the relation . . ." and a valid one, but his defense of the rationalist position is not fully developed in his 1772 letter to Herz. The details of his argument are missing, presumably because Kant had not yet given them the precise formulation such arguments require.[93] What we find in Kant's correspondence, notes, and lectures from this period are indications of the direction he thought he might take, rather than drafts of the arguments he would later include in the "Transcendental Deduction" of the *Critique of Pure Reason*.[94] This reflects a more general feature of Kant's approach to philosophy. When we look at his plans for works like *The Proper Method of Metaphysics, The Bounds of Sensibility and Reason*, and the *Critique of Pure Reason*, it becomes clear that Kant often knew what he wanted to argue and then tried to find ways to reach that conclusion. Being self-aware and philosophically responsible, Kant was willing to admit when his arguments were inadequate. That is why he abandoned so many works during the 1760s and 1770s. Yet there is an important difference between these earlier works and the critique of pure reason that Kant announced in 1772, since he remained convinced for more than a decade that his critique contained "the key to the whole secret of metaphysics," despite the many challenges he faced as he tried to formulate arguments that would support his claims.

Kant's letter to Herz gives us a good indication of the direction he intended to take in 1772 and why it was so different from the other works he had planned. It shows that Kant thought he could locate the ground of the relation between representations and objects "in us"—he mentions "the nature of the soul" and "our inner activity" as possible sources—while avoiding the idealism often associated with this position.[95] From the beginning, Kant rejects the idealist claim that intellectual representations "bring the object itself into being."[96] Later, in the *Critique of Pure Reason*, he will reserve this relation to objects for the divine understanding, "which would not represent given objects, but through whose representation the objects would themselves at the same time be given or produced."[97] In the same passage, he makes it clear that divine understanding has nothing to do with human understanding, since human understanding "cannot form for itself the least concept of another possible understanding, either one that would intuit itself or one that, while possessing a sensible intuition, would possess one of a different kind than one grounded in space and time."[98] The distinction between divine and human understanding informs Kant's answer to the question concerning "the ground of the relation . . ." in his 1772 letter to Herz, leading him to ask "how a representation that refers to an object without being in any way affected by it can be possible."[99]

Kant suggests that mathematics offers a possible answer to this question, because it provides an unproblematic example of how intellectual representations can stand in a valid relation to their objects. Kant tells Herz the objects of mathematics are "quantities and can be represented as quantities only because it is possible for us to produce their mathematical representations."[100] This does not commit Kant to mathematical idealism, because he does not think the production of mathematical representations creates mathematical objects. In his inaugural dissertation, Kant argues that the production of mathematical representations merely actualizes mathematical concepts—numbers, figures—that already exist.[101] "By taking numerical units a given number of times," Kant thinks we construct representations that allow us to determine a priori the properties of the objects of our representations.[102] Because all of this takes place in pure intuition, and pure intuition belongs to the faculty of sensibility, there is no need to appeal to intellectual intuition to guarantee the correspondence between mathematical representations and their objects.[103] The construction of mathematical representations allows us to demonstrate a priori that our representations are valid.

Demonstrating the validity of our representations of nonmathematical objects is more troublesome. Kant writes "in the case of relationships involving qualities—as to how my understanding may form for itself concepts of things completely *a priori*, with which concepts the things must necessarily agree, and as to the possibility of such concepts, with which principles of experience must be in exact agreement and which nevertheless are independent of experience—this question, of how the faculty of the understanding achieves this conformity with the things themselves, is still left in a state of obscurity."[104] Kant rejects the Platonic idea of a "previous intuition of divinity," Malebranche's suggestion of a "stillcontinuing perennial intuition of this primary being," as well as Crusius's suggestion that there are "certain implanted rules for the purpose of forming judgments and ready-made concepts that God implanted in the human soul just as they had to be in order to harmonize with things" as possible explanations of the correspondence of intellectual representations and their objects.[105] While he specifically identifies Crusius's position as a "*deus ex machina*" that would "encourage all sorts of wild notions and every pious and speculative brainstorm," Plato and Malebranche are subject to the same objection, because they both appeal to intellectual intuition and divine intervention to explain the relation between representations and objects. Their accounts of that relationship fail, because their explanations are even more dubious than the relations they are trying to explain.

Instead of relying on intellectual intuition and divine intervention to establish the validity of the relation between representations and objects, Kant turns to the understanding itself. In his 1772 letter to Herz, he says "while I was searching in such ways for the sources of intellectual cognition, without which one cannot determine the nature and limits of metaphysics, I divided this science into its naturally distinct parts, and I sought to reduce the transcendental philosophy (that is to say, all concepts belonging to completely pure reason) to a certain number of categories, but not like Aristotle, who, in his ten predicaments, placed them side by side as he found them in a purely accidental juxtaposition. On the contrary, I arranged them according to the way they classify themselves by their own nature, following from a few fundamental laws of the understanding."[106] By reducing "all concepts belonging to completely pure reason" to a few categories, and then classifying these categories "according to the way they classify themselves by their own nature" as they follow from "a few fundamental laws of the understanding," Kant turns away from empiricist and idealist accounts of the validity of our representations that he had discussed earlier in his letter. In their place, he begins to develop an immanent account of the validity of that relation within the understanding. He begins to see that the pure concepts of the understanding are not simply representations of purely intelligible objects. They are categories that serve as the ground of valid representations of objects. Implicit in these claims is the view that Kant would later defend in the *Critique of Pure Reason*: the pure concepts of the understanding are the universal and necessary conditions of objectively valid representation.

Kant excuses himself from providing any more details about his insights into the categories in his letter to Herz, but he assures his former student that "so far as my essential purpose is concerned, I have succeeded and that now I am in a position to bring out a critique of pure reason that will deal with the nature of theoretical as well as practical knowledge—insofar as the latter is purely intellectual."[107] This claim is reminiscent of a claim Kant made in his June 7, 1771, letter to Herz, where he boasted that he had already "considered, weighed, and harmonized" everything he would need to make *The Bounds of Sensibility and Reason* a more conclusive and convincing statement of his views on metaphysics than his inaugural dissertation.[108] Yet there are a number of significant differences between Kant's claims about *The Bounds of Sensibility and Reason* in 1771 and the announcement of his critique of pure reason in 1772. First of all, they relate to his inaugural dissertation in very different ways. *The Bounds of Sensibility and Reason* was intended as a reformulation and extension of the inaugural dissertation, while the critique of pure reason represents an entirely new approach to metaphysics. The difference between these two approaches is also significant. Instead of trying to found metaphysics on the distinction between sensible and intellectual cognition, the critique of pure reason locates the ground of relations between representations and objects in the laws of the understanding.[109] This approach would ultimately lead Kant to conclude that the pure concepts of the understanding are the universal and necessary conditions of objectively valid representation. Before rushing headlong into Kant's defense of that position in the *Critique of Pure Reason,* however, it should be noted that Kant was already calling his answer to the question concerning "the ground of the relation" a critique in 1772. Even in his letter to Herz, Kant recognized that critique was the title best suited to an inquiry into the ground of the relation between representations and objects.

The significance of this fact has been overlooked by generations of Kant scholars, much to the detriment of our understanding of the 1772 letter to Herz and the *Critique of Pure Reason* that Kant published in 1781. If we wish to understand why Kant's philosophy is critical, we will have to look more closely at Kant's conception of critique and the answer it provides to the question concerning "the ground of the relation . . ."

## What Is a Critique of Pure Reason?

The *Critique of Pure Reason* that Kant published in 1781 includes a transcendental deduction of the pure concepts of the understanding, which provides a more sophisticated answer to the question concerning "the ground of the relation . . ." than Kant could have imagined in the early 1770s. Even if the deduction was not yet a glimmer in Kant's eye when he wrote to Herz, the structure of his 1772 letter makes it clear that Kant's attempts to answer the question concerning "the ground of the relation . . ." had already led him to abandon his plans for *The Bounds of Sensibility and Reason.* Kant was so confident that his critique of pure reason would definitively answer the question concerning "the ground of the relation . . ." that he never mentioned *The Bounds of Sensibility and Reason* again.

The 1772 letter to Herz gives us some idea what Kant thought his plans for *The Bounds of Sensibility and Reason* were missing. Kant planned to extend the method he had proposed in his inaugural dissertation in *The Bounds of Sensibility and Reason*, distinguishing what belonged to the facts, what belonged to sensibility, and what belonged to the understanding. After his debate with Herz in Königsberg, Kant realized that he could not use these distinctions to demonstrate that there is a valid relation between intellectual representations and their objects. It is simply beyond the scope of an account of the "bounds" (*Grenzen*) of sensibility and reason to explain how a valid relation between intellectual representation and its objects is constituted. This forced Kant to reexamine the "ground" (*Grund*) of the relation between representations and objects. In his 1772 letter to Herz, Kant maintains that the ground of the relation between representations and objects is something "in us." He even suggests it can be derived from "a few fundamental laws of the understanding."[110] But he also realizes that he will have to show how those laws give rise to valid relationships between intellectual representations and objects, without resorting to a theological deus ex machina or a special faculty of intellectual intuition.[111] The arguments for these claims took much longer to formulate than Kant anticipated. Indeed, they did not assume their final form until 1781 or 1787, depending on one's view of the (A) and (B) versions of the deduction of the first *Critique*. Yet they are predicated on the same insight that led Kant to abandon his plans for *The Bounds of Sensibility and Reason* in 1772: the "grounds" of objectively valid representation cannot be derived from the "bounds" of sensible and intellectual cognition.

Kant was so confident that the critique he announced in his letter to Herz in 1772 would definitively answer the question concerning "the ground of the relation . . ." that he called it "the key to the whole secret of metaphysics, hitherto still hidden from itself."[112] His subsequent correspondence with Herz describes the difficulties Kant faced as he tried "to formulate and carry out to completion an entirely new conceptual science."[113] It also helps us track the evolution of the structure of Kant's critique. In a letter to Herz from 1776, for example, Kant suggests that, in addition to a critique, a discipline, canon, and architectonic of pure reason will be necessary "to lay the road marks so that in the future one can know for sure whether one stands on the floor of true reason or on that of sophistry."[114] These claims are worthy of more attention than we can devote to them here, as are the studies of the *Duisburg Nachlaß*, which Wolfgang Carl regards as early "drafts" of the transcendental deduction, and the other documents from Kant's "silent decade," such as his lecture transcripts, notes, and fragments.[115] Unfortunately, none of these sources explain why Kant thought a "critique" of pure reason was necessary to answer the question concerning "the ground of the relation . . ."

Throughout his life, in all the works he published after he abandoned his plans for *The Bounds of Sensibility and Reason*, Kant remained committed to the idea that metaphysics must begin with a critique. In the first (A) and second (B) editions of the *Critique of Pure Reason* (1781/1787), as well as in the *Prolegomena to Any Future Metaphysics* (1783), the *Critique of Practical Reason* (1788), the *Critique of the Power of Judgment* (1790), and polemical pieces like *On a Discovery Whereby Any New Critique of Pure Reason Is to Be Made Superfluous by an Older One* (1790), *What Real Progress Has Metaphysics Made in Germany Since the Time of Leibniz and Wolff* (1793/1804), and his *Proclamation of the Imminent Conclusion of a Treaty of Perpetual Peace in Philosophy* (1796), Kant insists that the "critical path" is the only one that remains open to philosophy.[116] Yet he never takes the time, in any of these works, to answer the question "What is a critique of pure reason?" as clearly and compellingly as he answered the question "What is enlightenment?" in his article in the *Berlinische Monatsschrift* in 1784. For that reason, we will have to explore the various definitions and justifications Kant offers for his critique in greater detail in the chapters that follow.

# 4

# The Critique of Pure Reason Itself

Kant did not publish anything on metaphysics for eleven years after the publication of his inaugural dissertation. When he finally announced the publication of the *Critique of Pure Reason* in May 1781, Kant thought his struggles were over. He had finished a long and difficult project that he thought would "bring about a complete change of thinking in this part of human knowledge, a part of knowledge that concerns us so earnestly."[1] He even hoped his *Critique* might become popular, though the book's reception soon disabused him of that notion. Hamann told Herder that Kant's book "all comes down to pedantry and empty verbiage."[2] Mendelssohn set the *Critique of Pure Reason* aside until he was well enough to deal with such a "nerve-juice consuming book."[3] Christian Garve wrote a relatively sympathetic review for *Göttingischen Anzeigen von gelehrten Sachen*, but the text was rewritten by Johann Georg Heinrich Feder, who compared Kant to Berkeley and accused him of radical idealism.[4] As a result, Kant had to spend the next few years responding to reviews, restating his position in works like the *Prolegomena to Any Future Metaphysics* (1783), and revising the second (B) edition of the *Critique of Pure Reason* (1787). All of these works were meant to "to remove as far as possible those difficulties from which may have sprung several misunderstandings into which acute men, perhaps not without some fault on my part, have fallen in their judgment of this book."[5]

Today, few scholars believe Kant's responses to his critics and the revisions he made to his arguments left the substance of the first *Critique* unchanged. Most scholarly reflection on the difference between the first (A) and second (B) editions of the *Critique* has centered on the changes Kant made to the "Deduction of the Pure Concepts of the Understanding."[6] In the "Preface" to the first (A) edition of the *Critique of Pure Reason*, Kant said he knew "no investigations more important for getting to the bottom of that faculty we call the understanding, and at the same time for the determination of the rules and boundaries of its use" than those he had undertaken "in the second chapter of the Transcendental Analytic, under the title Deduction of the Pure Concepts of the Understanding."[7] Because Kant placed such great emphasis on the "Deduction," many regard the changes he made to its central arguments in the second (B) edition as the key to understanding the first *Critique*. Yet scholars have also noted the significance of the changes Kant made to the "Transcendental Aesthetic," the "Analytic of Principles," and the "Paralogisms of Pure Reason," as well as the addition of the "Refutation of Idealism" to the second (B) edition of the *Critique of Pure Reason*. Like the changes to the "Deduction," these changes appear to be more than mere improvements to the mode of presentation of the work.[8]

While many suppose them to be of still less philosophical consequence than the changes he made to other parts of the *Critique*, the differences in the way Kant defines the nature and purpose of his critique in the "Preface" and "Introduction" to the first (A) and the second (B) editions are as striking as those he made to any other part of the work. There are, of course, a number of similarities in the way Kant characterizes the critique of pure reason in the two editions. He uses many of the same adjectives to describe his critique, calling it strict (*streng*), just (*gerecht*), sober (*nüchtern*), acute (*scharf*), complete (*vollendet*), and mature (*reif*).[9] Kant also promises that his critique will treat its subject with completeness (*Vollständigkeit*), comprehensiveness (*Ausführlichkeit*), and certainty (*Gewißheit*) in both the first (A) and second (B) editions.[10] Yet there are also important differences in the definitions Kant proposes, the ways in which he tries to explain them, and the context in which he discusses them. By examining these differences, I hope to shed new light on Kant's understanding of his critique.

In the pages that follow, I will consider four different definitions of a critique of pure reason that appear in the prefaces and introductions to the first (A) and second (B) editions of the first *Critique*. The first is the identification of the critique of pure reason with a "court of justice" that will secure reason's rightful claims and dismiss its groundless pretensions in the "Preface" to the first (A) edition.[11] A second and quite different definition appears in the very next sentence, where Kant calls his critique "a critique of the faculty of reason in general, in respect of all the cognitions after which reason might strive independently of all experience, and hence the decision about the possibility and impossibility of a metaphysics in general, and the determination of its sources, as well as its extent and boundaries, all, however, from principles."[12] While this definition succinctly states the goals and methods of Kant's critique, he replaces it in the preface to the second (B) edition with another definition. Kant now says his critique is an "attempt to transform the accepted procedure of metaphysics . . . according to the model of the geometers and natural scientists."[13] Finally, in the introduction, Kant calls his critique "a special science . . . serving not for the amplification, but only for the purification of our reason, and for keeping it free of errors."[14] Examining these definitions will help us understand exactly what Kant's critique is and what it is supposed to do for metaphysics.

## A Court of Justice

The "Preface" to the first (A) edition of the *Critique of Pure Reason* is a peculiar document. It begins with an account of the peculiar fate of human reason, explaining how the descent of human reason into perplexity has made metaphysics a battlefield of endless controversies.[15] In the next few paragraphs, Kant presents a pseudo-historical and quasi-political narrative about how metaphysics lost its title as the queen of all the sciences.[16] After that, Kant announces the institution of a "court of justice, by which reason may secure its rightful claims while dismissing its groundless pretensions, and this not by mere decrees, but according to its own eternal and unchangeable laws."[17] Because he identifies that court with "the critique of pure reason itself," the context in which this claim appears is worth considering.

At the beginning of the "Preface," Kant describes the "peculiar fate" (*besondere Schicksal*) of human reason as a kind of tragedy in which human reason loses its natural innocence and becomes corrupted. "In the beginning," Kant says, human reason employed principles "whose use is unavoidable in the course of experience and at the same time sufficiently warranted by it."[18] But then it "takes refuge in principles that overstep all possible use in experience," because the questions it attempts to answer drive human reason to rise "ever higher, to more remote conditions."[19] As a result, human reason loses any touchstone in experience, against which it can test the validity of its principles.[20] Without realizing that it is "proceeding on the ground of hidden errors," human reason is eventually led into "obscurity and contradiction" by the principles it employs.[21] It is finally left in a state of perplexity because human reason does not know how to identify the source of its errors without appealing to experience.

At the end of his discussion of the peculiar fate of human reason, Kant says "the battlefield of these endless controversies is called metaphysics."[22] He moves on quickly, but we should pause when we realize that Kant's account of human reason's descent into "perplexity" (*Verlegenheit*) makes no reference to "controversies" (*Streitigkeiten*). It is reasonable to suppose that perplexity leads to controversy, especially when there are philosophers who compulsively argue about the things that perplex them. Their controversies would be especially pointless when the origins of their perplexity remain unclear. However, claiming that these controversies are "endless" (*endlosen*) is even more arresting than Kant's leap from perplexity into controversy. Calling the controversies that have made metaphysics a battlefield "endless" suggests that human reason can never escape its peculiar fate. It is condemned to fall into obscurity and contradiction whenever it appeals to principles that go beyond the bounds of experience, even though the appeal to those principles is both natural and necessary.[23] If that is really the fate of human reason, then it is more tragic than peculiar.

Kant's claim that metaphysics is a battlefield of endless controversy is all the more surprising, because he claims "there was a time when metaphysics was called the queen of all the sciences" in the very next sentence.[24] How could metaphysics have been the queen of all the sciences, if its tragic fate condemns it to fall into endless controversies? Kant answers that metaphysics deserved its title because of "the preeminent importance of its objects."[25] The objects of metaphysics—which he will later identify as God, freedom, and the immortality of the soul—surpass the bounds of all experience, but Kant does not condemn metaphysics for concerning itself with things of that nature.[26] The preeminent importance of the objects of metaphysics justifies and even necessitates the risk human reason runs in going beyond experience. That explains why human reason cannot be satisfied with principles whose use is sufficiently warranted by experience—they do not answer the questions that are most important to human reason. It also explains why Kant denies that empirical principles can play any role in metaphysics—in the "Introduction" to the *Critique of Pure Reason*, he explains that experience can give neither guidance nor correction with respect to the investigation of reason. [27] Consequently, we must rely on pure principles, which are "clear and certain for themselves, independently of experience" and "have the character of inner necessity" if we are to make any progress in metaphysics.[28] These principles are indispensable, because the objects with which metaphysics is concerned are not subject to the same conditions as ordinary experience.

Despite the importance of its objects and the necessity of its principles, Kant thinks metaphysics has lost the title of honor it once enjoyed. [29] Now "the queen proves despised on all sides" and "the matron, outcast and forsaken, mourns like Hecuba."[30] Kant blames the decline of metaphysics on the dogmatists, who he presents as the ministers to metaphysics, the queen of the sciences, in a kind of political drama.[31] Kant describes how the rule of the queen under the administration of the dogmatists was "despotic" and "gradually degenerated through internal wars into complete anarchy."[32] Kant also mentions skepticism, but denies that it played a significant role in the decline of metaphysics. Skeptics are characterized as "a kind of nomad who abhor all permanent cultivation of the soil," but there are "fortunately only a few" of them, so even if they "shattered civil unity from time to time," Kant says they "could not prevent the dogmatists from continually attempting to rebuild, though never according to a plan unanimously agreed to among themselves."[33]

It is the lack of agreement among the dogmatists and the internal conflicts of their administration, rather than the attacks of the skeptics or the struggles between dogmatism and skepticism, that caused metaphysics to lose its title of honor.

Kant does not deny that metaphysics could one day regain its title, but he does not think much of recent attempts to restore its authority. The restoration has "fallen back into the same old worm-eaten dogmatism, and thus into the same position of contempt out of which the science was to have been extricated."[34] The most troubling example is Locke's attempt to trace the genealogy of metaphysical principles back to "the rabble of common experience."[35] Kant is convinced that Locke's genealogy is false—he does not think the principles necessary to address the questions most important to human reason can be derived from experience—but he also thinks refuting Locke would do little to extricate metaphysics from the position of contempt into which it has fallen. Arguments with dogmatists are pointless battles in an endless war. They eventually give rise to "tedium and complete indifferentism."[36]

Kant calls tedium and indifferentism "the mother of chaos and night in the sciences."[37] They are far worse for metaphysics than either dogmatism or skepticism, because they deny the importance of the objects with which metaphysics is concerned. Still, Kant says they are "at the same time also the origin, or at least the prelude, of their incipient transformation and enlightenment."[38] When sciences have become obscure, confused, and useless, it is only reasonable to concern oneself with other things. Similarly, when metaphysics has become a battlefield of endless controversy, it makes sense to ignore the claims of dogmatists and skeptics. When metaphysics has lost its title of honor, tedium and indifferentism suggest that the "ripened power of judgment" of the age will "no longer be put off with illusory knowledge."[39] Kant is confident that this same power of judgment will force human reason to "take on anew the most difficult of all its tasks, namely that of self-knowledge." [40] And this will eventually lead human reason to recognize that metaphysics is a science "to whose objects human nature cannot be indifferent."[41]

Like Etienne Gilson, who said that philosophy always buries its undertakers, Kant thinks it is impossible to avoid metaphysics.[42] "However much they may think to make themselves unrecognizable by exchanging the language of the schools for a popular style," he writes, "these so-called indifferentists, to the extent that they think anything at all, always unavoidably fall back into metaphysical assertions, which they professed so much to despise."[43] This should not be surprising. Any claim we make about anything at all presupposes that something exists, that it is not contradictory, that it has a cause, and so forth. Consequently, our everyday understanding of ordinary objects depends on the same meta-physical principles as the most abstract philosophical system. But that is not the only reason metaphysics is unavoidable. Kant thinks human nature compels us to try to answer metaphysical questions, because of the preeminent importance of the things those questions are about.[44] He does not think we can afford to be indifferent to metaphysics, because its "objects" (*Gegenstandes*) and "results" (*Kenntnisse*) are essential for the well-being of humanity. Indeed, Kant says that indifferentism must be re-futed, because it is "directed precisely at those sciences whose results (if such are to be had at all) we could least do without."[45]

In order to determine whether the objects and results of metaphys-ics can ever be won, Kant introduces a court of justice (*Gerichtshof*) "by which reason may secure its rightful claims while dismissing all its ground-less pretensions, and this not by mere decrees, but according to its own eternal and unchangeable laws."[46] Judicial metaphors like this one were relatively common in the early modern period. In his author's replies to objections to the *Meditations on First Philosophy* (1641/1642), Descartes appeals to the judgment of the court of pious and orthodox theologians to show that his views were not threatening to religion; Hobbes says the laws of nature are only binding in the court of conscience in *On the Citizen* (1642); Spinoza brings his objections against anthropomorphic concep-tions of God before the bar of reason in the *Ethics* (1677); and, in the *Theodicy*, Leibniz maintains that the tribunal of reason can be used to confirm the authority of the holy scriptures.[47] Still, Kant's court differs from the other tribunals of early modern philosophy because he identi-fies his court with "the critique of pure reason itself."[48]

Kant does not explain how the critique of pure reason will secure reason's rightful claims and dismiss its groundless pretensions, but some answers can be found in his discussion of the peculiar fate of human reason, his account of the loss of metaphysics' title of honor, and his re-jection of indifferentism earlier in the "Preface." Kant's discussion of the peculiar fate of human reason shows that his critique cannot call reason back to principles whose use is sufficiently warranted by experience, be-cause the appeal to principles that transcend the bounds of experience is both natural and necessary for human reason. His account of metaphys-ics' lost title of honor proves that the critique of pure reason will not end the controversies that have made metaphysics a battlefield by mediating between the dogmatists and skeptics and giving each of their claims its due. Kant simply does not think the claims of skeptics are worth consider-ing, much less refuting. He also thinks an enlightened age demonstrates its "ripened power of judgment" by ignoring the claims of dogmatists. Finally, Kant's rejection of indifferentism shows that his court cannot dismiss metaphysics as one of the groundless pretensions of human reason. Kant's critique cannot do any of these things, because it is charged with a very different task. The context of Kant's "Preface" makes it clear that his critique must determine which errors are responsible for human reason's descent into perplexity and which principles can be used to secure the objects and results that we seek in metaphysics. That is what it means for Kant's critique to secure reason's rightful claims and dismiss its groundless pretensions.

A passage from the "Discipline of Pure Reason" in which Kant repeats the judicial metaphor he employs in the first (A) "Preface" can also help us understand how his critique will secure reason's rightful claims. Crucial for this passage is the distinction between the "rightful claims" (*gerechten Ansprüchen*) of reason and claims secured through "mere decrees" (*Machtsprüche*) that Kant mentions in the "Preface.'[49] In the "Discipline," Kant explains this distinction in greater detail, by describing the condition of human reason without a critique of pure reason. He compares this condition to the state of nature, which he characterizes as "a state of violence and injustice."[50] The only way to assert a claim in such a state is through "force" (*Macht*). Yet even superior force, which leads to victory in a contest of claims, is inadequate to guarantee the validity of decrees, since "each can take advantage of the exposure of his enemy" and renew the conflict when he is strong enough to overwhelm his opponents.[51] For this reason, Kant thinks a claim has to be asserted by "right" (*Recht*) rather than by "force" (*Macht*) if it is really to be made secure. In the "Preface," Kant says the critique of pure reason will determine the rightfulness of reason's claims through its own laws.[52] He expands on this claim in the "Discipline," where he says his critique is "set the task of determining and judging what is lawful in reason in general in accordance with the principles of its primary institution," "derives all decisions from the ground rules of its own constitution, whose authority no one can doubt," and "grants the peace of a state of law, in which we should not conduct our controversy except by due process."[53] Because it judges reason's claims according to "law" (*Gesetz*), in a way that is consistent with the "primary institutions" (*Grundsätzen*) and "ground rules" (*Grundregeln*) of reason, and through "due process" (*Prozeß*), Kant is confident that his critique will establish what is "rightful" (*gerecht*) and "lawful" (*rechtsam*) in reason's claims. He even boasts that the "verdict" (*Sentenz*) of his critique will bring an end to the "endless controversies" of metaphysics, leading to perpetual peace in philosophy![54]

Before concluding, I would like to point out the republicanism implicit in Kant's appeals to the rightfulness and lawfulness of reason's claims. Although he says metaphysics had been the queen of all the sciences before the internal conflicts of the dogmatist regime forced her to surrender her title, Kant does not actually claim that this title of honor should be returned to metaphysics. It could be argued that Kant meant to replace a failed philosophical monarchy and its despotic administration with a new republican metaphysics, governed by the rule of law, in the first *Critique*. His claim in the first (A) "Preface" that the critique of pure reason distinguishes reason's rightful claims from its groundless pretensions through "its own eternal and unchangeable laws" supports this reading, since Kant often describes monarchy as autocratic rule by violence (*Gewalt*), decree (*Machtsprüch*), and command (*Befehl*), while identifying republicanism with the self-government of rational beings through laws of their own making.[55] The passage from the "Discipline" also supports the republican interpretation of Kant's critique, because it argues that self-government belongs to "the original right of human reason, which recognizes no other judge than universal human reason itself, in which everyone has a voice."[56] Even Kant's reference to perpetual peace in the "Disciple" supports the republican interpretation of the critique of pure reason, since he says perpetual peace can only be achieved by a cosmopolitan federation of republican states in his late essay *Towards Perpetual Peace* (1795).[57] If Kant really did intend his critique to bring an end to the controversies that have made metaphysics a battlefield, as Kant suggests in the first (A) "Preface," in the "Discipline," and in his *Proclamation of the Imminent Conclusion of a Treaty of Perpetual Peace in Philosophy* (1796), then it should not be surprising that he would extend his republicanism to metaphysics as well as politics.[58]

## A Critique of the Faculty of Reason

Kant presents a second definition of the critique of pure reason in the sentence immediately following the one in which he defines his critique as a "court of justice." The second definition could be taken to clarify the first; yet the two definitions do not appear to have very much in common. In the first definition, Kant claims that the critique of pure reason is a court of justice that will secure reason's rightful claims and dismiss its groundless pretensions through its own eternal and unchangeable laws. In the second definition, Kant argues that his critique is not "a critique of books and systems," but a "critique of the faculty of reason in general, in respect of all the cognitions after which reason might strive **independently of all experience**, and hence the decision about the possibility or impossibility of a metaphysics in general, and the determination of its sources, as well as its extent and boundaries, all, however, from principles."[59] Although this second definition differs considerably from the first definition Kant proposes, it could be argued that it more accurately describes what a critique of pure reason is and does than the metaphor of a court of justice.

The first part of Kant's second definition, where he denies that his critique is "a critique of books and systems," is rather surprising. Few readers would leap from the claim that the critique of pure reason is a court of justice to the idea that it is a critique of books and systems, but Kant seems to have worried that they expected him to evaluate the works of other philosophers and point out their shortcomings.[60] He disabuses readers of this notion in the "Preface" to the first (A) edition and "Introduction" to the second (B) edition of the *Critique of Pure Reason*. Both texts affirm the distinction between "a critique of the faculty of human reason" and "a critique of the books and systems of pure reason" that Kant introduces in the first (A) "Preface.'[61] In the "Introduction" to the second (B) edition, Kant adds a remark that explains the relation between them. He says "a critique of the faculty of reason" provides "a secure touchstone for appraising the philosophical content of old and new works."[62] Without this touchstone, Kant says "the unqualified historian and judge assesses the groundless assertions of others through his own, which are equally groundless."[63] His reference to "the unqualified historian and judge" is significant, because it relates Kant's rejection of a critique of books and systems to the distinction between historical and philosophical cognition. In his lectures, Kant complains that studying the history of philosophy only teaches us what philosophers have said and written. Acquainting ourselves with the published works and stated opinions of philosophers might help us understand "the history of the use of our reason," but it cannot provide us with properly philosophical cognition.[64] Philosophical cognition involves knowledge of the nature of things, their grounds, and their consequences.[65] And Kant thinks that can only be achieved by actively philosophizing, by thinking for ourselves, and by working our own way through philosophical problems.[66] Consequently, we must go beyond historical accounts of what philosophers have said and written, if we are to judge the claims of philosophical books and systems.

Saying that the *Critique of Pure Reason* is more than a critique of books and systems does not really explain why Kant says his critique is a critique of "the faculty of reason in general."[67] Many readers will assume this is a reference to the faculty of reason that Kant distinguishes from the faculties of sensibility and the understanding in the "Transcendental Dialectic." There he says the faculty of reason is "the faculty of the unity of the rules of the understanding under principles" and claims that reason "never applies directly to experience to any object, but instead applies to the understanding, in order to give unity *a priori* through concepts to the understanding's manifold cognitions, which may be called the unity of reason."[68] In the first book of the "Dialectic," Kant goes on to say that "metaphysics has as the proper end of its investigation only three ideas: God, freedom, and immortality . . . the insight into these ideas would make theology, morals, and, through their combination, religion, thus the highest ends of our existence, dependent solely on the faculty of speculative reason and on nothing else."[69] It is of course possible that Kant had this conception of reason in mind when he called the critique of pure reason a critique of the faculty of reason in general in the first (A) "Preface," but we would be forced to exclude much of the a priori cognition that he tries so hard to demonstrate in the "Transcendental Aesthetic" and the "Transcendental Analytic" if we understood "the faculty of reason in general" as the faculty that Kant describes in the "Transcendental Dialectic."

Because Kant says his critique is "a critique . . . of the faculty of reason in general, in respect of all the cognitions after which reason might strive independently of all experience," a broader interpretation of the faculty of reason in the second definition is needed. Only this broader interpretation can account for the a priori cognition of the pure forms of intuition (space and time) and the pure concepts of the understanding (the categories) that Kant discusses in the "Transcendental Aesthetic" and "Transcendental Analytic."[70] This a priori cognition derives from the faculties of sensibility and the understanding, rather than the faculty of reason; yet there is evidence from the text that suggests Kant meant to include the a priori cognition originating in these faculties among the objects of his critique. In the "Introduction," Kant says reason is "the faculty that provides the principles of cognition *a priori*," which is a more general description of the faculty of reason than the one he presents in the "Dialectic," but which includes a priori cognition of the pure forms of sensible intuition and the pure concepts of the understanding.[71] Later, in the "Architectonic of Pure Reason," Kant also says that his critique can be called metaphysics, because it includes "the investigation of everything that can ever be cognized *a priori* as well as the presentation of that which constitutes a system of pure philosophical cognitions of this kind."[72] These remarks suggest that the critique of pure reason is addressed to all a priori cognition and not just the a priori cognition associated with the faculty of reason as it is described in the "Transcendental Dialectic."

Even if we adopt a broader interpretation of the faculty of reason, we must still determine why Kant's critique is concerned with "all the cognitions after which reason might strive **independently of all experi-**

ence."[73] Kant could have addressed his critique to the cognition we derive from experience, like many of his empiricist predecessors. Yet he takes on a more ambitious critique of the cognition that reason seeks independently of experience. His reasons become clear in the first section of the "Introduction," where he identifies cognition sought independently of experience as "*a priori* cognition."[74] A priori cognition is "clear and certain" and also possesses "true universality" and "inner necessity" that is lacking from the a posteriori cognition we derive from experience.[75] The fact that a priori cognition is not derived from experience and possesses clarity and certainty, universality and necessity does not mean that a priori cognition has nothing to do with experience. "Even among our experiences," Kant says, "cognitions are mixed in that must have their origin *a priori* and that perhaps serve only to establish connection among our representations of the senses."[76] We know this a priori cognition is a part of the cognition we derive from experience, because the concepts and judgments that we use to cognize an object are still present in our minds when we remove all the sensations that are produced when an object affects us.[77] While the content of that sensation is a posteriori, the concepts we use to think of the object, and which connect our representations to one another and give them order, must be a priori. Otherwise we would be forced to determine how the sensible qualities of an object go together before we could even think of that object. Because we cannot have an experience of an object about which we cannot think, a priori cognition is a universal and necessary condition of the possibility of experience.

In the "Introduction," Kant also says a critique of a priori cognition is necessary, because some of our cognitions "go beyond the world of the senses, where experience can give neither guidance nor correction."[78] Instead of warning us about transcendental illusion and the impossibility of knowing things in themselves, Kant reminds us of the importance of the objects with which these cognitions are concerned. He acknowledges that we take the object of these cognitions to be "far more preeminent in their importance and sublime in their final aim than everything that the understanding can learn in the field of appearances" and notes that "we would rather venture everything, even at the risk of erring, than give up such important investigations because of any sort of reservation or from contempt and indifference."[79] But he cautions his readers against making claims about these objects "on the credit of principles one does not know" and constructing a philosophical system out of them "without having first assured oneself of its foundation through careful investigations."[80] Before making any claims about objects that go beyond the world of experience, Kant thinks we must determine "how the understanding could come to all these cognitions *a priori* and what domain, validity, and value they might have," so that we do not fall into the endless controversies that plague the history of metaphysics.[81] The answers Kant's critique provides to these questions may not be reassuring to readers seeking support for claims about the nature of God, the freedom of the will, or the immortality of the soul. Yet they are necessary to avoid the perplexity into which human reason so often descends, when it tries to answer questions that "surpass the bounds of all experience."[82]

Kant's defense of a priori cognition as a condition of the possibility of experience and his rejection of a priori cognition of objects that transcend experience are indicative of a significant change in his views on metaphysics. This change does not have to do with a shift from ontology to epistemology, because Kant had regarded metaphysics as "the science of the first principles of our cognition" as early as his *New Elucidation of the First Principles of Metaphysical Cognition* (1755).[83] He defended the same view in his *Inquiry Concerning the Distinctness of the Principles of Natural Theology and Morality* (1764), where he says "metaphysics is nothing other than the fundamental principles of our cognition."[84] Kant does not specify that the principles of metaphysics are a priori in either the *New Elucidation* or the *Inquiry*, but his inaugural dissertation *On the Form and Principles of the Sensible and the Intelligible World* (1770) makes it very clear that a posteriori cognition derived from experience has no place in metaphysics.[85] Kant even says "the concepts met with in metaphysics are not to be sought in the senses," because metaphysics is "the philosophy which contains the *first principles* of the use of the *pure understanding*."[86] The first principles of the use of the pure understanding must be a priori, because Kant defines the understanding (*intelligentia, intellectus, rationalitas*) as "the faculty of a subject in virtue of which it has the power to represent things which cannot come before the senses of that subject."[87] Purely intellectual cognition, arising from a faculty that represents purely intelligible objects, which cannot be perceived through the senses—this is the caricature of a priori cognition that is most maligned by the empiricists, but it is the one that Kant defends in his inaugural dissertation, and he insists it is essential to metaphysics.

Kant's views had changed considerably by the time he published the *Critique of Pure Reason* in 1781. While he insisted that sensible and intellectual cognition had to be separated and denied that the first principles of the pure understanding have anything to contribute to sensible cognition in his inaugural dissertation, Kant now asserts that there is a priori cognition "mixed in among" our experience that makes it possible for us to cognize the object of our experience.[88] In the "Transcendental Aesthetic," he even argues that some of that a priori cognition is sensible, because he sees that "the pure form of sensible intuitions in general is to be encountered in the mind *a priori*, wherein all of the manifold of appearances is intuited in certain relations."[89] When Kant says, in the "Introduction" to the "Transcendental Logic," that cognition can only arise from the unification of intuitions and concepts, because "the understanding is not capable of intuiting anything and the senses are not capable of thinking anything," his rejection of the epistemology of his inaugural dissertation is almost complete.[90] Yet his commitment to the idea that metaphysics is a "pure" (*rein, purus*) science remains. His critique addresses a priori cognition, because that is the kind of cognition with which metaphysics is concerned. Throughout the critique, in both the "Transcendental Aesthetic" and the "Transcendental Logic," Kant dismisses questions about the matter of sensation and the empirical content of our cognition, because he is convinced that they are a posteriori, empirical cognitions derived from experience.[91] As such, they have no place in metaphysics, which contains only "the cognitions after which reason might strive **independently of all experience**."[92]

Kant promises that his survey of all the a priori cognition that belongs to metaphysics will render a decision about "the possibility or impossibility of a metaphysics in general."[93] He does not explain how his critique will determine the possibility or impossibility of metaphysics in the first (A) "Preface," but Kant devotes the third part of the *Prolegomena* to the question "How is metaphysics in general possible?"[94] There he argues that metaphysics differs from mathematics and natural science because it is concerned with "pure concepts of reason that are never given in any possible experience whatsoever" and "assertions whose truth or falsity cannot be confirmed or exposed by any experience."[95] This echoes Kant's claim that his critique is addressed to a priori cognition; yet what follows merely repeats Kant's distinction between categories ("pure concepts of the understanding," *reinen Verstandesbegriffen*) and ideas ("pure concepts of reason," *reinen Vernunftbegriffe*), reiterates the argument that they arise from different faculties, and summarizes the claims of the "Transcendental Dialectic" before concluding with a discussion of the boundaries of pure reason.[96] While these discussions help to clarify many of the problems Kant addresses in the *Critique of Pure Reason*, they do not explain why or how metaphysics is possible. Indeed, it is not until the very end of part 3 of the *Prolegomena* that he says anything that sounds like an answer to the question with which he began. In the very last sentence of the chapter, Kant says he has already answered the question about the possibility of metaphysics, because he has "ascended from the place where its use is actually given, at least in the consequences, to the grounds of its possibility."[97] Because the critique of pure reason proves that a priori cognition exists and also that this cognition is "constitutive and law-giving with respect to experience," metaphysics must be possible.[98]

In addition to surveying all the a priori cognition possessed by the faculty of reason and using it to demonstrate the possibility of metaphysics, Kant claims that his critique will determine the sources, extent, and boundaries of a priori cognition.[99] It is worth noting that Kant emphasizes the "sources" of a priori cognition in the second definition, relegating discussion of the "extent" and "boundaries" of our a priori cognition to a dependent clause. This makes sense, since Kant's critique is a critique of the faculty of reason, understood as the faculty of a priori cognition. It must show how a priori cognition arises from the faculties of sensibility, understanding, and reason. Kant undertakes this demonstration in the "Transcendental Aesthetic," where he tries to show that the pure forms of intuition must "lie ready in the mind *a priori*," as well as the "Transcendental Analytic," where he explains how the categories emerge spontaneously from the thinking of the understanding, using the "logical forms of judgment" as a "guiding thread."[100] He argues that the pure concepts of reason emerge from the inferences of reason in the "Transcendental Dialectic," but here Kant touches on questions of the boundaries and extent of reason's a priori cognition. Unlike the pure forms of intuition and the pure concepts of the understanding, which are a priori cognitions that are "mixed into" experience, a pure concept of reason is a transcendental idea that goes beyond the bounds of possible experience.[101] This poses a special problem, because Kant uses the necessity of the a priori cognitions of sensibility and the understanding for experience to prove that our cognition of objects is objectively valid. Transcendental ideas go beyond the bounds of possible experience, so they do not possess the same necessity, leaving us without any "touchstone for their correctness."[102] They are all the more dangerous because of the "natural and unavoidable dialectic" through which reason extends the application of its concepts to the unconditioned totality of all experience, producing paralogisms, antinomies, and merely speculative ideals along the way.[103] Kant calls these errors transcendental illusions and warns that they will lead to "the death of a healthy philosophy," unless they are "checked by criticism" and "put to the fiery test of critique."[104]

Despite his warnings about transcendental illusion, we should not mistake Kant's attempt to define the boundaries of a priori cognition for the primary objective of his critique. This mistake was common among Analytic and Continental philosophers in the twentieth century, united as they were by their shared distaste for metaphysics.[105] By emphasizing Kant's account of the boundaries of a priori cognition, they tried to enlist him in their own campaigns to eliminate or overcome metaphysics.[106] But this effort led them to ignore the emphasis Kant places on the source of a priori cognition in the faculty of reason. It also leads them to forget his account of the extent of a priori cognition, which may not reach as far as the pure concepts of reason, but certainly includes the pure forms of intuition, the pure concepts of the understanding, and the principles Kant enumerates in the "Analytic of Principles." As we will see in the next chapter, Kant's critique even extends a priori cognition to the practical use of pure reason, which cannot be constrained by the bounds of sense without contradicting itself.[107] That is quite enough for Kant to demonstrate the validity of transcendental idealism, secure the principles of theoretical and practical philosophy, and make metaphysics a science.

Finally, a few words about the last words in Kant's second definition are in order. After explaining that his critique is not "a critique of books and systems," but "a critique of the faculty of reason in general, in respect of all the cognition after which reason might strive independently of all experience, and hence the decision about the possibility or impossibility of metaphysics in general, and the germination of its sources, as well as its extent and boundaries," Kant claims that everything contained in his critique will be derived from principles.[108] His appeal to principles (*Principien*) is intriguing, since Kant says he will refer to reason as "the faculty of principles" in the "Introduction" to the "Transcendental Dialectic."[109] Yet he often refers to principles in parts of the *Critique of Pure Reason* that have nothing to do with the faculty of reason. At the beginning of the second chapter of the "Analytic of Principles," for example, Kant mentions "the principles of the transcendental aesthetic" and calls the principle of contradiction "the principle of all analytic cognition," even though they have nothing to do with the faculty of reason. Given the latitude with which Kant employed the language of "principles," it seems wise not to impose such a strict interpretation on the second definition. In the second definition, Kant's promise to derive everything in his critique from principles is best taken as an elaboration of the claim that the critique of pure reason will secure reason's rightful claims and dismiss its groundless pretensions, "not by mere decrees but according to its own eternal and unchangeable laws" in the first definition.[110] Kant's appeal to the laws of reason in the first definition shows that he is more interested in "right" (*Recht*) than "might" (*Macht*), while his appeal to principles in the second definition shows that his critique does not proceed in an arbitrary and haphazard fashion, like the "dogmatically enthusiastic lust for knowledge" that can only be satisfied through "magical powers."[111]

## A Transformed Procedure

In the "Preface" to the second (B) edition of the *Critique of Pure Reason,* Kant abandons the judicial metaphor for the critique of pure reason that he employs in the first definition he proposes in the "Preface" to the first (A) edition.[112] He also steps back from the claim he makes in the second definition, where he calls his critique a critique of the faculty of human reason. Instead, Kant calls his critique an "attempt to transform the accepted procedure of metaphysics, undertaking an entire revolution according to the example of the geometers and natural scientists."[113] He thought the revolutionary transformation that his critique proposed would finally make metaphysics the science it had struggled for so long to become.

To understand this transformation, it is helpful to remember that Kant placed a great deal of emphasis on the relationship between mathematics, natural science, and metaphysics in the *Prolegomena to Any Future Metaphysics That Will Be Able to Come Forward as Science* (1783). The *Prolegomena* was published in the years between the publication of the first (A) and second (B) editions of the first *Critique*. It was supposed to present a popular and accessible account of the critical philosophy that would "convince all of those who find it worthwhile to occupy themselves with metaphysics that it is unavoidably necessary to suspend their work for the present, to consider all that has happened until now as if it had not happened, and before all else to pose the question: *whether such a thing as metaphysics is even possible at all.*"[114] In the course of answering that question, Kant points out that metaphysics must be possible if mathematics and physics are possible, because the possibility of pure mathematics and pure natural science depends on metaphysics.[115] Kant then uses the actuality of pure mathematics and pure natural science to argue that a scientific metaphysics is possible because of the actuality of his critique.[116]

The "Preface" to the second (B) edition of the *Critique of Pure Reason* has many things in common with the discussion of the possibility of pure mathematics and pure natural science in the *Prolegomena*. It refers to the same sciences in the same order, though it begins with a discussion of the scientific status of logic, which is not discussed in the *Prolegomena*. Another significant difference is that Kant contrasts the scientific achievements of logic, mathematics, and natural science with the scientific failures of metaphysics in the second (B) "Preface," instead of showing how the possibility of these sciences depends on metaphysics, as he had in the *Prolegomena*.[117] By showing that logic, mathematics, and natural science are already sciences, and, at least in the case of logic and mathematics, have been since antiquity, Kant is able to drive home the point that the accepted procedures of metaphysics need to be changed. Kant maintains that metaphysics is "older than all the other sciences" and "would remain even if all the others were swallowed up by an all-consuming barbarism," but the methods it has employed have not allowed it to advance beyond "a mere groping, and what is the worst, a groping among mere concepts."[118] In the second (B) "Preface," Kant argues that his critique will bring this groping to an end by following the example of mathematics and natural science.

In the short histories of logic, mathematics, and natural science that follow, Kant explains how logic was the first to become a science, because it had the easiest and most certain path to follow.[119] "Since the time of Aristotle," Kant claims, logic "has not had to go a single step backwards, unless we count the abolition of a few dispensable subtleties or the more distinct determination of its presentation, which improvements belong more to the elegance than to the security of that science."[120] That is because logic concerns only "the formal rules of all thinking."[121] Because it is solely concerned with the understanding and the form of its thinking, however, logic can be no more than "the outer courtyard, as it were, of the sciences."[122] Sciences like mathematics, physics, and metaphysics resemble logic, inasmuch as they are rational sciences in which something "must be cognized *a priori*," but they also differ from logic, insofar as they concern different kinds of objects. There are material conditions for the cognition of the objects of mathematics, natural science, and metaphysics that go beyond the formal rules of the use of the understanding.[123] The determination of these objects and their conditions requires the understanding to consider something other than itself, even when the object in question is determined entirely a priori. The means of achieving this determination, the determination of an object other than the understanding by the understanding entirely a priori, poses unique difficulties for sciences like mathematics, natural science, and metaphysics.

Mathematics was able to make swifter progress as a science than natural science or metaphysics because it is able to construct its objects for itself. Kant thinks the properties of mathematical objects follow directly from the rules of their construction, so they can be derived from the construction of figures in pure intuition.[124] However, this does not mean the properties of mathematical objects are analytically contained in the concepts of those objects. If the properties of mathematical objects were contained in their concepts, then mathematicians could determine the properties of mathematical objects simply by examining the content of those concepts. They would not have to construct figures in order to know which properties belonged to mathematical objects. Kant rejects this possibility, following a long tradition in mathematical practice that holds that mathematicians must demonstrate which properties belong to objects by actually constructing their figures. However, Kant also broke with that tradition by arguing that one could demonstrate the properties that belong to a mathematical object by exhibiting "*a priori* the intuition which corresponds to the concept" instead of drawing a complex figure with paper and pencil.[125] In Kant's view, the simplicity of this procedure allowed "the happy inspiration of a single man" to bring about a revolution in mathematical thinking very early in its history, so "the road to be taken onward could no longer be missed, and the secure course of a science was entered on and prescribed for all time and to an infinite extent."[126]

Natural science was not able to become a science as early as logic or mathematics because it had to deal with nature, which is something very different from the formal laws of the understanding and the construction of figures in pure intuition. Yet Kant says natural science became a science by applying the same insights that allowed logic and mathematics to become sciences. According to Kant, natural science became a science when it realized that "reason has insight only into what it itself produces according to its own design."[127] This insight was the foundation for the experimental method, which encouraged natural scientists to approach their object "with its principles in one hand, according to which alone the agreement among appearances can count as laws, and, in the other hand, the experiments thought out in accordance with these principles."[128] Kant also says a scientist must approach nature "not like a pupil, who has recited to him whatever the teacher wants to say, but like an appointed judge who compels witnesses to answer the questions he puts to them." This claim is striking, not just because of the return of the judicial metaphors Kant employed in the "Preface" to the first (A) edition, but also because of the rationalism of Kant's understanding of natural science. Empiricists claim that the sciences take what is given in experience and then abstract general principles from those experiences. Some empiricists think scientific theories are produced by imaginatively rearranging the contents of experience, so that they form elaborate systems.[129] Yet Kant does not think the revolution that made natural science a science begins with experience; on the contrary, he thinks natural science only became a science when it started using experience to test rational principles that had been formulated independently of experience.

Kant thought metaphysics could follow a course similar to the one natural science had followed, but he was also aware of the differences between natural science and metaphysics.[130] Because "propositions of pure reason . . . admit of no test by experiment with their objects," he argues metaphysics can only experiment with "concepts and principles."[131] If we assume these concepts and principles a priori, Kant says, "by arranging the latter so that the same objects can be considered from two different sides, on the one side as objects of the senses and the understanding for experience, and on the other side as objects that are merely thought at most for isolated striving beyond the bounds of experience," then we will find "there is agreement with the principle of pure reason when things are considered from this twofold standpoint, but that an unavoidable conflict of reason with itself arises with a single standpoint."[132] In one sense this is a thought experiment analogous to many other thought experiments in the history of early modern science. But it is worth noting that Kant's experiment is solely concerned with the conditions under which concepts, principles, and experience can be made to agree in principle, entirely a priori, without relying on experience or a posteriori cognition derived from experience. This is consistent with Kant's claim that metaphysics is solely concerned with "the cognitions after which reason might strive independently of all experience" in the first (A) "Preface," but it is noticeably different from experiments in the natural sciences, which apply principles to experience in order to test the validity of scientific explanations.[133]

The experiment Kant uses to determine the a priori conditions under which concepts, principles, and experience agree has come to be known as Kant's Copernican revolution. Yet the phrase "Copernican revolution" does not appear anywhere in the second (B) "Preface."[134] Kant calls the change he plans to bring about "revolutionary" and compares his argument to "the first thoughts of Copernicus, who, when he did not make good progress in the explanation of the celestial motions if he assumed that the entire celestial host revolves around the observer, tried to see if he might not have greater success if he made the observer revolve and left the stars at rest," but this is merely an analogy for the critique of pure reason, which Kant calls "a transformation in the accepted procedure of metaphysics."[135] He goes on to boast that his critique will bring about "an entire revolution" in metaphysics, "according to the example of the geometers and natural scientists."[136]

Kant presents the transformation in the accepted procedure of metaphysics and the scientific revolution brought about by his critique "merely as a hypothesis."[137] This is curious, because it contradicts his declaration in the first (A) "Preface" that "anything that even looks like a hypothesis is a forbidden commodity, which should not be put for sale at even the lowest price, but must be confiscated as soon as it is discovered."[138] Kant's attitude towards hypotheses had apparently softened between 1781 and 1787, perhaps because of his work on the *Metaphysical Foundations of Natural Science* (1786). And though he assures readers that the hypothesis proposed by his critique will be "proved not hypothetically but rather apodictically from the constitution of our representations of space and time and from the elementary concepts of the understanding," Kant readily admits that it will not be proven in the "Preface."[139] Readers would have to make their way through the text of the *Critique of Pure Reason* to understand why his critique succeeds. They might even have to wait until Kant had carried out his plans for "the metaphysics of nature and morals," which he regarded as the final "confirmation of the correctness of the critique both of theoretical and practical reason."[140]

Despite the incompleteness of his arguments in the second (B) "Preface," Kant presents an outline of the course his critique will take. Like the Copernican hypothesis that Galileo discusses in the *Dialogue on the Two Chief World Systems*, the hypothesis proposed by Kant's critique is controversial. It flies in the face of traditional metaphysics, which assumes that "all our cognition must conform to the objects."[141] Kant thinks metaphysics has come to nothing by assuming that our cognition must conform to objects, so he is willing to take the opposite assumption—"objects must conform to our cognition"—as a new experimental hypothesis.[142] This hypothesis is counterintuitive, like the Copernican claim that the Earth revolves around the Sun. It is also easily misunderstood, leading many to assume that Kant's idealism is more radical than the transcendental idealism he actually defends.[143] Still, Kant thinks metaphysics will be better able to demonstrate the possibility of a priori cognition by assuming "objects must conform to our cognition" than it had under the assumptions of traditional metaphysics.[144] And he tries to prove the superiority of his critical hypothesis by applying the traditional hypothesis and the critical hypothesis to intuitions, concepts, and objects of pure reason in the paragraphs that follow.

When the traditional hypothesis is applied to intuition, Kant thinks it fails to produce a priori cognition. "If intuition has to conform to the constitution of objects," he writes, "then I do not see how we can know anything of them *a priori*."[145] Intuition would have to be derived from experience of the object in order to conform to that object. And that would make our intuition of that object a posteriori. Kant thinks the critical hypothesis produces better results: "If the object (as an object of the senses) conforms to the constitution of our faculty of intuition, then I can very well represent that possibility to myself."[146] This is reasonable, because nothing could be given through the senses unless we already possessed a faculty of sensible intuition.[147] The possibility of sensible intuition is therefore determined by the faculty of sensible intuition. Moreover, this faculty can be considered a kind of a priori cognition, since it precedes any intuition that is actually given in experience. Kant even thinks it makes our receptivity to what is given in sensible intuition possible, because it contains the formal conditions under which sensible intuition is given.[148]

The results are similar when the traditional hypothesis and the critical hypothesis are applied to the understanding and its concepts. Kant thinks the understanding is more fundamental than the faculty of intuition, because intuitions have to be referred "as representations" to something "as their object" by the understanding.[149] In order to refer intuitions to objects, we must assume either "that the concepts through which I bring about this determination also conform to the objects" or "that the objects, or what is the same thing, the *experience*, in which alone they can be cognized (as given objects) conforms to those concepts."[150] The assumption that our concepts conform to objects, which corresponds to the traditional hypothesis, leads to the same difficulty Kant faced when he assumed that intuitions conform to objects: a priori cognition of objects is impossible, because we must derive our concepts from objects and that can only be achieved a posteriori, after we have experience of objects. Therefore, no a priori cognition is possible if we follow the traditional hypothesis.[151] Kant thinks the critical hypothesis, the assumption that objects must conform to our concepts, fares much better. The critical hypothesis provides "an easier way out of the difficulty, since experience itself is a kind of cognition requiring the understanding."[152] The idea that experience is a kind of cognition is important, because it means that objects of experience must also be objects of thought. So, in order to experience an object, I must be able to think of it, and in order to think of that object, I must have a concept of it. That requires me to presuppose pure concepts of the understanding "in myself, before any object is given to me, hence *a priori*."[153] This confirms the critical hypothesis, because it makes the pure concepts of the understanding the a priori condition of any cognition we might have of any object we might experience.[154]

Applying the critical hypothesis to intuitions and concepts shows just how much progress can be made in metaphysics when we abandon the traditional hypothesis. Yet Kant is still concerned about one of the consequences that seem to follow from his experiment. When we apply the critical hypothesis to problems like God, freedom, and the immortality of the soul, Kant thinks we encounter a contradiction that is both "a splendid touchstone of what we assume as the altered method of our way of thinking" and a "check" on the extension of metaphysical principles "beyond the bounds of possible experience."[155] He explains some of the reasons for this contradiction in a footnote, where he argues that objects must be considered "from two different sides."[156] When we think of objects as both "objects of the senses and understanding" and "objects that are merely thought," Kant thinks "there is agreement with the principle of pure reason."[157] But we confront "an unavoidable conflict of reason with itself" whenever we consider an object from a single standpoint.[158] This means that every object of possible experience must be able to be thought and every object of thought must also be an object of possible experience. The idea that an object of possible experience could not be thought is obviously absurd, since the object in question would have to be logically impossible to be unthinkable. No object of possible experience can be logically impossible, so the correspondence of "objects of the senses and the understanding" and "objects that are merely thought" makes sense. The conclusion that every object of thought be an object of possible experience is more troublesome, because it suggests that an object cannot be thought unless it is also possible for that object to be given in experience. If an object that cannot be given in experience also cannot be thought, then metaphysics must be restricted to the "boundaries of possible experience."[159]

Restricting metaphysics to the "boundaries of possible experience" seems to pose a threat to practical philosophy, because it excludes the possibility of determining the will through pure practical reason. That possibility is central to the *Groundwork of the Metaphysics of Morals* (1785), where Kant argues that morality requires the will to be determined by pure practical reason, rather than sensible intuition or inclination.[160] Because Kant thinks reason necessarily contradicts itself whenever it attempts to go beyond the bounds of possible experience, he must show that pure practical reason does not fall into that contradiction when it determines the will. Kant has various ways of addressing this problem in his practical philosophy, most of which follow from the demonstration of the possibility of freedom in the "Antinomy of Pure Reason."[161] He refers to these arguments in the second "Preface" when he affirms that it is indeed possible for human reason to determine "the transcendent rational concept of the unconditioned, in such a way as to reach beyond the boundaries of all possible experience, in accordance with the wishes of metaphysics."[162] Yet Kant also insists that this determination is only possible "from a practical standpoint."[163]

If the objects of speculative or theoretical philosophy cannot be determined through pure reason alone, then Kant thinks the concepts of the "thing in itself" and the "unconditioned" have to be excluded from metaphysics.[164] Metaphysics has to deny knowledge of things in themselves, because they cannot be considered objects of the senses and the understanding. Considering them as objects of the senses and the understanding would be contradictory, since every object of the senses and the understanding is conditioned by the cognitive faculties we use to sense or think of them. Things in themselves have to be unconditioned by our cognitive faculties to be "in themselves," so we can only know them if it is possible to think of them solely as objects of reason. And even that might not be possible, since considering things in themselves as objects of reason seems to make them "beings of reason" rather than things in themselves.[165] That point is, however, immaterial for Kant. What matters is that things in themselves cannot be regarded as objects of the senses and the understanding, which means they cannot even be thought without contradiction, according to the footnote in the second (B) "Preface" to the *Critique of Pure Reason.*

If reason cannot consider things in themselves without contradiction, then the only reasonable conclusion is the one Kant draws: "Our representation of things as they are given to us does not conform to these things as they are in themselves but rather that these objects as appearances conform to our way of representing."[166] This conclusion marks a considerable change in the accepted procedure of metaphysics, because the traditional hypothesis assumes that our representations conform to objects, no matter what kind of objects they are. Whether objects are objects of the senses, the understanding, or pure reason does not matter for traditional metaphysics, so long as our representations can be made to correspond to the objects they are supposed to represent. Kant rejects this assumption, but he does not insist that the objects of pure reason must conform to "our way of representing." In fact, he argues that they cannot be made to conform to our cognition. If our cognitive faculties require us to consider objects from two different sides—as objects of the senses and the understanding and objects of reason—then there may be some objects that cannot be made to conform to our cognition. And if it is impossible for us to think of those objects as they are in themselves without contradiction, then metaphysics has nothing to tell us about those objects.

Although it restricts metaphysics to "the bounds of possible experience," the critical hypothesis confirms that a priori cognition of intuition (pure intuition) and concepts (pure concepts of the understanding) is possible. This is not inconsistent, because pure intuition and the pure concepts of the understanding are not objects of pure reason. They are the universal and necessary conditions of the possibility of experience. The arguments supporting that conclusion are not presented until the "Transcendental Aesthetic" and the first division of the "Transcendental Logic," but Kant assures us that that the experiment undertaken in his critique "succeeds as well as we could wish."[167] This is significant, because it proves that "we can cognize of things a priori only what we have put into them."[168] Just as mathematics constructs its objects in pure intuition and natural science formulates the principles that guide its experiments, metaphysics generates for itself the a priori principles that make experience possible. It cannot abstract them from experience, because that would make them a posteriori. Metaphysics is concerned solely with a priori cognition—the conditions under which it is possible, in principle, for concepts, principles, and experience to agree—so it must derive its principles a priori from the faculties of sensible intuition and the understanding. Once it has done that, Kant says, metaphysics will be able to "fully embrace the entire field of cognitions belonging to it and thus can complete its work and lay it down for posterity as a principal framework that can never be enlarged, since it has to do solely with principles and the limitations of their use, which are determined by the principles themselves."[169]

## A Propaedeutic to a System That Does Not Exist?

The last definition of a critique of pure reason that I will consider in this chapter can be found in the "Introduction" to the first (A) and second (B) editions of the first *Critique*.[170]

After noting that reason is "the faculty that provides the principles of cognition *a priori*" and "contains the principles for cognizing something entirely a priori," Kant says that "a system of pure reason" could be constructed through the "exhaustive application" of the "sum total of all those principles in accordance with which all pure *a priori* cognition can be acquired and actually brought about."[171] Constructing such a system "requires a lot, and it is still an open question whether such an amplification of our cognition is possible at all and in what cases it would be possible," so Kant prefers to regard his critique as a "special science" devoted to "the mere estimation of pure reason, of its sources and boundaries."[172] As a "special science," the critique of pure reason would serve as a "propaedeutic" to the system of pure reason, but it would not have to contain all the concepts and principles that would have to be included in that system.

The definition Kant proposes in the "Introduction" limits the scope of his critique. While he called the critique of pure reason a "critique of the faculty of reason in general, in respect of all the cognitions after which reason might strive independently of all experience" in the "Preface" to the first (A) edition, he acknowledges in the "Introduction" that there is some a priori cognition that lies beyond the scope of his critique.[173] Kant explains what kind of a priori cognition he has omitted from his critique in the *Leitfaden* chapter of the "Analytic of Concepts," where he tries to show how the pure concepts of the understanding can be derived from the logical forms of judgment. In the *Leitfaden* chapter, Kant admits that there are numerous "pure derivative concepts" that can be added to the list of "true ancestral concepts of pure understanding" that he presents in the "Table of Categories."[174] These derivative concepts can be produced by combining the fundamental "ancestral concepts" with one another or with "the *modis* of sensibility."[175] And while Kant says he would like to be in possession of a complete list of the pure derivative concepts, he leaves their enumeration for a later work. "In a system of pure reason one could rightly demand these of me," he writes, "but here they would only distract us from the chief point of the investigation by arousing doubts and objections that can well be referred to another occasion without detracting from our essential aim."[176] Kant concludes that it is sufficient to mention that such pure derivative concepts are possible, but denies that he is under any obligation to catalog them in his critique, because a critique of pure reason is solely concerned with "the ancestral concepts that comprise the pure cognition in question."[177]

The limitations Kant imposed on his critique have significant consequences for his understanding of system, but they also affect his conception of transcendental philosophy. A few sentences after he defines the critique of pure reason as a propaedeutic to the system of pure reason in the "Introduction," Kant says that transcendental cognition is "occupied not so much with objects but rather with our *a priori* concepts of objects."[178] He goes on to say that "a system of such concepts would be called transcendental philosophy," but denies that this philosophy is contained in the *Critique of Pure Reason*. Kant realizes that "such a science would have to contain completely both analytic as well as synthetic *a priori* cognition," so he claims it is "too broad in scope" for his "transcendental critique."[179] Again, Kant limits the scope of his critique, claiming it only needs to go "as far as is indispensably necessary in order to provide insight into the principles of *a priori* synthesis in their entire scope, which is our only concern."[180] And while he insisted that the *Critique of Pure Reason* contains "everything that constitutes transcendental philosophy," and even includes "the complete idea of transcendental philosophy," he is forced to admit that his critique is "not yet this science itself."[181]

Kant hoped to supplement the contributions of his critique in a work called *The Metaphysics of Nature*, which would contain "a system of pure (speculative) reason" and complete the "transcendental philosophy" he had promised.[182] In the "Preface" to the first (A) edition, Kant says he could not include all the contents of this system in the first *Critique*, because he first had to "display the sources and conditions of its possibility, and needed to clear and level a ground that was completely overgrown" before proceeding in the *Metaphysics of Nature*, which would enumerate all the derivative concepts he had to omit from his critique and demonstrate analytically what he had already proved synthetically.[183] Because he never completed the *Metaphysics of Nature*, the limitations Kant imposed on the scope of his critique had fateful consequences. Karl Leonhard Reinhold seized on the claim that the *Critique of Pure Reason* was only a propaedeutic to argue that Kant's system was incomplete.[184] And he used the incompleteness of Kant's system to position his own *Elementarphilosophie*, elaborated in works like *Attempt at a New Theory of the Human Faculty of Representation* (1789) and *On the Foundation of Philosophical Knowledge* (1791), as the only possible foundation for the sciences.[185] Fichte adopted this strategy as well, arguing that his *Wissenschaftslehre* would complete the system of pure reason that neither Kant nor Reinhold had been able to provide.[186] Kant responded to these charges indignantly in his *Declaration concerning Fichte's Wissenschaftslehre* (1799), declaring that he finds their assumption that he only intended to publish "a *propaedeutic* to transcendental philosophy and not the actual system of this philosophy" to be "incomprehensible," since he had clearly indicated that he intended to complete the system for which his critique was to serve as a propaedeutic.[187]

# 5

# What Sort of Treasure Is It?

Most of Kant's critics focused on the claims of the "Transcendental Aesthetic" and the "Transcendental Analytic" in the debates following the publication of the *Critique of Pure Reason* (1781/1787). They accused Kant of denying the reality of space and time, exaggerating the difference between the pure forms of intuition and the pure concepts of the understanding, giving specious arguments for the necessity of a priori categories and synthetic a priori judgments, and endorsing radical idealism.[1] Kant responded to these accusations with peevish defenses of the doctrines to which his critics had objected. He explained again and again that he did not deny the reality of space and time, even though he affirmed their transcendental ideality; he asserted that there are fundamental differences between the faculty of sensibility and the faculty of understanding, despite the fact that cognition arises from the unification of intuitions and concepts; he defended the objective validity of the categories and the necessity of synthetic a priori judgments; and he tried repeatedly to explain the differences between Berkley's dogmatic idealism, the problematic idealism of Descartes, and his own transcendental idealism.[2] At one point, Kant even considered abandoning the language of the "transcendental" idealism, because it seemed to invite exaggeration and misunderstanding.[3] Since his first critics focused their attention elsewhere, Kant generally did not feel the need to defend the claim that a critique of pure reason was needed to demonstrate the possibility of metaphysics and set it on the sure path of science.

By the time Reinhold and Fichte claimed that his critique was a propaedeutic to a system that did not exist, Kant was in no position to complete the *Metaphysics of Nature* he had promised in the first (A) edition of the first *Critique*. He was already worried about his ability to finish this work when he wrote the "Preface" to the second (B) edition, where he warns that "I must proceed frugally with my time if I am to carry out my plan of providing the metaphysics both of nature and of morals, as confirmation of the correctness of the critique both of theoretical and practical reason."[4] Twelve years later, when he was in his mid-seventies, Kant was even more concerned. He had brought his critical philosophy to an end in the *Critique of the Power of Judgment* (1790).[5] And he had managed to complete the progression from the *Groundwork of the Metaphysics of Morals* (1785) and the *Critique of Practical Reason* (1788) to the *Metaphysics of Morals* (1797) just as he had promised.[6] Yet there is little evidence that he had made similar progress on the *Metaphysics of Nature*. Kant had become preoccupied with "the unpaid bill of my uncompleted philosophy," but the gap he tried to close in his system was not the enormous opening left by the absence of the *Metaphysics of Nature*.[7] Instead, it was the gap between the science of physics and his *Metaphysical Foundations of Natural Science* (1786), which he had described as a "mere application" of the principles of the *Metaphysics of Nature*, even though he had not yet written the work in which he intended to lay out those principles.[8] The delays, deferrals, and detours that prevented Kant from completing both the *Metaphysics of Nature* and the transition from *Metaphysical Foundations of Natural Science* to physics seem to have contributed to the view that Kant's critique was a propaedeutic without a system, which was common among the early German idealists. Although Kant denied that he had only intended to publish a propaedeutic in his *Declaration Concerning Fichte's Wissenschaftslehre* (1799), his failure to publish the rest of his system left his critics unsatisfied.[9]

Although Kant was not always willing to defend his conception of critique, there are a few instances in which he argued forcefully for its originality, utility, and necessity. The first can be found in the "Appendix" to the *Prolegomena to Any Future Metaphysics* (1783), where Kant insists that a critique of pure reason is necessary, if metaphysics is to become a science. The second is a passage from the "Preface" to the second (B) edition of the *Critique of Pure Reason*, where he explains the negative and positive utilities of his critique. The third is *On a Discovery Whereby Any New Critique of Pure Reason Is to Be Made Superfluous by an Older One* (1790), where Kant tries to refutes Eberhard's claim that he had merely repeated the conclusions of an earlier Leibnizian critique of pure reason. Finally, in his unfinished essay *What Real Progress Has Metaphysics Made in Germany Since the Time of Leibniz and Wolff* (1793/1804) and his *Proclamation of the Imminent Conclusion of a Treaty of Perpetual Peace in Philosophy* (1796), Kant tries to show that his critique represents the culmination of philosophical history. Although they are not nearly as extensive or well-developed as his arguments for the transcendental ideality of space and time, his deductions of the pure concepts of the understanding, or his explanations of transcendental idealism, Kant's accounts of the value of a critique of pure reason deserve serious consideration.

## The Possibility and Necessity
## of Metaphysics

Shortly after the first (A) edition of the *Critique of Pure Reason* was published, Kant began work on an abstract of his critique.[10] The abstract was meant to help the public, who were unlikely to read and even less likely to understand Kant's critique. Hamann reports that Kant even thought his abstract would help make his critique popular, though a series of negative reviews soon disabused him of that notion.[11] By the time he published the *Prolegomena to Any Future Metaphysics That Will Be Able to Come Forward as Science* (1783), Kant realized that he would have to do more than explain the method and conclusions of his critique to the public. He would have to demonstrate the merits of his work "to all of those who find it worthwhile to occupy themselves with metaphysics."[12] And he would have to defend the *Critique of Pure Reason* against critics who treated the length of his work with "impatience" and his attempt to reform metaphysics with "ill-temper."[13]

The structure of the *Prolegomena* plays an important role in that defense. Kant presents the *Prolegomena* as a response to two general questions that ask "Is metaphysics possible at all?" and "How is cognition from pure reason possible?" The answers to these questions are contained in the three parts devoted to the main transcendental question, which ask "How is pure mathematics possible?" "How is pure natural science possible?" and "How is metaphysics in general possible?" Kant then concludes with his "solution to the general question of the *Prolegomena*" and an appendix, "On What Can Be Done in Order to Make Metaphysics as Science Actual." When one considers all these questions, their solutions, and the proposals contained in the appendix, it becomes apparent that the *Prolegomena* is much more than a simplified summary of the first *Critique*. It is actually an extended account of "the decision about the possibility or impossibility of metaphysics in general" that Kant had mentioned in the second definition of a critique of pure reason in the first (A) "Preface."[14]

In the *Prolegomena*, the decision begins with Kant's formulation of "general questions" asking about the possibility of metaphysics. He writes "If a metaphysics that could assert itself as science were actual, if one could say: here is metaphysics, you need only to learn it, and it will convince you of its truth irresistibly and immutably, then this question would be unnecessary, and there would remain only that question which would pertain more to a test of our acuteness than to a proof of the existence of the subject matter itself, namely: *how is it possible*, and how reason should set about attaining it."[15] Because "a metaphysics that could assert itself as science" is not actual, however, a demonstration of its possibility is necessary. That demonstration is the answer to the critical question: "*How is metaphysics possible at all?*"[16] Kant claims that he has answered that question in the *Critique of Pure Reason*, though he has done so "synthetically, namely by inquiring within pure reason itself, and seeking to determine within this source both the elements and the laws of its pure use, according to principles."[17] That has made the work difficult to understand, perhaps too difficult for the average reader, so Kant presents the answer in the *Prolegomena* according to the analytic method. The analytic method presupposes the correctness of Kant's critique and then explains the reasons why metaphysics is possible. Along the way, Kant says his *Prolegomena* will prepare the way for a future metaphysics by indicating what needs to be done to transform the possibility of metaphysics into an actual science.[18]

In order to answer the question about the possibility of metaphysics and lay out the path metaphysics will have to take if it is to become a science, Kant formulates another "general question" about the possibility of cognition from pure reason. This question is actually very helpful in demonstrating the differences between the second definition and the *Prolegomena*, as well as the synthetic and analytic methods. While the second definition suggests that Kant's critique of the faculty of reason would use its inquiry into "all the cognition after which reason might strive **independently of all experience**" in order to reach a decision about the possibility or impossibility of metaphysics in general, the *Prolegomena* starts with the question about the possibility of metaphysics and then answers it with an account of the possibility of a priori cognition and synthetic a priori judgments. That account is contained in Kant's answers to the transcendental questions "How is pure mathematics possible?" "How is pure natural science possible?" and "How is metaphysics in general possible?" While many scholars have assumed that Kant intended to lay the foundations of mathematics and physics with his answers to the first two questions, they are both intended to provide answers to the third question about the possibility of metaphysics. If a priori cognition and synthetic a priori judgments make mathematics and natural science possible, then cognition through pure reason is possible, and metaphysics must be possible as well. Once the possibility of metaphysics has been demonstrated, then its actuality as science will follow.

The part of the *Prolegomena* devoted to the question "How is pure mathematics possible?" demonstrates the possibility of a priori cognition and synthetic a priori judgments by reversing the arguments of the "Transcendental Aesthetic" of the first *Critique*. In the *Prolegomena*, Kant argues that pure mathematics is possible because it is possible to "present" or "exhibit" mathematical concepts a priori in pure intuition.[19] The presentation of mathematical concepts in pure intuition allows geometers to determine that "full-standing space (a space that is itself not the boundary of another space) has three dimensions and that space in general cannot have more" without referring to experience.[20] It also makes it possible for mathematicians to calculate the quantity of units that are presented successively, without relying on a concept.[21] Kant thinks the immediate certainty with which a geometer proves that "no more than three lines can cut each other at right angles in one point" proves that geometry "bases itself on the pure intuition of space," just as he thinks the proposition $7 + 5 = 12$ proves that arithmetic "forms its concepts of numbers through successive addition of units in time."[22] Because the "Transcendental Aesthetic" proves that space and time are pure forms of sensible intuition that precede "all actual impressions through which I am affected by objects," Kant takes it as proof of the possibility of pure mathematics.[23]

In his answer to the question about the possibility of pure mathematics, Kant notes that pure mechanics depends on the pure forms of sensible intuition, since it "can form its concepts of motion only by means of the representation of time."[24] However, pure natural science requires something more than the pure intuition of space and time. In his answer to the question about the possibility of pure natural science, Kant argues that in addition to "mathematics applied to appearances," there are "discursive principles (from concepts) which make up the philosophical part of pure cognition of nature."[25] These principles are discursive because their objects are not given directly, concretely, and immediately like intuitions. Discursive principles provide only indirect, abstract, and mediate cognition of objects, because they cognize objects through concepts.[26] These concepts are necessary for the "pure cognition of nature" because they are the a priori concepts that lie "at the foundation of all empirical use of the understanding."[27] Without these concepts, we could not guarantee that our cognition of the objects we encounter in nature is objectively valid, since sensible intuition only provides freely associated perceptions.[28] Freely associated perceptions do not require that "all judgments of the same object must also agree with one another," so Kant appeals to "concepts originally generated in the understanding" to ensure the agreement of our judgments and their objects.[29] Natural science confirms that this agreement is regular and lawful, though Kant thinks that is already guaranteed by the universality and necessity of the categories he lays out in the "Transcendental Table of Concepts of the Understanding" in the *Critique of Pure Reason*.[30] The arguments he presents in the *Prolegomena* merely confirm what he has already demonstrated.

Having answered the first two "transcendental" questions, Kant turns to the third question, "How is metaphysics in general possible?" in the next section of the *Prolegomena*. Most of the section is devoted to a summary of the arguments of the "Transcendental Dialectic" of the first *Critique*, but at the beginning Kant explains how the possibility of pure mathematics and pure natural science help demonstrate the possibility of metaphysics. He maintains that "pure mathematics and pure natural science would not have needed, *for the purpose of their own security* and certainty, a deduction of the sort that we have hitherto accomplished for them both."[31] The possibility of mathematics does not need to be demonstrated, since it is supported by the intuitive certainty that 7 + 5 = 12 and the sum of the angles of a triangle is 180 degrees. The possibility of natural science also does not need to be demonstrated, because the regularity and lawfulness of nature are constantly confirmed by experience. The only reason Kant discusses their possibility is because they establish the existence of the pure forms of intuition and the pure concepts of the understanding, which Kant takes to be the elements of metaphysical cognition. Proving that they are a priori, universal, and necessary is enough to prove that metaphysics in general is possible.

Of course, the fact that metaphysics is possible in general does not mean that all metaphysical claims are valid. As he rehearses the arguments of the "Transcendental Dialectic" in the *Prolegomena*, Kant is eager to show that the pure forms of intuition and the pure concepts of the understanding do not provide knowledge of things in themselves or anything that might lie beyond the bounds of possible experience. He insists, for example, that "all the pure cognitions of the understanding are such that their concepts can be given in experience and their principles confirmed by experience."[32] This distinguishes the categories from "the transcendent cognitions of reason," which "neither allow what relates to their *ideas* to be given in experience, nor their *theses* ever to be confirmed or refuted through experience."[33] Without the distinction between categories and ideas, Kant warns that "metaphysics is utterly impossible, or at best is a disorderly and bungling endeavor to patch together a house of cards, without knowledge of the materials with which one is preoccupied and their suitability for one or another end."[34] The possibility of metaphysics therefore depends on more than the transcendental ideality of space and time and the deduction of the pure concepts of the understanding. It also depends on the restriction of their application to objects of possible experience and a clear demarcation of the boundaries of the validity of metaphysical claims. An examination of the "dialectical endeavors of pure reason" is helpful, because it serves "not only actually to show us the boundaries of reason's pure use, but also to show us the way to determine such boundaries; and that too is the end and use of this natural predisposition of our reason, which bore metaphysics as its favorite child."[35]

Kant's reference to the "natural predisposition of our reason" in the last quotation is important for his account of the transition from the possibility to the actuality of metaphysics as science. The claim that metaphysics is a "natural predisposition" of human reason is familiar from the second (B) edition of the *Critique of Pure Reason* and from Kant's later works, but it first appears in the *Prolegomena*. It can be understood as a kind of shorthand for the first paragraph of the "Preface" to the first (A) edition of the first *Critique*, where Kant says that human reason "has the peculiar fate in one species of its cognitions that it is burdened with questions which it cannot dismiss, since they are given to it as problems by the nature of reason itself, but which it also cannot answer, since they transcend every capacity of human reason."[36] Since these problems are unavoidable and follow from the nature of human reason, it makes sense to call them a natural predisposition of reason. It also makes sense to say that metaphysics is a natural predisposition of human reason, since it is our rational desire to answer questions that lie beyond our capacities that leads to the endless controversies of metaphysics.[37] Because these controversies concern matters that go beyond the bounds of experience, Kant concludes that metaphysics as a natural predisposition of human reason is "dialectical" and "deceitful" in the "Solution to the General Question of the *Prolegomena*: How Is Metaphysics Possible as Science?"

The dialectical and deceitful nature of metaphysics as a natural predisposition of human reason has prevented metaphysics from becoming a science like mathematics and natural science, but Kant thinks his critique provides the solution to that problem. "In order that metaphysics might, as a science, be able to lay claim, not merely to deceitful persuasion, but to insight and conviction," he argues, "a critique of pure reason itself must set forth the entire stock of *a priori* concepts, their division according to the different sources (sensibility, understanding, and reason), further, a complete table of those concepts, and the analysis of all them along with everything that can be derived from that analysis; and then, especially, such a critique must set forth the possibility of synthetic cognition *a priori* through a deduction of these concepts, it must set forth the principles of their use, and finally also the boundaries of that use; and all of this in a complete system."[38] This passage can be read as an elaboration of the claims of the second definition that Kant proposes in the "Preface" to the first (A) edition of the *Critique of Pure Reason*, since it says that a critique will catalog "all the cognitions after which reason might strive independently of all experience" and explain the sources, nature, and boundaries of that cognition from principles. Yet it also differs from the second definition, because it uses the critique of pure reason to transform metaphysics from a natural predisposition of human reason into a science, instead of using it to demonstrate the possibility of metaphysics in general. In the *Prolegomena*, Kant concludes that "a critique, and that alone, contains within itself the whole well-tested and verified plan by which metaphysics as science can be achieved, and even all the means for carrying it out; by any other ways or means it is impossible."[39]

The *Prolegomena* ends with an appendix, "On What Can Be Done in Order to Make *Metaphysics as Science* Actual," which contains a "Specimen of a judgment about the *Critique* which precedes the investigation" and a "Proposal for an investigation of the *Critique*, after which the judgment can follow." It is in these sections that Kant most directly responds to the Garve-Feder review published in the *Göttingischen Anzeigen von gelehrten Sachen*. While he acknowledges that it is reasonable to expect that his critique will be subjected "to an exact and careful examination" by the reading public, Kant thinks the Göttingen review proceeds from "*a judgment that precedes the investigation.*"[40] In other words, he thinks the judgment of the review is biased, because the reviewer judges Kant's critique based on his own prejudices about metaphysics, instead of considering the demonstration of the possibility of metaphysics the critique contains or the consequences of that demonstration. As an alternative, Kant proposes "a different *judgment that comes after the investigation.*"[41] He was satisfied that one review published in the *Gothaische gelehrte Zeitung* had presented a "clear and candid presentation of a portion of the first principles of my work," but Kant did not believe it had investigated his critique carefully enough.[42] Only a thoroughgoing investigation of the *Critique of Pure Reason*, "examined piece by piece from its foundation," could really judge its merits.[43] Because that critique is necessary for demonstrating the possibility of metaphysics in general and making metaphysics actual as science, Kant did not think such an investigation was too much to ask from his readers.

## The Utility of a Critique of Pure Reason

The "Preface" to the second (B) edition of the first *Critique* is closely related to the end of the *Prolegomena*. Both texts argue that a critique of pure reason is necessary to make metaphysics a science.[44] Even the revised definition of a critique of pure reason that Kant presents in the second (B) "Preface" announces that the methods of metaphysics will be transformed "according to the example of the geometers and natural scientists," so that metaphysics can attain similar heights of scientific achievement.[45] Yet the paragraphs following Kant's revised definition go far beyond the necessity of a critique of pure reason that Kant describes in the *Prolegomena*. Kant responds to those who wondered "what sort of treasure it is that we intend to leave to posterity, in the form of a metaphysics that has been purified through criticism," with an extensive account of the negative and positive "utilities" of his critique. [46]

The fact that Kant emphasizes the negative and positive utilities of his critique is significant, because he had suggested that the utility of his critique "would really be only negative" in the "Introduction" to the first (A) edition of the *Critique of Pure Reason*.[47] And though he had also insisted that "a great deal is already won" by this negative utility, some of Kant's critics rejected the positive implications of his critique.[48] The infamous *Göttingen Review* (1782) claims that the first *Critique* "can certainly serve to expose the most considerable difficulties of speculative philosophy," but rejects virtually all of the positions Kant defends in the "Transcendental Aesthetic" and "Transcendental Analytic."[49] Christian Garve provides a more charitable account of the positive contributions of Kant's critique in the review he published in the *Allgemeine deutsche Bibliothek* (1783), but still claims that the *Critique of Pure Reason* is intended "to determine the limits of reason."[50] These interpretations of Kant's critique have proven to be very influential in the reception of his work; yet it is impossible to reduce the critical philosophy to a condemnation of the speculative excesses of metaphysics or a patrol along the borders of reason. Doing so leaves out those parts of Kant's critique that he worked hardest to articulate and thought were the most valuable.

In the second (B) "Preface," Kant still maintains that the utility of his critique is primarily negative, because the first lesson the critique of pure reason teaches is "never to venture with speculative reason beyond the boundaries of experience."[51] But he goes on to argue that this negative utility immediately gives way to a positive utility. In the second (B) "Preface," Kant explains the benefits of a critique of pure reason for practical philosophy, theoretical philosophy, and even the general welfare of the public in much greater detail than he had in the first (A) "Introduction." So emphatic is Kant about the positive utility of his critique that he compares its denial to the claim "that the police are of no positive utility because their chief business is to put a stop to the violence that citizens have to fear from other citizens, so that each can carry on his own affairs in peace and safety."[52]

Kant's discussion of the positive utility of the critique of pure reason for practical philosophy is so extensive in the "Preface" to the second (B) edition of the first *Critique* that it often obscures his account of the positive utility of his critique for theoretical philosophy.[53] Kant even incorporates a discussion of "the analytical part of the critique," which includes his defense of the transcendental ideality of space and time and the distinction between appearances and things in themselves, into the account of the positive utility of the critique of pure reason for practical philosophy.[54] These are doubtless some of the main theoretical contributions of the *Critique of Pure Reason*, but Kant acts as though he had come to these positions in an effort to save practical philosophy from the "unfounded groping" and "frivolous wandering" of speculative metaphysics.[55] Because theoretical philosophy "would have to help itself to principles that in fact reach only to objects of possible experience, and which, if they were to be applied to what cannot be an object of experience, then they would actually transform it into an appearance," Kant argues that theoretical philosophy would have to "declare all practical extension of pure reason to be impossible" if it were not strictly limited by the bounds of possible experience.[56] By showing that these bounds do not affect the practical extension of pure reason, Kant thinks his critique preserves the possibility of "an absolutely necessary practical use of pure reason (the moral use), in which reason unavoidably extends itself beyond the boundaries of sensibility, without needing any assistance from speculative reason, but in which it must also be made secure against any counteraction from the latter, in order not to fall into contradiction with itself."[57] Kant assumes this possibility whenever he claims that the will is determined by pure reason, so it is imperative that the *Critique of Pure Reason* does not declare such determination impossible.

Kant's defense of the positive utility of his critique for practical philosophy is so enthusiastic that he even claims he found it necessary "to deny knowledge in order to make room for faith."[58] Although this claim is often cited in discussions of the first *Critique*, there is actually very little evidence that Kant intended to make room for faith in his critique. Kant's notes, his lectures, his correspondence, and the works associated with the development of the critical philosophy all suggest that Kant's critique was motivated by theoretical concerns about the status of metaphysics. These concerns led him to devote more than a decade to the composition of a critique that would secure reason's rightful claims, demonstrate the possibility of a priori cognition and synthetic a priori judgments, answer the question about the possibility of metaphysics, and radically transform the method it employs. Practical philosophy and the philosophy of religion remained an abiding concern throughout Kant's life, and he wrote important works on the subject in the years between the publication of the first (A) and second (B) editions of the *Critique of Pure Reason*, as well as the years that followed; yet it is not clear that they motivated him to deny knowledge or make room for faith in the *Critique of Pure Reason*. It is also unclear why Kant thinks denying knowledge and making room for faith should be considered a positive utility of the critique of pure reason for practical philosophy, since morality requires the determination of the will through pure practical reason and not through faith.[59]

In the second "Preface," Kant maintains his commitment to the positive utility of the critique of pure reason for theoretical philosophy, despite the emphasis he now places on practical philosophy. He begins his defense of the positive utility of his critique for theoretical philosophy by identifying the parts of theoretical philosophy that are affected by its negative utility. "With this important alteration in the field of the sciences, and with the loss of its hitherto imagined possessions that speculative reason must suffer," Kant says, "everything yet remains in the same advantageous state as it was before concerning the universal human concern and the utility that the world has so far drawn from the doctrines of pure reason."[60] By checking the excesses of "the dialectic that is natural to reason" and depriving it of "all disadvantageous influence," the negative utility of the critique of pure reason disabuses metaphysics of the fantasy of its "imagined possessions."[61] Because the loss of imagined possessions is not a real loss, Kant does not think the negative utility of his critique does metaphysics any harm. In fact, he thinks his critique serves a positive utility, because it helps reason make progress in metaphysics, while "blocking off the source of the errors."[62]

Because the critique of pure reason helps keep reason free from error, Kant thinks it will allow metaphysics to employ "the dogmatic procedure of reason in its pure cognition as science" in a way that avoids dogmatism.[63] Because Kant thinks science "must always be dogmatic" if it is to "prove its conclusions strictly *a priori* from secure principles," metaphysics cannot entirely reject the "dogmatic procedure of reason."[64] However, it must reject "dogmatism," which Kant defines as "the presumption of getting on solely with pure cognition from (philosophical) concepts according to principles which reason has always been using for a long time without first inquiring in what way and by what right it has obtained them."[65] Dogmatism is essentially a form of prejudice that assumes the authority of the principles it employs without questioning them or demonstrating their legitimacy. The critique of pure reason undermines this prejudice, because it challenges metaphysics to undertake "fundamental investigations of the rights of speculative reason."[66] In the process, it paves the way for a positive statement of the doctrine of transcendental philosophy, which may become dogma without being dogmatic.

What is perhaps most surprising about Kant's defense of the dogmatic procedure of reason is the proximity it establishes between Kant and Wolff. Christian Wolff is often decried as a dogmatic rationalist and a scholastic metaphysician, so much so that his importance for eighteenth-century German philosophy has often been the subject of ridicule and caricature. Kant sometimes encouraged the view that his critical philosophy was the antithesis of the Leibnizian-Wolffian philosophy, identifying Wolffianism and dogmatism in a number of texts.[67] In the second (B) "Preface," he even suggests that one of the positive utilities of the critique of pure reason is undermining the "the monopoly of the schools" and the "ridiculous despotism" of Wolffianism in the universities.[68] Yet he also praises the rigor of Wolff's method and calls Wolff "the greatest among all dogmatic philosophers" because he "gave us the first example (an example by which he became the author of a spirit of well-groundedness in Germany that is still not extinguished) of the way in which the secure course of a science is to be taken."[69] The only mistake Wolff made, according to the second (B) "Preface," was to overlook the importance of supplementing "the dogmatic procedure of pure reason" with "an antecedent critique of its own capacity."[70] "Through the regular ascertainment of the principles, the clear determination of concepts, the attempt at strictness in the proofs, and the prevention of audacious leaps in inferences," Kant says, Wolff proved that he "had the skills for moving a science such as metaphysics into this condition," the condition of a science which Kant hoped to establish for metaphysics with his critique.[71] "If only it had occurred to him to prepare the field for it by a critique of the organ, namely pure reason itself," Kant says that Wolff would have discovered the critical philosophy himself.[72]

Kant's comments are not entirely fair to Wolff, who also recommends a preliminary examination of the cognitive powers of human beings in the "Preliminary Discourse" to the *German Logic* (*Rational Thoughts on the Powers of the Human Understanding*, 1712).[73] Yet they are meant to serve a good greater than the positive utility of a critique of pure reason for theoretical philosophy. Kant thinks undermining the monopoly of the schools and the dogmatic Wolffianism that dominates the universities helps promote the dignity of humanity and the enlightenment of the public. To demonstrate this point, he asks "whether the proof of the continuation of our soul after death drawn from the simplicity of substance, or the proof of freedom of the will against universal mechanism drawn from the subtle though powerless distinction between subjective and objective practical necessity, or the proof of the existence of God drawn from the concept of a most real being (or from the contingency of what is alterable and the necessity of a first mover), have ever, after originating in the schools, been able to reach the public or have the least influence on its convictions?"[74] Such a rhetorical question can only be answered in the negative, but Kant thinks his critique can do much more than reveal the origins of scholastic error and dogmatic inefficacy. He claims that it teaches those in the schools "to pretend to no higher or more comprehensive insight on any point touching human concerns than the insight that is accessible to the great multitude (who are always most worthy of our respect)."[75]

While Kant acknowledges that the critique of pure reason "can never become popular," he thinks it serves the public "even without their knowledge" by recognizing the intellectual powers of all human beings, respecting their basic equality, and rejecting claims of privilege and authority. These claims have a long history in early modern philosophy, dating back to Descartes and Hobbes, who were among the first philosophers to defend human equality.[76] But they have a special significance for Kant, who notes in the remarks he wrote in his copy of *Observations on the Feeling of the Beautiful and the Sublime* (1764–65) that Rousseau set him right at a time when he "despised the rabble who knows nothing."[77] Because he is "a researcher by inclination," Kant thought "the entire thirst for cognition and the eager restlessness to proceed further in it, as was the satisfaction at every acquisition" constituted "the honor of humankind."[78] But then he read Rousseau, which taught him "to honor human beings" and to work "to establish the rights of humanity."[79] These comments are usually taken as evidence of Kant's growing disaffection with metaphysics or the primacy he grants to practical reason; yet their influence is as apparent in the *Critique of Pure Reason* as any of Kant's other works.[80] When Kant calls metaphysics a "natural predisposition" (*Naturanlage*) of human reason in the *Prolegomena* and the "Preface" and "Introduction" to the second (B) edition of the first *Critique*, he acknowledges that all human beings share his desire for knowledge. When he says that the answers to metaphysical questions are matters of "universal human concern," he recognizes that the public is harmed by the monopoly of the schools and the falsehoods they promote "in the absence of criticism."[81] For the same reason, he thinks they will share the benefits of his critique.

The account of the positive and negative utilities of a critique of pure reason in the second (B) "Preface" allows us to see a number of things. First, it confirms that the utility of the critique of pure reason is not entirely negative. Its "first usefulness" may be negative, but that is not its only utility. Kant's critique also makes positive contributions to practical philosophy, by showing that there is no contradiction in a practical extension of reason beyond the bounds of possible experience; theoretical philosophy, by demonstrating the possibility of a priori cognition and synthetic a priori judgments, the availability of the dogmatic procedure for metaphysics, and the failures of scholastic metaphysics;

as well as the general public, by affirming the equality of human beings and the universal human concerns to which metaphysics is addressed. If these are the outcomes of "a metaphysics that has been purified through criticism," then no one can doubt the value of a critique of pure reason.

## The Originality of a Critique of Pure Reason

Kant had to contend with a rather different set of criticisms in the years following the publication of the second (B) edition of the *Critique of Pure Reason*. While his first critics had raised empiricist objections against his arguments for the transcendental ideality of space and time and the pure concepts of the understanding, the objections raised by Johann August Eberhard derived from a rationalist perspective. In a series of articles published in the *Philosophisches Magazin* (1788–92), Eberhard argues that everything worthwhile in Kant's critique could already be found in Leibniz, whose philosophy contains "just as much of a critique of reason as the more recent one, whereby it nevertheless introduces a dogmatism grounded in a careful analysis of the cognitive faculties, therefore containing everything that is true in the latter, but still more besides in a grounded extension of the domain of the understanding."[82]

Eberhard's claims are likely to surprise readers who think the author of the *Monadology* (1714) gave free reign to rational speculation.[83] They also surprised Kant, who wondered "how it came to pass that these things were not long ago already seen in the great man's philosophy and in its daughter, the Wolffian philosophy."[84] Kant regarded Eberhard's discovery with suspicion, asking "how many discoveries that are regarded as new are seen now by unskilled interpreters in the ancients, after they have been shown what they should look for," but he was not terribly concerned with the challenge Eberhard's newly discovered critique posed to the "originality" (*Neuigkeit*) of his own.[85] Kant was much more concerned about its conclusions, because they were "the exact opposite" of his critique.[86] Eberhard claims that the Leibnizian critique shows "that there is indeed an extension of cognition beyond objects of the senses" whose possibility can be demonstrated "*a priori*, through synthetic propositions."[87] Kant denied that these conclusions were valid in *On a Discovery Whereby Any New Critique of Pure Reason Is to Be Made Superfluous by an Older One* (1790), but we will have to say more about the nature of the critique that Eberhard attributes to Leibniz before we can judge the merits of Kant's response, the originality of his critique, and the validity of its conclusions.

In the first piece he published in the *Philosophisches Magazin*, "On the Limits of Human Knowledge," Eberhard praises Kant for trying to determine the limits of human understanding more precisely, but asks whether his critique has really "drawn the line" properly.[88] After reviewing some alternative accounts of what is within the reach of human reason and what lies beyond its scope, Eberhard comes to Leibniz's account of the "domain" (*Gebiet*) of human understanding, which he praises for expanding the limits of human knowledge while defending common sense.[89] Unlike the ancient skeptics, who denied that there is any certain knowledge; Descartes, who recognized that the comprehensible (*Begreifliche*) is true, but did not explain how it could be known; Locke, who relied on the senses and overlooked the contributions of the understanding and reason; or Kant, who "throws out" the pure concepts of the understanding because they do not contain any content derived from sensible intuition and also because they do not correspond to any objects, Leibniz recognizes that the human understanding is capable of certain knowledge, that this knowledge extends beyond the objects of the senses to pure concepts of the understanding, and that the pure concepts of the understanding allow us to demonstrate truths about concepts and objects a priori and a posteriori.[90] Eberhard contends that this makes Leibniz's system "critical" (*kritisch*) and he denounces Kant for denying, "through a mere decree, without a shred of proof," that Leibniz's "critique" (*Kritik*) had already achieved everything proposed in the *Critique of Pure Reason*.[91]

Eberhard mentions his comparison of the Leibnizian and Kantian critiques of reason at the beginning of his next article in the *Philosophisches Magazin*, "On the Logical Truth or the Transcendental Validity of Human Cognition," but he explains their differences in the greatest detail in two later articles, "On the Domain of the Pure Understanding" and "On the Origin of Human Cognition." In these articles, Eberhard places what he takes to be the central claims of each critique side by side in tables (see pp. 105–7 in this book), so that readers can draw their own conclusions.[92]

Much could be said about Eberhard's characterization of the Kantian and Leibnizian critiques in these tables. The table from "On the Domain of the Pure Understanding" is supposed to support the conclusion that the Leibnizian critique is superior to the Kantian critique, because the Kantian critique grounds appearances in an incomprehensible transcendental object, which we cannot know and whose possibility we cannot confirm. The Leibnizian critique avoids these difficulties, because it regards phenomena as instances of noumena, whose general characteristics can be known, and which are only modified by the particular conditions under which our senses are affected. In the table from "On

the Origin of Human Cognition," Eberhard suggests that the Kantian critique is a radical form of idealism, because it denies that our concepts of
space and time have both subjective and objective grounds. The Leibnizian critique provides a more reasonable alternative, because it relates the
particular determinations of our concepts to objective grounds outside of
us, as well as the subjective conditions of our constitution, making them
"well-founded phenomena" (*phaenomena bene fundata*). Whether these
are accurate representations of the differences between the Kantian and
Leibnizian critiques is debatable, though most scholars agree that Eberhard's articles contain a host of misunderstandings, misrepresentations,
and equivocations.[93] However, there can be no question that Kant took
great offense at Eberhard's claims about his critique and responded with
a polemical force that is mostly absent from his replies to his empiricist
critics.

Kant's initial reaction to Eberhard's articles is described in a series
of letters to Karl Leonhard Reinhold, who had informed Kant of their
publication and planned to write an article responding to Eberhard on
Kant's behalf.[94] Kant provided Reinhold with material for his response
in their subsequent correspondence, noting that Eberhard had turned
his definition of a synthetic a priori judgment into a tautology; conflated
the logical principle of the determining ground with the metaphysical
principle of causality; misapplied the principles of contradiction and sufficient reason; distorted Kant's account of the relation between intuitions
and concepts; misrepresented his arguments about the ideas of reason;
and provided a host of incorrect and misleading references to cover his
errors.[95] Kant was so irritated by these mistakes and misrepresentations
that he eventually decided to publish his own response to the "fraud"
(*Falschheit*) that Eberhard had perpetrated.[96] *On a Discovery* appeared a
year later, denouncing the use Eberhard made of the principles of contradiction and sufficient reason; his misrepresentation of Kant's account
of space and time; his attempt to distinguish phenomena and noumena
by degrees of clarity and distinctness; his failure to appreciate the differences between appearances and things in themselves; and especially his
claim that the validity of synthetic a priori judgments can be determined
without reference to pure sensible intuition.[97] In the course of his arguments, Kant accuses Eberhard of rank incompetence and deliberate obfuscation; refutes virtually all of the charges against the *Critique of Pure
Reason* that Eberhard had raised; and turns the tables on the defender
of Leibnizian-Wolffian orthodoxy by claiming his critique "might well be
the true apology for Leibniz, even against those of his disciples who heap
praises upon him that do him no honor."[98]

Unfortunately, Kant does not pay much attention to Eberhard's

**"On the Domain of the Pure Understanding"***

| Kantian Critique of Pure Reason | Leibnizian Critique of Pure Reason |
|---|---|
| 1. Something must correspond to the appearance, which is not an appearance. | 1. An appearance must have an ultimate ground, which is not an appearance. |
| 2. I know nothing about this something. | 2. I do not differentiate between determinations belonging to the individuality of this something; I do not have a clear idea of them. |
| 3. I have absolutely no concept of it. | 3. I have only a concept of the determinations that belong to its genus. I can render this concept distinct through a definition and then deduce from that concept a set of predicates, which contain essential parts and attributes of the thing. |
| 4. This something, to which the appearance refers, cannot therefore be called a *noumenon*. | 4. This something, which is not an appearance, not a phenomenon, can therefore be called a *noumenon*. For I can define it, and deduce several truths from its definition, which are eternal truths. I can distinguish an infinite being, a finite mind like the human soul, and the elements of bodies, according to their genus concepts by way of definitions, and I can hence perceive (out of the definitions) different attributes that are in part common to all, in part peculiar to each genus, and by distinguishing them, I know what they have in common and what the peculiar attributes of each genus are. The cognitive faculty that knows this is the *understanding*, and the objects of the understanding are *noumena*, just as the objects of the senses are *phenomena*. |
| 5. If this something were to be an object that would be a *noumenon*, then it would have to be given through a different kind of intuition than sensible intuition. | 5. The nonsensible intuition is called representation; for that is the simplest object of inner sense and the simplest matter of concrete time. |
| 6. Because in every object there has to be an intuition. However, we cannot prove that there is another kind of intuition than sensible intuition, even though we cannot prove the opposite either. | 6. Even if we had no intuitive idea of this simplest matter, we could still prove many things from its general determinations. This is the path taken by Wolff with regard to the elements of bodies; Leibniz believed he was able to determine this matter, and it is for him the simplest object of inner sense, the simplest element of concrete time, which is representation. |
| 7. The something, which must correspond to appearances, is only a transcendental object, a something = x, about which we know absolutely nothing nor can know anything (given the present constitution of our understanding). | 7. This something, which is the ultimate ground of appearances, contains general determinations = a, which are knowable to us, and determinations belonging to the individuality = x, which are not clearly knowable to us. Thus, from the perspective of its knowability the entire something = a + x. |

* *Philosophisches Magazin*, pt. 3, no. 2, pp. 284–88.

**"On the Origin of Human Cognition"***

| Kantian Critique of Pure Reason | Leibnizian Critique of Pure Reason |
|---|---|
| 1. Sensible intuitions are singular representations, which depend on the constitution of the representing subject. | 1. The representations of the singular have their ground in the object, as well as in the representing subject. |
| 2. They do not, therefore, relate to things in themselves, but to appearances. | 2. They are appearances (*Philosophisches Magazin*, pt. 3, pp. 299ff.) and have, as such, no recognizable similarity to objects, because they do not distinguish the latter's singular realities. The general determinations of the manifold of the object are distinguished through the understanding; those determinations belonging to the object's individuality are not knowable by the finite power of representation (*Vorstellungskraft*). But what does it mean to refer to appearances?—That is what we have presupposed here.—Or, does it mean: their objects are appearances? That would mean: the objects of appearances are appearances, which is absurd. |
| 3. That which allows the manifold of appearance to be intuited, is the form of appearance (*Critique of Pure Reason*, pg. 20). | 3. The limits of the representing subject are the subjective ground or the form of appearance. |
| 4. The pure forms of intuition are space and time. | 4. Space and time are appearances; for they have subjective grounds in the finite power of representation (*der endlichen Vorstellungskraft*). The limits of this finite power of representation are thus (1) the forms of the appearances of space and time. (2) But space and time can be thought without the modifications and distinctions of things, which are their ultimate objective grounds. They can also be thought without a determined magnitude, without determined limits and degrees, like movement without a determined speed. Then they are abstract, general space and time, that is, from the perspective of their inner determinations as well as from the perspective of their outer limits: undetermined space, undetermined time. I am not entirely certain in which sense critical idealism uses the expression "pure form of intuition," whether in sense (1) or (2). (c. pg. 378). |
| 5. These forms of sensible appearance are in the mind a priori, for (1) they are: the receptivity of the subject to be affected by objects, and this must necessarily precede all intuitions of these objects. | 5. If we are to understand the form of sensible intuition as the receptivity of the subject, then it is the subjective ground of appearances, and, in a comprehensible explanation of the appearance, this must be thought before the appearance itself, not in the sense of the priority of time, but in the sense of the priority of the grounds of appearance. (See *Philosophisches Magazin*, pt. 2, pp. 124ff.) |
| 6. Nevertheless, (2) they must, as forms of all appearances, be given before all actual perception. | 6. If perceptions are sensations with consciousness, then they are representations of real and therefore particular fully determined things. These lower things cannot be without the determinations of higher things, to which they belong; in the subordination of things, the higher precede the lower. The lower |

things, on the other hand, cannot be thought without the higher things: they succeed the higher things in the subordination of things. But from this it does not follow that the former must precede the latter in time; for in the development of concepts towards clarity, the order is reversed. Thus, if one understands the pure form of intuition as general time and general space, then in this development of concepts perceptions precede form.

7. That can mean (1) no extended or spatially real thing is a thing in itself; that is indeed true, and was first taught by Leibniz. (2) The extended or spatially real thing has no objective grounds, which are things in themselves, and that is false, since the extended thing is, like every appearance, a *well-founded phenomenon*, that is, it has subjective and objective grounds. What we know about these grounds through the understanding has already been indicated on pg. 284.

8. Apperception, or the clear concept of space, is indeed an empirical concept, or such a concept, which is derived from external experience. For all of our sensible concepts become clear through sensation. Otherwise, the clear concept would have to be innate to us, which no one would maintain. (For the refutation of the arguments against the empirical origin of the clear concept of space, see, in this *Philosophisches Magazin* innate, are the grounds of our concept of space, which, prior to all sensation through the external senses, are obscure, as was proven in no. 2 of the present essay; and therefore must first become clear through sensation and abstraction. There is, therefore, no contradiction between the propositions: (1) the pure intuitions, or the simplest marks of cognition through the senses, precede all perception or sensation, and (2) they are abstracted from them. For as *obscure* concepts they precede perception and sensation, while as *clear* concepts they are abstracted from them.

9. The coexistence of simple substances according to the principle of continuity can be thought without their modifications and effects, (Number 4), and therefore the soul has the grounds of space in itself and can have an obscure general concept of space without color and impenetrability; certainly, if an actual extended thing is not visible and tangible, like the air, then the soul knows space through its visible and tangible boundaries. Once actual space is visible, the soul cannot sense it without color. Since the colors are sensed through their effects on the face, they also cannot be sensed without an extended thing, for activities must be in the substances and powers, and their continuous coexistence, if it is sensed, is the objective ground of the appearance of extension. That is the reason why extension can be represented without color, but not color without extension.

7. Nothing that is intuited in space is a thing in itself.

8. Space is not an empirical concept, which can be derived from external experience. For in order to refer certain sensations to something outside of me (i.e., to something in a location in space other than where I am); similarly, in order for me to be able to represent them as external to one another, that is, not simply as different, but rather as in different places, the representation of space must already be in place.

9. Space is the only a priori intuition of the outer sense; for no one can have a priori a representation of a color or any taste.

10. Space and time is an intuition, which is originally in the soul.

* *Philosophisches Magazin*, pt. 4, no. 1, pp. 393–405.

comparison of the Kantian and Leibnizian critiques of pure reason in *On a Discovery*. He rejects the positions Eberhard associates with the Leibnizian critique, especially the claim that noumena are the ground of phenomena, because he thinks this view turns phenomena into confused representations of things in themselves and also makes noumena into clear and distinct representations of phenomena.[99] Kant thinks this position misrepresents the relationship between appearances and things in themselves, because our concept of a thing in itself must be completely empty, if sensible intuition supplies the content of our concepts, and our concept of a thing in itself is the concept of something that does not correspond to any sensible intuition.[100] It follows from this conception of a thing in itself that the understanding cannot know its general characteristics, since it is an empty concept devoid of any characteristics. It also follows from this conception of a thing in itself that appearances and things in themselves must differ in kind and not just in degrees of clarity and distinctness, since an appearance is a cognition whose content is provided by sensible intuition, and the concept of a thing in itself is completely empty without a corresponding intuition.[101] An appearance can be confused or clear and distinct, but it can never be empty, so long as an intuition supplies its content. Kant could have presented this argument as the vindication of his critique against the Leibnizian alternative; yet he prefers "to leave the great man out of the picture and consider the propositions which Mr. Eberhard ascribes to his name as his own assertions," because "in justifiably parrying the blows which he administers to us in the other's name, we might hit a great man, thereby drawing upon ourselves the odium of those who admire him."[102]

The only exceptions to this rule seem to be the first paragraph of the "Introduction" to *On a Discovery*, where Kant expresses his surprise at Eberhard's alleged discovery of a Leibnizian critique of reason; the conclusion, where Kant denies that Eberhard understands that critique, if it even exists, and then asserts that the *Critique of Pure Reason* is the true apology for Leibniz; and the title (*On a Discovery Whereby Any New Critique of Pure Reason Is to Be Made Superfluous by an Older One*), which contains an interesting ambiguity I have not yet mentioned. If the Leibnizian critique is the older critique to which the title refers, then Kant's claim that the *Critique of Pure Reason* is the "true apology for Leibniz" would make his critique a continuation of Leibniz's philosophy. This would mean that Kant's critique is unoriginal, but that would still not make it superfluous, since Kant believes his critique provides a better account of the peculiarities of Leibniz's metaphysics than the works of his "would-be followers and interpreters."[103] If Kant's critique is the older critique of pure reason referred to in the title, then there can be no question of its "originality"

(*Neuigkeit*). Yet that would make Eberhard's Leibnizian critique something worse than superfluous. It would be an insult to attribute to a philosopher as great as Leibniz a critique so full of confusions, mistakes, and fallacious arguments as the one Eberhard presents.

## The Historical Necessity of a Critique of Pure Reason

The last defense Kant offers for his critique builds on a claim he makes in the "History of Pure Reason" with which he concludes the *Critique of Pure Reason*. The brief history of philosophy Kant presents in this chapter is unusual, because it departs from the other narratives Kantians have used to explain the virtues of the critical philosophy. Instead of casting his critique as a successor to dogmatism, a refutation of skepticism, a challenge to rationalism, or a supplement to empiricism, Kant distinguishes three phases in the history of philosophy. In antiquity, Kant says, philosophers like Plato and Epicurus divided the world into intellectual concepts and sensible objects, debating which one was the proper object of philosophical inquiry.[104] In the early modern period, philosophers disagreed about the origin of human cognition. Locke and the empiricists argued that all our cognition derives from experience, while Leibniz and the noologists maintained that our cognition has its origins in reason.[105] In Kant's own time, philosophers were distinguished by the method they employed. The philosophical naturalists follow common sense, while the scientific philosophers proceed systematically on the basis of principles (dogmatism) or against principles (skepticism).[106] Kant considers himself a scientific philosopher, but his method is different from the methods of the dogmatists and the skeptics. This is of considerable importance, since Kant thinks dogmatism and skepticism are self-refuting approaches to philosophy.[107] He says "the critical path alone is still open," not because his critique has refuted dogmatism and skepticism, but because it is the only philosophy that can "bring human reason to full satisfaction in that which has always, but until now vainly, occupied its lust for knowledge" without contradicting itself.[108] One need not follow the path Kant blazed in his critique, but any other route is certain to lead to "the total failure of all attempts in metaphysics."[109]

After arguing that a critique of pure reason is necessary to demonstrate the possibility of metaphysics and its actuality as science in the *Prolegomena* and the second (B) edition of the first *Critique*, Kant began making even stronger claims about its historical necessity in the 1790s.

A number of these claims can be found in the drafts for an essay he planned to submit to the Prussian Royal Academy's prize-essay competition in 1792/1795, which was devoted to the question "What real progress has metaphysics made in Germany since the time of Leibniz and Wolff?"[110] Kant never finished his essay, but it is clear from his drafts that he planned to argue that the different periods in the history of metaphysics are founded on "the nature of man's cognitive capacity," so that their "temporal sequence" reflects the progress of human reason.[111] At the beginning of this sequence, during the period that he calls the "Theoretico-Dogmatic" stage, Kant says metaphysics extended the use of pure reason to objects that lie beyond the bounds of sense, because it was unaware of the limits of its capacities.[112] The next stage in the history of metaphysics, which Kant associates with skepticism, is an advance on the first stage, because it recognizes the psychological, cosmological, and theological antinomies that arise when we extend pure reason beyond the bounds of possible experience.[113] And while he thinks it is possible for metaphysics "to vacillate for many centuries, leaping from an unlimited self-confidence of reason to boundless mistrust, and back again" after passing the first two stages in its history, Kant also thinks that metaphysics must go beyond the opposition between dogmatism and skepticism and make progress towards its "ultimate purpose" (*Endzweck*), which is the extension of pure reason "from the limits of the sensible to the field of the super-sensible."[114] Kant acknowledges that making the transition from the sensible to the super-sensible may be a dangerous leap for reason to take, but he also says progress towards this goal is unavoidable from a "morally practical" and "practico-dogmatic" point of view.[115] Metaphysics simply needs a critique of pure reason to explain the conditions under which such a transition might be possible. "If this critique has performed what it promises, namely to determine the scope, the content, and the bounds of such knowledge—if it has done this in Germany, and done it since the days of Leibniz and Wolff—then," Kant writes, "the problem of the Royal Academy of Sciences will have been resolved."[116]

In addition to helping metaphysics achieve its ultimate purpose, Kant also maintains that his critique would put metaphysics "into a condition of stability, both external and internal, in which it would need neither increase nor decrease, nor even be capable of this" in the drafts of his essay on the progress of metaphysics.[117] A similar claim lies at the foundation of Kant's *Proclamation of the Immanent Conclusion of a Treaty of Perpetual Peace in Philosophy* (1796). Written in response to the "Letter to a Young Man Who Wanted to Study the Kantian Philosophy" (1796) by Johann Georg Schlosser, which was itself a response to Kant's earlier attack on Schlosser in "On a Recently Prominent Tone of Superiority in Philosophy" (1796), Kant's *Proclamation* is polemical and sarcastic. Kant considered Schlosser a mystical fanatic and denounced his injunction "*to philosophize through feeling*" as antithetical to philosophy as "wisdom of life" and "the pursuit of wisdom."[118] In the *Proclamation*, he even compares the advice Schlosser offers the recipient of his letter to "the assurance of those good friends who proposed to the sheep that, if only the latter would get rid of the dogs, they might live like brothers."[119] Still, there is an earnestness in Kant's *Proclamation* when he says "it is thus a mere misunderstanding, or a confusion of the morally-practical principles of ethics with those of theory—of which only the former can provide knowledge as to the super-sensible—if a quarrel is still raised about what philosophy affirms, as a doctrine of wisdom."[120] Since the critical philosophy has surpassed dogmatism and skepticism, as well as the "moderatism" that "proceeds from halfway and thinks to find the philosopher's stone in subjective *probability*," Kant thinks there is good reason to think that metaphysics will achieve its ultimate purpose in the very near future.[121] When that happens, there will be no more reason for strife, and philosophers will finally be able to "procure eternal peace" and "assure it for all time to come."[122]

Kant may have been too optimistic about the prospects for perpetual peace in philosophy, but his claims about the originality, utility, and necessity of his critique were eagerly repeated by his followers. And though Karl Ameriks has recently argued that Reinhold is "the best candidate for the honor of being regarded as the prime inaugurator, or at least the major catalyst, of the momentous 'historical turn' that Western philosophy has taken in the last two centuries," it is important to remember that Kant asserted the historical necessity of his critique long before Reinhold began to claim that the *Critique of Pure Reason* could secure "a better future for our descendants."[123] Indeed, Kant's claim that the critical path was the only one still open to philosophy; that his critique was the only way for metaphysics to achieve its ultimate purpose; and that his critique would settle once and for all the "endless controversies" that had made metaphysics a battlefield served as models for those who wished to promote Kant's achievements, as well as those who wished to present their own work as the culmination of philosophical history. Fichte, Schelling, and Hegel are the most obvious examples of this tendency, because they described the history of philosophy as a series of stages that ended with their own systems; yet a number of contemporary philosophers are just as guilty of treating the past as "a royal road to me."[124] It is unfortunate that so many historians of philosophy have taken these philosophers at their word, because the force of their historical claims has tended to obscure the nature of their contributions to philosophy. Perhaps that is why there have been so few studies of Kant's critique, even in a time when everyone recognizes the historical significance of the critical philosophy.

# Conclusion

In the "Preface" to the first (A) edition of the *Critique of Pure Reason* (1781), Kant calls his age "the genuine age of criticism, to which everything must submit."[1] His subsequent comments about the holiness of the church and the majesty of the state suggest that Kant's time was defined by a particular kind of criticism—a critique that questions the legitimacy of our most deeply held beliefs, long-standing traditions, practices that have almost become second nature, and powerful institutions. Yet there were more and different conceptions of critique at play in Germany in the eighteenth century than Kant's footnote suggests.

Very different conceptions of critique can be found in early modern philology, literary criticism, aesthetics, and logic. Philological critique was used to achieve an authentic understanding of ancient languages and texts, their authors and the cultures that produced them, as well as the historical and political contexts in which they were written. Literary criticism employed a number of different conceptions of critique, but critics in Kant's time were especially interested in identifying "those excellencies that should delight a reasonable reader."[2] Aesthetics was understood as a critique of taste, which included the general principles for judging music, poetry, painting, sculpture, and architecture. In the *ars critica* tradition in logic, critique provided the standards of practical judgment and determined the conditions under which different kinds of principles could be applied. All of these different conceptions of critique could be said to have some bearing on Kant's critique, since he does not explicitly connect his critique to the Enlightenment critique of church and state, or specify which kind of critique is most similar to his own.

The search for authentic knowledge often required philologists to identify errors in the transcription, corruption in the transmission, and even clever forgeries of ancient texts. Similarly, the pursuit of literary excellence sometimes compelled critics to censure what Dryden called "slips of the pen." There were times when the guardians of good taste found it necessary to denounce crimes against elegance and refinement, just as there were times when logicians had to declare certain judgments false or the application of certain principles inappropriate. Yet none of this suggests that critique was an essentially negative concept during the eighteenth century. For every critique that condemned corrupt texts, poor writing, bad taste, and erroneous judgment, there was another that was concerned with authenticity, literary excellence, artistic beauty, and good judgment. Whether the critique of pure reason is more like the former or the latter can only be determined by looking more closely at the development of Kant's critique and the definitions he provides.

Many accounts of Kant's intellectual development and the evolution of his critical philosophy suggest that Kant became disillusioned with metaphysics during the 1760s and then made a dramatic return to metaphysics at the beginning of the 1770s.[3] Some even claim that Kant came to doubt "not only the possibility but even the desirability of metaphysics" during the 1760s and then reversed his position in the 1770s, when he tried to "revive speculative metaphysics" in his inaugural dissertation.[4] These accounts are generally unconvincing and their strongest claims are almost certainly false. Kant's correspondence and the works he published after the success of his *Inquiry Concerning the Distinctness of the Principles of Natural Theology and Morality* (1764) in the prize-essay competition sponsored by the Prussian Royal Academy in 1763 show that he remained committed to metaphysics during the 1760s. Kant even announced the publication of a new work called *The Proper Method of Metaphysics*, which he discussed in his correspondence with Johann Heinrich Lambert in 1765. When that work became too difficult, Kant decided to publish essays that would serve as examples of the method metaphysics should follow. His studies of the method of metaphysics continued in another work published a few months later, *Dreams of a Spirit-Seer, Elucidated by the Dreams of Metaphysics* (1766). Although *Dreams of a Spirit-Seer* is said to represent "the height of Kant's growing disaffection with metaphysics," it is actually an attempt to purge metaphysics of the erroneous judgments and mistaken procedures that have prevented it from making better progress.[5]

Kant thought his inaugural dissertation *On the Form and Principles of the Sensible and the Intelligible World* (1770) would provide metaphysics with a new foundation, but he was disappointed by its reception. Convinced that his work did not win the approval of philosophers like Lambert, Sulzer, and Mendelssohn because it lacked "clarity, self-evidence, or even something more essential," Kant began work on a new book that would reformulate and extend the principles he had proposed in his dissertation.[6] In the end, his plans for *The Bounds of Sensibility and Reason* suffered the same fate as *The Proper Method of Metaphysics*. After a debate with Marcus Herz in Königsberg, Kant realized that metaphysics could not be founded on the distinction between sensible and intellectual cognition, as he had claimed in his inaugural dissertation. That distinction could not answer the question concerning the ground of the relation between representations and objects. And while it seemed plausible that sensibility could explain the relationship between representations and objects, Kant concluded that there was no way to guarantee the validity of representations derived from sensible affection. So, he traced the ground of the relation between representations back to "principles that are derived from the nature of our soul" and tried "to reduce transcendental philosophy (that is to say, all the concepts belonging to completely pure reason) to a certain number of categories."[7] Kant would attempt something similar in the "Transcendental Deduction of the Pure Concepts of the Understanding" several years later, but he abandoned his plans for the *Bounds of Sensibility and Reason* long before he began work on the deduction, because he realized the distinction between sensible and intellectual cognition could never explain the validity of those categories.[8]

Kant described the work he planned to answer the question concerning "the ground of the relation . . ." as "a critique of pure reason."[9] Unfortunately, there is little evidence from the period between 1772 and 1781 that explains why Kant thought this was an appropriate title for his new work. Because he never published an essay called "An Answer to the Question: What is a Critique of Pure Reason?" we are forced to look at the definitions of a critique of pure reason that Kant provides in the work bearing that title, if we want to understand what Kant's critique is and why he thought it was the only way to set metaphysics on the sure path of science. Unfortunately, Kant does not provide one standard definition of a critique of pure reason in any of his works. In the "Preface" and "Introduction" to the first (A) and second (B) editions of the first *Critique*, Kant actually provides four different definitions of a critique of pure reason, which emphasize radically different aspects of his critique.

In the "Preface" to the first (A) edition of the *Critique of Pure Reason*, Kant calls his critique a "court of justice, by which reason may secure its rightful claims while dismissing all its groundless pretensions, and this not by mere decrees but according to its own eternal and unchangeable laws."[10] In the very next sentence, Kant provides a very different account of his critique. "Yet by this I do not understand a critique of books and systems," he writes, "but a critique of the faculty of reason in general, in respect of all the cognitions after which reason might strive **independently of all experience**, and hence the decision about the possibility or impossibility of a metaphysics in general, and the determination of its sources, as well as its extent and boundaries, all, however, from principles."[11] Both of these definitions are very helpful for understanding Kant's critique. The first ("court of justice") definition shows that Kant's critique is intended to secure the "rightful claims" of reason and dismiss its "groundless pretensions." The second ("critique of the faculty of reason") definition explains how Kant's critique will secure reason's "rightful claims" by examining the sources, extent, and limits of a priori cognition and using them to determine the possibility of metaphysics.

The definition Kant proposes in the "Preface" to the second (B) edition of the *Critique of Pure Reason* (1787) goes beyond the task he sets for his critique in the "Preface" to the first (A) edition. Kant says his critique is concerned with "that attempt to transform the accepted procedure of metaphysics, undertaking an entire revolution according to the example of the geometers and natural scientists."[12] He is careful to note that his critique is merely "a treatise on method" and does not contain a complete system of the science of metaphysics, because he argues, in the "Introduction" to the first (A) and second (B) editions of the first *Critique*, that the critique of pure reason is a "special science" that serves as a "propaedeutic" to a system of transcendental philosophy.[13] "To the critique of pure reason," he writes, "there accordingly belongs everything that constitutes transcendental philosophy, and it is the complete idea of transcendental philosophy, but is not yet this science itself, since it goes only so far in the analysis as is requisite for the complete estimation of synthetic *a priori* cognition."[14] Together, the third ("transformed procedure") and fourth ("propaedeutic to a system") definitions suggest that the critique of pure reason will provide metaphysics with a new method that will allow it to become a science like mathematics or physics, though we cannot expect to find a complete system of the science of metaphysics in a mere critique. The critique of pure reason is only the idea, the method, and the outline of transcendental philosophy.

These four definitions tell us a great deal about Kant's critique. The first confirms that Kant's critique is not a polemic against traditional metaphysics, because it is just as concerned with the "rightful claims" of reason as its "groundless pretensions." The second definition explains how the rightful claims of reason can be secured by a critique of "the faculty of reason" that determines the sources, extent, and boundaries of our a priori cognition. The a priori cognition derived from that critique can be used to demonstrate the possibility of metaphysics, though the third definition stipulates that a scientific metaphysics will need the new and better method, which is also supplied by the critique of pure reason. That method allows us to begin formulating the principles of a system of the science of metaphysics. And while the fourth definition reminds us that the completion of that system lays beyond the scope of a critique of pure reason, Kant's critique is still the first step towards that goal.

At first, Kant's *Critique of Pure Reason* did not fare much better than his inaugural dissertation. The most important philosophers in Germany did not read, review, or promote the book as Kant had hoped. Things became even worse when a series of negative reviews began to appear in leading journals. Instead of acknowledging that his critique must have "lacked something essential" and moving on to the next project, as he had done with his earlier works, Kant defended his critique in a series of revisions and polemical works published during the 1780s and 1790s. In the *Prolegomena to Any Future Metaphysics That Will Be Able to Come Forward as Science* (1783), Kant summarized many of the arguments he had presented in the "Transcendental Aesthetic," "Transcendental Analytic," and "Transcendental Dialectic." He also responded to critics who alleged that he denied the reality of space and time and conflated his transcendental idealism with Berkeley's dogmatic idealism. Yet Kant emphasized that a critique of pure reason was necessary to demonstrate the possibility of metaphysics. He also argued that a critique of pure reason was necessary to make metaphysics something more than a mere possibility. If metaphysics was to become an actual science, Kant thought it would have to pass through the fire of his critique.

Kant repeated many of his arguments about the necessity of a critique of pure reason in the "Preface" and "Introduction" to the second (B) edition of the first *Critique* (1787). The second (B) "Preface" begins with a history of the sciences, which shows that metaphysics has still not found its way onto "the secure path of science," even though it is older than logic, mathematics, or physics.[15] Because it has not undertaken a critique of pure reason, Kant says metaphysics has remained a "natural predisposition" (*Naturanlage*) of human reason and has not made the same kind of progress as the other sciences.[16] In addition to making metaphysics a science, Kant also claims that his critique will have a number of valuable "utilities" (*Nutzen*). The first of these utilities is negative, because it teaches us "never to venture with speculative reason beyond the boundaries of experience."[17] But that negative utility is hardly the only utility the critique of pure reason possesses. Kant maintains that his critique also makes positive contributions to practical philosophy, because it shows that the extension of the moral use of reason beyond the bounds of possible experience does not involve a contradiction; theoretical philosophy, because it demonstrates the ideality of space and time, the objective validity of the pure concepts of the understanding; and the public, by undermining the monopoly of the schools, calling philosophy back to matters of "universal human concern," and forcing it to recognize the dignity and equality of mankind.[18] Denying these positive utilities and emphasizing only the negative utility of his critique would be like saying "the police are of no positive utility because their chief business is to put a stop to the violence that citizens have to fear from other citizens, so that each can carry on his own affairs in peace and safety."[19]

Kant defended the originality of his critique in a polemical work called *On a Discovery Whereby Any New Critique of Pure Reason Is to Be Made Superfluous by an Older One* (1790). Written in response to a series of articles by Johann August Eberhard, who claimed that Leibniz's philosophy contains "just as much of a critique of reason" as Kant's critical philosophy, most of *On a Discovery* is devoted to the correction of Eberhard's misunderstanding and misrepresentation of the claims of Kant's critique.[20] In the end, Kant concludes that there never was any Leibnizian critique of pure reason or, if there was, "it was at least not granted to Mr. Eberhard to see it, to understand it, or at any other point to satisfy this need of philosophy, even at second hand."[21] Interestingly, Kant goes on to argue that his critique "might well be the true apology for Leibniz," since it does better justice to the peculiarities of Leibniz's metaphysics—the principle of sufficient reason, the doctrine of monads, and the doctrine of preestablished harmony—than the critics who did not understand him or would-be followers like Eberhard, who neglect "the key to all accounts of what pure reason produces from mere concepts," which is nothing other than "the critique of reason itself."[22]

The last line of argument Kant used to defend his critique concerns its historical necessity. Building on a claim he first made in the "History of Pure Reason" at the end of the first *Critique*, where he declares "the critical path alone is still open," Kant drafted an essay answering the question posed by the Prussian Royal Academy for its prize-essay competition in 1792/1795: "What Real Progress Has Metaphysics Made in Germany since the Time of Leibniz and Wolff?"[23] Kant never completed his essay, but his drafts show that he intended to focus on the various stages metaphysics had to traverse in order to determine the possibility and extent of a priori cognition. He maintains that the sequence of these stages is "founded in the nature of man's cognitive faculty," but argues that the last stage in this process is a critique of that faculty, which will bring metaphysics "into a condition of stability, both external and internal, in which it would need neither increase nor decrease, nor even be capable of this."[24] In a short essay published in 1796, Kant even compares this condition to a state of "perpetual peace" in philosophy, whose treaty would be secured by his critique.

Unfortunately, neither the definitions of a critique of pure reason Kant proposed in the first (A) and second (B) editions of the first *Critique* nor the defense that he mounted in his later works determined the reception of Kant's critique. Kant's conception of critique was appropriated by those who wished to promote his achievements, those who wished to criticize them, and those who wished to go beyond them, according to their own needs. That makes the interpretation of Kant's critique even more difficult, because our view of that critique has been shaped by their interests as well as our own.

Kant's empiricist and rationalist critics both saw the critique of pure reason as an attempt to define the limits of reason. While the infamous *Göttingen Review* (1782) criticizes Kant for denying the reality of space and time and for his idealism, it actually praises the first *Critique* for exposing "the most considerable difficulties of speculative philosophy" and providing "much material for salutary reflection to all those builders and defenders of metaphysical systems who all too proudly and boldly depend on their imagined pure reason."[25] Christian Garve, in his review of the *Critique of Pure Reason* in the *Allgemeine deutsche Bibliothek* (1783), says "the real purpose of this work is to determine the limits of reason, and its content consists in showing that reason goes beyond these limits whenever it asserts something about the actuality of any one thing."[26] Even a Wolffian like Eberhard saw the determination of the limits of reason as the primary contribution of Kant's critique. Eberhard simply objected to the particular way in which Kant had "drawn the line" with respect to the limits of reason and promoted a different critique that affirms the possibility of extending reason beyond the bounds of possible experience.[27]

The defenders of the critical philosophy, especially Johann Schultz and Jacob Sigismund Beck, did not see the determination of the limits of reason as the primary contribution of Kant's critique. In his *Exposition of Kant's Critique of Pure Reason* (1784), Schultz presents Kant's critique as "a system, which has been deeply thought through, down to its smallest constituent parts."[28] The purpose of that system is, Schultz argues, "to lead reason to true self-cognition, to investigate the legitimacy of reason's claim to possess metaphysical cognitions, and precisely through such an examination, to mark off the true limits beyond which reason may not venture in its speculations, if it does not want to stray into an empty realm of nothing but phantoms of the brain."[29] Beck also calls Kant's critique a system at the beginning of his *The Only Possible Standpoint from Which the Critical Philosophy Must Be Judged* (1796), though he usually uses the words "critical" and "critique" to distinguish Kant's philosophy from the speculative and dogmatic systems it renders obsolete.[30] For Schultz and Beck, Kant's critique is "the one true philosophy" that will answer every question, once its principles have been freed from Kant's convoluted arguments and his unintelligible prose.[31]

Reinhold and Fichte were no less enthusiastic about Kant's philosophy than Schultz and Beck, but they did not think his critique constituted a system. Referring to the definition of a critique of pure reason that Kant presents in the "Introduction" to the first (A) and second (B) editions of the first *Critique*, Reinhold insisted that a critique of pure reason is merely a propaedeutic to a system Kant had failed to complete.[32] He presented his own *Elementarphilosophie* (1789–91) as a reformulation and extension of the principles of the critical philosophy, that built on the foundation Kant had laid and made philosophy into a complete and unified whole. Fichte followed suit, arguing that Kant may have entertained the idea of a science and the thought of a system in his critique, but never actually constructed the system he envisioned.[33] This allowed Fichte to position his own *Wissenschaftslehre* (1794/1795) as the culmination of Kant's transcendental idealism, even though Kant regarded it as "a totally indefensible system."[34]

Like Reinhold and Fichte, Schelling and Schopenhauer thought Kant's critique was incomplete and imperfect. Yet they accepted the distinction Kant and his defenders had drawn between dogmatism and criticism. In his *Philosophical Letters on Dogmatism and Criticism* (1795/1804), Schelling presents the *Critique of Pure Reason* as "a negative refutation of dogmatism" that demonstrates "the theoretical *indemonstrability* of dogmatism."[35] He nevertheless denies that Kant's critique can "ascend to the absolute" and "rise to that absolute unity" that is the ultimate foundation of philosophy, since "criticism proceeds from the point it has in common with dogmatism."[36] This distinguishes the critical philosophy from philosophy itself, which must proceed from an absolute first principle and articulate its system without reference to the principles and presuppositions of other philosophies.[37] Schopenhauer actually adopts a very similar attitude towards Kant's critique in the "Critique of the Kantian Philosophy" that he added to the first volume of *The World as Will and Representation* (1818/1844). According to Schopenhauer, Kant's achievement "rests on the fundamental distinction between dogmatic and critical or transcendental philosophies."[38] Critical philosophy assumes the standpoint, principles, and assumptions of dogmatic philosophy in order to demonstrate their falsehood.[39] And while Kant failed to see that "appearance is the world as representation, and the thing in itself is the will," because he "pursued his symmetrical, logical system without giving enough thought to the objects he was dealing with," he was at least able to show that the dogmatic conception of metaphysics is impossible.[40]

Just as there were those who questioned the correctness and completeness of Kant's philosophy, there were also those who did not think the critical philosophy was so different from the dogmatic philosophy it claimed to overcome. In one of the fragments published in the *Athenaeum* (1798), Friedrich Schlegel said "the philosophy of the Kantians is probably termed critical *per antiphrasin;* or else it is an *epitheton ornans.*"[41] Using critique as an *epitheton ornans* suggests that there is no essential difference between critical philosophy and dogmatic philosophy. Saying that Kantians used the word "critical" *per antiphrasin* means they are just as dogmatic as the dogmatists they oppose. Hegel held a similar view of Kant's critique, which he outlined in his *Lectures on the History of Philosophy* (1840). According to Hegel, Kant's philosophy is critical because "its aim . . . is first of all to supply a criticism of our faculties of knowledge; for before obtaining knowledge we must inquire into the faculties of knowledge."[42] While this might seem like an important pursuit, Hegel points out that inquiring into the faculties of knowledge requires knowledge of them, so that it becomes unclear how we are "to know without knowing" and "apprehend the truth before the truth."[43] He denies that Kant's critique can ever attain the knowledge it seeks, because that knowledge is "already with itself."[44] In the end, critical philosophy is no different than dogmatic philosophy, because they both presuppose what they eventually conclude.

The interpretation and appropriation of Kant's critique did not end with Hegel. Indeed, it continues to this day. In this book, I have tried to reconstruct Kant's reasons for calling the *Critique of Pure Reason* a critique and explain the significance of that decision for his critical philosophy To do that, I have outlined the different ways in which the word "critique" was used in Kant's time, which prevents us from seeing his critique of pure reason as an entirely negative undertaking. My account of the development of Kant's critique supports this view, because it shows that Kant wanted to define the proper method of metaphysics, just as much as he wanted to purge metaphysics of the erroneous judgments and mistaken procedures that prevented it from making better progress as a science. The definitions of a critique of pure reason that Kant provides in the "Preface" and "Introduction" to the first (A) and second (B) editions of the first *Critique* also support this view, because they suggest that Kant thought his critique would secure reason's rightful claims; demonstrate the possibility of metaphysics; provide metaphysics with a new and better method; and pave the way for a complete system of transcendental philosophy. Kant's defense of the originality, utility, and necessity of his critique in the works he published after 1781 also provides evidence that Kant's critique was intended to provide metaphysics with a new foundation, instead of denying its possibility or desirability. Kant's critics, defenders, or successors did not always accept the definitions or justifications that Kant offered for his critique, but that simply means there are more conceptions of critique at play in German philosophy than the one associated with Kant.

# Notes

## Introduction

1. The exception to this rule seems to be Claus von Bormon, Helmut Holzhey, and Giorgio Tonelli, "Kritik," in *Historisches Wörterbuch der Philosophie,* vol. 4, ed. Joachim Ritter, Karlfried Gründer and Gottfried Gabriel (Basel: Schwabe Verlag, 1976), 1250–82.

2. The reasons these claims are false will be described more fully in what follows, but careful attention to the "Preface" to the first (A) edition of the *Critique of Pure Reason* shows that Kant intended to refute indifferentism, not dogmatism or skepticism, with his critique. There can also be no question that Kant thought he had demonstrated the possibility and necessity of metaphysics, and helped make metaphysics a science, through his critique. The *Prolegomena* and the "Preface" and "Introduction" to the second (B) edition also show that the critique of pure reason is important to Kant because it provides a foundation for a scientific metaphysics, not because it provides a foundation for other sciences. See Immanuel Kant, *Critique of Pure Reason,* trans. Paul Guyer and Allen W. Wood (New York: Cambridge University Press, 1998), 100–101, 109–14, 146–48 (Ax–Axii, Bxiv–Bxxiv, B19–B24). See also Immanuel Kant, *Prolegomena to Any Future Metaphysics That Will Be Able to Come Forward as a Science,* trans. Gary Hatfield, in *Theoretical Philosophy after 1781,* ed. Henry Allison and Peter Heath (New York: Cambridge University Press, 2002), 53–60 (IV:255–64).

3. Unavoidable misunderstanding and justifiable misrepresentation have most often been discussed under the heading of "hermeneutic violence." The necessity of hermeneutic violence is usually derived from *Being and Time* (1926), where Heidegger argues that interpretation "constantly has the character of *doing violence.*" See Martin Heidegger, *Being and Time,* trans. John Maquarrie and Edward Robinson (New York: Harper Perennial, 1962), 359 (§63, 311). See also John D. Caputo, *Radical Hermeneutics: Repetition, Deconstruction, and the Hermeneutic Project* (Bloomington: Indiana University Press, 1987), 63–64.

4. One of the most egregious periodizations imposed on Kant's intellectual development can be found in Hans Vaihinger's commentary on the *Critique of Pure Reason.* Vaihinger divides Kant's intellectual development into two separate "development processes" (*Entwicklungsprocesse*). He divides the first of these processes into a Leibnizian dogmatic period (1750–60), a Humean empiricist period (1760–64), and a critical period associated with Kant's *Dreams of a Spirit-Seer* (1766). In the second period, Vaihinger claims that Kant goes through another

Leibnizian dogmatic period (1770) and a period of Humean skepticism (1772) before he finally arrives at his critical philosophy. See Hans Vaihinger, *Commentar zu Kants Kritik der reinen Vernunft,* vol. 1 (Stuttgart: Spemann Verlag, 1881), 49. Erdmann repeats Vaihinger's periodization at the beginning of his edition of Kant's notes (*Reflexionen*) to the *Critique of Pure Reason,* and even uses Vaihinger's account of Kant's intellectual development to divide the notes into the categories "Kritischer Empirismus," "Kritischer Rationalismus," and into different periods of "Kriticismus." See Benno Erdmann, *Reflexionen Kants zur kritischen Philosophie, aus Kants Handschriftlichen Aufzeichnungen,* vol. 2: *Reflexionen zur "Kritik der reinen Vernunft"* (Leipzig: Feues Verlag, 1884), XII–LX. In the end, I have to agree with Manfred Kuehn that these kinds of accounts need to be taken (at best) *cum grano salis.* See Manfred Kuehn, *Kant: A Biography* (Cambridge: Cambridge University Press, 2001), 178–79. I might even go farther and suggest that periodizations like the ones proposed by Vaihinger and Erdmann presuppose which characteristics make Kant's philosophy critical, rather than explaining them.

5. On this point, I disagree with Frederick Beiser and Martin Schönfeld, who maintain that Kant intended to provide a complete philosophy of nature, by which they mean a metaphysical foundation for modern natural science, in his pre-critical works. See Frederick C. Beiser, "Kant's Intellectual Development: 1746–1781," in *The Cambridge Companion to Kant,* ed. Paul Guyer (Cambridge: Cambridge University Press, 1992), 30–31. See also Martin Schönfeld, *The Philosophy of the Young Kant* (Oxford: Oxford University Press, 2000), 3–8.

6. Kant, *Critique of Pure Reason,* 101 (Axii).

7. Immanuel Kant, *Correspondence* (Kant to Lambert, December 31, 1765), trans. Arnulf Zweig (Cambridge: Cambridge University Press, 1999), 82 (X:56).

8. Kant, *Correspondence* (Kant to Herz, February 21, 1772), 133 (X:130).

9. Kant, *Critique of Pure Reason,* 101 (Axiii)

10. Kant, *Critique of Pure Reason,* 113 (Bxxii).

11. Kant, *Critique of Pure Reason,* 111 (Bxviii).

12. Immanuel Kant, *On a Discovery Whereby Any New Critique of Pure Reason Is to Be Made Superfluous by an Older One,* trans. Henry Allison, in *Theoretical Philosophy after 1781,* ed. Henry Allison and Peter Heath (New York: Cambridge University Press, 2002), 283 (VIII:187).

Chapter 1

1. Giorgio Tonelli, "Critique and Related Terms Prior to Kant: A Historical Survey," *Kant-Studien* 69 (1978): 119.

2. See the "Introduction" to this book.

3. Tonelli, "Critique and Related Terms Prior to Kant," 119.

4. Kant, *Critique of Pure Reason,* 100 (Axi).

5. Tonelli, "Critique and Related Terms Prior to Kant," 119.

6. Tonelli, "Critique and Related Terms Prior to Kant," 119–20.

7. Tonelli, "Critique and Related Terms Prior to Kant," 119.

8. Tonelli, "Critique and Related Terms Prior to Kant," 120. See also H.

G. Lidell and R. Scott, *A Greek–English Lexicon* (Oxford: Oxford University Press, 1996), 996.

9. Tonelli, "Critique and Related Terms Prior to Kant," 120.

10. Lidell and Scott, *A Greek–English Lexicon*, 996.

11. Diogenes Laertius, *Lives of the Eminent Philosophers*, vol. II.7: *Chrysippus*, trans. R. D. Hicks (Cambridge: Loeb Classical Library, 2000), 314–15 (200).

12. Hans von Arnim, *Stoicorum veterum fragmenta*, vol. 3 (Munich: KG Saur Verlag, 2005), 164 (*SVF* III.654). I would like to thank the late Dr. Steven Strange of Emory University for translating this fragment from the Greek.

13. John F. D'Amico, *Theory and Practice in Renaissance Textual Criticism* (Berkeley: University of California Press, 1988), 8–38. See also Benedetto Bravo, "*Critice* in the Sixteenth and Seventeenth Centuries and the Rise of Historical Criticism," in *History of Scholarship: A Selection of Papers from the Seminar on the History of Scholarship Held Annually at the Warburg Institute*, ed. Christopher Ligota and Jean-Louis Quantin (New York: Oxford University Press, 2006), 135–96.

14. See Anthony Grafton, *Defenders of the Text: The Traditions of Scholarship in an Age of Science, 1450–1800* (Cambridge, Mass.: Harvard University Press, 1991), 1–3. See also Anthony Grafton, "The New Science and the Traditions of Humanism," in *The Cambridge Companion to Renaissance Humanism*, ed. Jill Kraye (New York: Cambridge University Press, 1996), 203–23.

15. Francis Bacon, *The New Organon*, ed. Lisa Jardine and Michael Silverthorne (New York: Cambridge University Press, 2000), 225.

16. Francis Bacon, *Of the Dignity and Advancement of Learning*, in *The Works of Francis Bacon*, vol. 4: *Translations of the Philosophical Works, Volume I*, ed. James Spedding, Robert Leslie Ellis, and Douglas Denon Heath (New York: Garrett, 1870), 493.

17. Bacon, *Of the Dignity and Advancement of Learning*, 494.

18. Bacon *Of the Dignity and Advancement of Learning*, 494.

19. Bacon *Of the Dignity and Advancement of Learning*, 494.

20. For a helpful account of Scaliger's comparison of Homer and Virgil, see David Scott Wilson-Okamura, *Virgil in the Renaissance* (New York: Cambridge University Press, 2010).

21. Richard Simon, *A Critical History of the Text of the New Testament* (London: R. Taylor, 1689), ii.

22. Simon, *A Critical History of the Text of the New Testament*, ii.

23. Simon, *A Critical History of the Text of the New Testament*, iv–v.

24. See John D. Woodbridge, "Richard Simon's Reaction to Spinoza's *Tractatus Theologicco-Politicus*," in *Spinoza in der Frühzeit Seiner Religiösen Wirkung*, edi. K. Gründner and W. Schmidt-Biggemann (Heidelberg: Schneider, 1984), 201–26. See also Richard H. Popkin, *The History of Skepticism from Savonarola to Bayle*, rev. and exp. ed. (Oxford: Oxford University Press, 2003), 219–38.

25. Pierre Bayle, *Historical and Critical Dictionary*, ed. and trans. Richard H. Popkin (Indianapolis: Hackett, 1991), 195 (C).

26. Louis Moreri, *Le Grand Dictionnaire historique*, vol. 9 (Lyon, 1671), 541–42.

27. Bayle, *Historical and Critical Dictionary*, 295 (E).

28. Tonelli points out that "for Bayle the term *critique* properly meant *philology* and *erudition* only." See Tonelli, "Critique and Related Terms Prior to Kant," 131. Richard Popkin confirms this view, explaining that Bayle's dictionary "began as an attempt to eliminate errors in previous histories" by questioning the sources and the interpretations of other historians. See Popkin, *The History of Skepticism*, 270.

29. Tonelli, "Critique and Related Terms Prior to Kant," 132–33.

30. See, for example, Friedrich August Wolff, *Darstellung der Altertums-Wissenschaft* (Berlin: Realschulbuchhandlung, 1807), 38–39. See also Friedrich Schleiermacher, *"Hermeneutics and Criticism" and Other Writings*, trans. Andrew Bowie (New York: Cambridge University Press, 1998), 158–224.

31. Immanuel Kant, *Reflexionen zur Logik 1956* (XVI:170).

32. Kant, *Critique of Pure Reason*, 101, 150 (Axii, A13/B27).

33. Immanuel Kant, *Lectures on Logic*, ed. and trans. J. Michael Young (New York: Cambridge University Press, 1992), 327 (XXIV:878).

34. Kant, *Lectures on Logic*, 449–54 (XXIV:712–16).

35. Nicolas Boileau, "Critical Reflections on Some Passages out of Longinus, Wherein Answer Is Occasionally Made to Some Objections of Monsieur Perrault against Homer and Pindar," in *The Works of Mons. Boileau Despreaux*, vol. 2 (London: E. Sanger and E. Curll, 1711), 88–127. See also Joseph M. Levine, *The Battle of the Books: History and Literature in the Augustan Age* (Ithaca, N.Y.: Cornell University Press, 1991), 127–28.

36. Perrault deals with Homer in many places in the five dialogues of his *Parallèle des anciens et des modernes* (1688–98). For a helpful overview of his criticism of Homer, see Kirsti Simonsuuri, *Homer's Original Genius: Eighteenth-Century Notions of the Early Greek Epic (1688–1798)* (New York: Cambridge University Press, 2010), 37–45.

37. William Wotton, *Reflections upon Ancient and Modern Learning* (London: J. Leake and P. Buck, 1694), 310–21.

38. Wotton, *Reflections upon Ancient and Modern Learning*, 318.

39. William Temple, "Some Thoughts upon Reviewing the Essay of Ancient and Modern Learning," in *Miscellanea, The Third Part*, ed. Jonathan Swift (London: B. Looke, 1701), 258–59.

40. Jonathan Swift, *A Tale of a Tub: Written for the Universal Improvement of Mankind, To Which Is Added, An Account of a Battel between the Antient and Modern Books in St. James's Library* (London: J. Nutt, 1704), 79.

41. John Dryden, "Author's Apology for Heroic Poetry and Poetic License," in *The Works of John Dryden*, 2nd ed., vol. 5, ed. Sir Walter Scott (Edinburgh: Constable, 1821), 106.

42. "Criticism, n.," *OED Online*, December 2012, Oxford University Press.

43. Dryden, "Author's Apology for Heroic Poetry and Poetic License," 106.

44. Joseph Addison, "Qualities Necessary for a Just Critic of *Paradise Lost*," in Richard Steele and Joseph Addison, *Selections from "The Tatler" and "The Spectator"* (No. 291, February 2, 1712), ed. Angus Ross New York: Penguin Classics, 1982), 423.

45. Addison, "Qualities Necessary for a Just Critic of *Paradise Lost*," 423.

46. Alexander Pope, "An Essay on Criticism," in *Alexander Pope: The Major Works*, ed. Pat Rogers (New York: Oxford University Press, 2006), 3 (611–25).

47. Pope, "An Essay on Criticism," 36 (639–42).

48. Samuel Johnson, *A Dictionary of the English Language: An Anthology*, ed. David Crystal (New York: Penguin Classics, 2006), 164.

49. Samuel Johnson, *The Rambler* (No. 93, February 5, 1751), in *Samuel Johnson: Selected Essays*, ed. David Womersley (New York: Penguin Classics, 2003), 187.

50. Gotthold Ephraim Lessing, *Briefe, die neueste Literatur betreffend* (17. Brief), in *Sämtliche Schriften*, vol. 8, ed. Karl Lachmann (Berlin: Walter de Gruyter, 1892), 41–44.

51. Lessing, *Briefe, die neueste Literatur betreffend* (17. Brief), 43.

52. Gotthold Ephraim Lessing, *Hamburg Dramaturgy* (New York: Dover, 1962), 254.

53. Friedrich Nicolai, "Briefe über die itzigen Zustand der schönen Wissenschaften in Deutschland (17. Brief)," in *Kritik ist überall, zumal in Deutschland, nötig: Satiren und Schriften zur Literatur*, ed. Wolfgang Albrecht (Leipzig: Gustav Kiepenheuer, 1987), 197.

54. Immanuel Kant, *Observations on the Feeling of the Beautiful and Sublime*, trans. Paul Guyer, in *Anthropology, History, and Education*, ed. Robert B. Louden and Günter Zöller (Cambridge: Cambridge University Press, 2007), 24, 26–27 (II:209, 212–13).

55. Immanuel Kant, *Critique of the Power of Judgment*, ed. Paul Guyer, trans. Paul Guyer and Eric Matthews (New York: Cambridge University Press, 2000), 166–167 (V:286).

56. Francis Hutcheson, *An Inquiry into the Original of Our Ideas of Beauty and Virtue*, ed. Wolfgang Leidhold (Indianapolis, Ind.: Liberty Fund, 2004), 23 (I.I.10).

57. Hutcheson, *An Inquiry into the Original of Our Ideas of Beauty and Virtue*, 80 (I.III.5).

58. David Hume, *A Treatise of Human Nature*, ed. P. H. Nidditch (New York: Oxford University Press, 1978), xv–xvi.

59. Hume, *A Treatise of Human Nature*, xvi.

60. David Hume, "Of the Standard of Taste," in *Essays: Moral, Political, and Literary*, rev. ed., ed. Eugene F. Miller (Indianapolis, Ind.: Liberty Fund, 1987), 229.

61. Hume, "Of the Standard of Taste," 242.

62. Edmund Burke, *A Philosophical Enquiry into the Sublime and Beautiful*, ed. David Woimersley (New York: Penguin Books, 1998), 64.

63. Burke, *A Philosophical Enquiry into the Sublime and Beautiful*, 65.

64. Burke, *A Philosophical Enquiry into the Sublime and Beautiful*, 66–67, 147–48, 178–86.

65. Burke, *A Philosophical Enquiry into the Sublime and Beautiful*, 75.

66. See Norman Kemp Smith, *A Commentary to Kant's "Critique of Pure Reason"* (New York: Palgrave Macmillan, 2003), 1. Guyer and Wood repeat Kemp Smith's claim in the notes to their translation of the *Critique of Pure Reason*, as does Robert Louden in his notes to Kant's *Lectures on Anthropology*. See Kant, *Critique of Pure Reason*, 715. See also Immanuel Kant, *Lectures on Anthropology*, ed. Allen W.

Wood and Robert B. Louden (Cambridge: Cambridge University Press, 2012), 531. German scholars also seem to have adopted Kemp Smith's claim. See Georg Mohr, *Kant's Theoretische Philosophie: Texte und Kommentar*, vol. 3 (Frankfurt am Main: Suhrkamp Verlag, 2004), 40.

67. Henry Home, *Elements of Criticism* (Honolulu: University Press of the Pacific, 2002), 194.

68. Home, *Elements of Criticism*, xi.

69. Home, *Elements of Criticism*, xii

70. Kemp Smith's claim that "the term critique or criticism, as employed by Kant, is of English origin" is manifestly false, as is his claim that "Kant was the first to employ it in German." The words "Critic" and "Critick" were present in the German language for more than a century before Kant used them in his *Critique of Pure Reason*. And they are derived from French rather than English. See *Deutsches Wörterbuch von Jacob and Wilhelm Grimm*, vol. 11 (Munich: Deutschen Taschenbuch Verlag, 1991), 2333–34.

71. Kant, *Lectures on Logic*, 530 (IX:15). These quotations are taken from the *Logik Jäsche*, which was published as *Immanuel Kants Logic* by Gottlob Benjamin Jäsche in 1800. Because it was composed by Jäsche, the *Logik Jäsche* is unreliable as a source for Kant's view on logic. There are, however, two reasons I have chosen to cite from this text. First, it includes the passage Kemp Smith cites as evidence for his claim that Kant derived his conception of critique from Home. Second, they are not entirely apocryphal. Jäsche drew the material for *Kants Logic* from Kant's notes, and the claims found in the passage Kemp Smith cites are also found in a series of notes and lecture transcripts dating from the late 1760s and 1770s. See, for example, Immanuel Kant, *Reflexionen zur Logik 1585, 1587, 1588, 1901* (XVI:25–27, 152) and the *Logik Pölitz* (c. 1780), where Kant says "aesthetics cannot be a doctrine, therefore it can never be a science. Home is therefore better to call it critique." Kant, *Vorlesungen über Logik* (XXIV:506).

72. Kant, *Lectures on Logic*, 530 (IX:15).

73. Johann Christoph Gottsched, *Versuch einer critischen Dichtkunst vor die Deutschen* (Leipzig: Bernhard Christoph Breitkopf, 1730), 5. The foreword ("An den Leser") in which Gottsched makes this remark was excised from subsequent editions of the *Dichtkunst*. It is not the critical edition of Gottsched's *Ausgewählte Werke*, which includes the prefaces to the second, third, and fourth editions. See Johann Christian Gottsched, *Ausgewählte Werke*, vol. 6.1–4: *Versuch einer Critischen Dichtkunst* (Berlin: Walter de Gruyter, 1973).

74. Gottsched, *Versuch einer critischen Dichtkunst*, 5.

75. Johann Christoph Gottsched, *Versuch einer critischen Dichtkunst für die Deutschen (Zweyte und verbesserte Auflage)* (Leipzig: Bernhard Christoph Breitkopf, 1737), 7. Gottsched expands upon this argument in part I, chapter 2: "On the Character of a Poet," where he argues that even a poet must be a critic and a philosopher in order to determine what is beautiful, what is pleasing, and so forth. See Gottsched, *Versuch einer critischen Dichtkunst (Zweyte Auflage)*, 93.

76. Georg Friedrich Meier, *Beurtheilung der Gottschedischen Dichtkunst* (Hildesheim: Georg Olms Verlag, 1975), 2–6, 10–16 (§2–§3, §7–10).

77. Georg Friedrich Meier, *Anfangsgründe aller schönen Wissenschaften*

(Hildesheim: Georg Olms Verlag, 1976), 5–6 (§3). See also *Auszug aus der Vernunftlehre* (XVI:6, §19).

78. Alexander Baumgarten, *Ästhetik,* vol. 1, trans. into German by Dagmar Mirbach (Hamburg: Felix Meiner Verlag, 2007), 12–13 (§5).

79. Baumgarten, *Ästhetik,* vol. 1, 20–21 (§14).

80. Kant, *Lectures on Logic,* 530 (IX:15).

81. Kant, *Critique of Pure Reason,* 156, 173 (A21/B35).

82. Kant, *Correspondence* (Kant to Reinhold, December 28/31, 1787), 272 (X:515).

83. Tonelli, "Critique and Related Terms Prior to Kant," 141.

84. Tonelli, "Critique and Related Terms Prior to Kant," 147. In another essay, Tonelli claims that "the very title of Kant's work is, in its specific meaning, of logical extraction, or else we should assume that a very astonishing coincidence took place." See Giorgio Tonelli, *Kant's "Critique of Pure Reason" within the Tradition of Modern Logic,* ed. David H. Chandler (Hildesheim: Georg Olms Verlag, 1994), 8. See also Giorgio Tonelli, "Kant's *Critique of Pure Reason* within the Tradition of Modern Logic," in *Akten des 4. Internationalen Kant Kongresses,* vol. 3 (Berlin: Walter de Gruyter, 1975), 190.

85. Fortunato Da Brescia, *Philosophia mentis (Tomus Primus: Logicam Continens)* (Brixia: 1749), xiv–xv.

86. Da Brescia, *Philosophia mentis,* 89.

87. Da Brescia, *Philosophia mentis,* 89. See also Tonelli, "Critique and Related Terms Prior to Kant," 142.

88. Antonio Genovisi, *Elementorum Artis Logicocriticae Libri V* (Naples, 1753), 4. See also Tonelli, "Critique and Related Terms Prior to Kant," 142–43.

89. Genovisi, *Elementorum artis logicocriticae,* 5–6. See also Tonelli, "Critique and Related Terms Prior to Kant," 143.

90. Genovisi, *Elementorum artis logicocriticae,* 5–6. See also Tonelli, "Critique and Related Terms Prior to Kant," 143.

91. Genovisi, *Elementorum artis logicocriticae,* 252–331.

92. Hermann Osterreider, *Logica Critica* (Ratisbon: Joannis Michaelis Englerth, 1760), 37.

93. Osterrieder, *Logica Critica,* 374.

94. Osterrieder, *Logica Critica,* 385–463.

95. Tonelli, "Critique and Related Terms Prior to Kant," 141–47. It could be argued that Tonelli fails to note that works like Caspar Schoppe's *De arte critica* (1597) and Jean Le Clerc's *Ars Critica* (1697) were works on philology and biblical hermeneutics rather than logic. They probably served as models for the later *ars critica* that Tonelli discusses. See Rene Wellek, *Concepts of Criticism,* ed. Stephen G. Nicholas (New Haven, Conn.: Yale University Press, 1963), 23–24.

96. Alexander Baumgarten, *Acroasis Logica* (Halle, 1761), 120–50. See also Tonelli, "Critique and Related Terms Prior to Kant," 146.

97. Alexander Baumgarten, *Sciagraphia encylopaedia philosophia* (Halle, 1768). See also Tonelli, "Critique and Related Terms Prior to Kant," 146.

98. Alexander Baumgarten, *Metaphysics,* trans. Courtney D. Fugate and John Hymers (London: Bloomsbury, 2013), 224 (§607).

99. Baumgarten, *Metaphysics*, 224 (§607).

100. Tonelli, "Critique and Related Terms Prior to Kant," 147.

101. Tonelli lists da Brescia, Crousaz, Doria, Genovisi, Lumm, Mehler, Monteiro, Nicholai, Osterrieder, Siebert, Vico, and Ziegler as authors who regarded logic as an *ars critica* in "Critique and Related Terms Prior to Kant," 142–47. I have searched in the *Bonner Kant-Korpus*, the *Kant im Kontext* CD-Rom, and Norbert Hinske's *Kant-Index* to confirm the absence of references to any of these authors in any of Kant's works.

102. See, for example, Kant, *Reflexionen zur Logik* 1628 and 1635 (XVI: 44–45, 58).

103. Kant, *Lectures on Logic*, 8 (XXIV:20).

104. Kant, *Lectures on Logic*, 13 (XXIV:26).

105. See, for example, Kant, *Lectures on Logic*, 14, 181, 253, 432–34, 525, 530 (IX:8, 15; XXIV:26, 228, 695–96).

106. On the significance of these practices, see Anthony Grafton, *Worlds Made by Words: Scholarship and Community in the Modern West* (Cambridge, Mass.: Harvard University Press, 2009). See also Hans Ulrich Gumbrecht, *The Powers of Philology: Dynamics of Textual Scholarship* (Urbana: University of Illinois Press, 2003).

107. Pope, "An Essay on Criticism," 36 (639–42).

108. Nicolai, "Briefe über die itzigen Zustand der schönen Wissenschaften in Deutschland," 197.

109. Johann Gottfried Herder, *On Recent German Literature: Selections from the Second Collection of Fragments: Johann Gottfried Herder: Selected Early Works, 1764–1767*, ed. Ernest A. Menze and Karl Menges, trans. Ernest A. Menze and Michael Palma (University Park: Pennsylvania State University Press, 1992), 172–73.

110. Kant, *Lectures on Logic*, 32 (XXIV:45).

111. Kant, *Lectures on Anthropology*, 24 (XXV:179).

112. Immanuel Kant, "M. Immanuel Kant's Announcement of the Programme of His Lectures for the Winter Semester 1765–1766," trans. David Walford and Ralf Meerbote, in *Theoretical Philosophy, 1755–1770*, ed. David Walford and Ralf Meerbote (New York: Cambridge University Press, 1992), 296 (II:310). I have emended Walford and Meerbote's translation, which distinguishes between logic as "a critique and canon of sound understanding" (*eine Kritik und Vorschrift des gesunden Verstandes*) and logic as "a critique and canon of real learning" (*eine Kritik und Vorschrift der eigentlichen Gelehrsamkeit*), in order to reflect Kant's reference to logic as *Kritik und Vorschrift*. Translating *Vorschrift* as "canon" is misleading because it introduces a technical term into a context in which it does not appear. A more literal translation might be "prescription" or "precept."

113. Kant, "Announcement," 296 (II:310).

114. Karl Ameriks is one of the few commentators to have done justice to the ambiguity and complexity of the relation between Kant's "rejection of transcendent metaphysics" and his "attempt to resuscitate pure philosophy in the form of a metaphysics of experience." See Karl Ameriks, "The Critique of Metaphysics: Kant and Traditional Ontology," in *The Cambridge Companion to Kant*, ed. Paul Guyer (Cambridge: Cambridge University Press, 1992), 250. See also Karl Ameriks, *Interpreting Kant's Critiques* (Oxford: Oxford University Press, 2003), 113.

## Chapter 2

1. See, for example, Beiser, "Kant's Intellectual Development: 1746–1781," 42. See also John Zammito, *Kant, Herder, and the Birth of Anthropology* (Chicago: University of Chicago Press, 2002), 83–87.

2. Beiser, "Kant's Intellectual Development: 1746–1781," 43.

3. Beiser, "Kant's Intellectual Development: 1746–1781," 43–46. Beiser's claim that "all the critical forces that had been mounting in the earlier writings of the 1760s now reach their climax in a complete skepticism toward metaphysics" in *Dreams of a Spirit-Seer* (45) is similar to claims found in Michael N. Forster, *Kant and Skepticism* (Princeton, N.J.: Princeton University Press, 2008), 16–20.

4. Kant, *Correspondence* (Kant to Lambert, December 31, 1765), 82 (X:56).

5. Kant, *Correspondence* (Kant to Mendelssohn, April 18, 1766), 90 (X:70).

6. See Zammito, *Kant, Herder, and the Birth of Anthropology*, 214–16.

7. Kant wrote to Lambert on December 31, 1765, but printed copies of *Dreams of a Spirit-Seer* were already available by January 31, 1766. See Immanuel Kant, *Theoretical Philosophy, 1755–1770*, ed. David Walford and Ralf Meerbote (Cambridge: Cambridge University Press, 1992), lxvii.

8. See, for example, Kant, *Critique of Pure Reason*, 100, 117 (Ax, Bxxxii).

9. Kant, *Correspondence* (Kant to Lambert, December 31, 1765), 82 (X:56).

10. Beiser, "Kant's Intellectual Development: 1746–1781," 45.

11. See Kant, *Theoretical Philosophy, 1755–1781*, lxii.

12. Pierre-Louis Moreau de Maupertuis, *Examen philosophique de la preuve de l'existence de Dieu employée dans l'Essai Comologie. P.L.M. de Maupertuis: Oeuvres (I)*, ed. Giorgio Tonelli (Hildesheim: Georg Olms Verlag, 1974), 394–99 (XIII–XXIV).

13. Maupertuis, *Examen philosophique* 399 (XXIV).

14. See Thomas Ahnert, "Newtonianism in Early Enlightenment Germany, c. 1720 to 1750: Metaphysics and the Critique of Dogmatic Philosophy," *Studies in History and Philosophy of Science*, 35, no. 3 (2004): 471–91.

15. On the academy's anti-Wolffianism and its effect on the prize-essay competitions, see William Clark, "The Death of Metaphysics in Enlightened Prussia," in *The Sciences in Enlightened Europe*, ed. William Clark, Jan Golinski, and Simon Schaffer (Chicago: University of Chicago Press, 1999), 438–44.

16. The winner of the 1747 competition, Johann Justi, claims in his *Untersuchung der Lehre von den Monaden und Einfachen Dingen* (Leipzig, 1748) that "I cannot conceal the fact that I have seen nothing in the world so poorly tied together as the doctrine of the monads" (§62). Adolf Friedrich Reinhard, the winner of the 1755 competition, is similarly dismissive of the optimism of Leibniz and Pope in his *Vergleichung des Lehrgebäudes des Herrn Pope von der Vollkommenheit der Welt, mit dem System des Herrn von Leibnitz* (Leipzig, 1757).

17. Adolf Harnack, *Geschichte der königlich Preußischen Akademie der Wissenschaften zu Berlin*, vol. 1 (Berlin: Reichsdruckerei, 1900), 263.

18. Clark, "The Death of Metaphysics in Enlightened Prussia," 439.

19. See K.-R. Biermann, "Was Leonhard Euler Driven from Berlin by J. H. Lambert?" in *Euler and Modern Science*, ed. N. N. Bogolyubov, G. K. Mikhaïlov, and

A. P. Yuskevich, trans. Robert Burns (Washington, D.C.: Mathematical Association of America, 2007), 91–93.

20. It is possible that Euler was planning to leave Berlin when the academy voted on the winner of its 1763 prize-essay competition. The king began making overtures to D'Alembert to come to Berlin to assume the presidency of the academy around that time, and Euler and D'Alembert were not on good terms. See Thomas L. Hankins, *Jean D'Alembert: Science and Enlightenment* (New York: Gordon and Breach, 1990), 55–65.

21. In his first letter to Voltaire—written on August 8, 1736—Frederick praised Wolff as a philosopher "who has been cruelly accused of irreligion and atheism because he carried light into the most shadowy recesses of metaphysics and because he treated this difficult subject in a manner as elevated as it was clear and precise." Voltaire responded, with the deference due to a king, saying that he saw Wolff's "metaphysical ideas as things which do honor to the human mind" and "flashes in the midst of a dark night." Later, under the influence of Voltaire, Maupertuis, and Euler, Frederick came to believe Germans lacked "two things, language and taste," and that none of them had contributed anything to philosophy since "the genius of Leibnitz and the great monad Wolff." See *Letters of Voltaire and Frederick the Great*, ed. and trans. Richard Aldington (New York: Brentano's, 1927), 20, 26, 364.

22. On the tie-breaking vote by Sulzer, see Alexander Altmann, *Moses Mendelssohn: A Biographical Study* (London: Littman Library of Jewish Civilization, 1998), 116. See also Paul Guyer, "Mendelssohn and Kant: One Source of the Critical Philosophy," in *Kant on Freedom, Law, and Happiness* (Cambridge: Cambridge University Press, 2000), 17–18.

23. Moses Mendelssohn, "On Evidence in Metaphysical Sciences," in *Moses Mendelssohn: Philosophical Writings*, ed. and trans. Daniel O. Dahlstrom (New York: Cambridge University Press, 1997), 255.

24. Moses Mendelssohn and Gotthold Ephraim Lessing, *Pope, ein Metaphysiker!* in *Moses Mendelssohn: Gesammelte Schriften*, vol. 2: *Schriften zur Philosophie und Ästhetik I*, ed. Fritz Bamberger and Leo Strauss (Stuttgart-Bad Cannstatt, 1972), 48.

25. Mendelssohn, "On Evidence in Metaphysical Sciences," 255.

26. Mendelssohn, "On Evidence in Metaphysical Sciences," 255.

27. Mendelssohn, "On Evidence in Metaphysical Sciences," 268. Emily Grosholz has produced a wonderful study that suggests the relationship between mathematical notation and its objects are nowhere near as natural or necessary as Mendelssohn suggests. See Emily R. Grosholz, *Representation and Productive Ambiguity in Mathematics and the Sciences* (Oxford: Oxford University Press, 2007).

28. Mendelssohn, "On Evidence in Metaphysical Sciences," 267.

29. Mendelssohn, "On Evidence in Metaphysical Sciences," 272–73.

30. For Mendelssohn's views on verbal disputes, see Daniel O. Dahlstrom, "Verbal Disputes in Mendelssohn's *Morgenstunden*," in *Moses Mendelssohn's Metaphysics and Aesthetics*, ed. Reiner Munk (Dordrecht: Springer, 2011), 3–20.

31. Mendelssohn, "On Evidence in Metaphysical Sciences," 273.

32. Mendelssohn, "On Evidence in Metaphysical Sciences," 273.

33. Mendelssohn, "On Evidence in Metaphysical Sciences," 274.

34. Mendelssohn, "On Evidence in Metaphysical Sciences," 270.

35. Mendelssohn, "On Evidence in Metaphysical Sciences," 269.

36. Mendelssohn, "On Evidence in Metaphysical Sciences," 272.

37. Mendelssohn, "On Evidence in Metaphysical Sciences," 269.

38. Mendelssohn, "On Evidence in Metaphysical Sciences," 271. See also Immanuel Kant, *Inquiry concerning the Distinctness of Natural Theology and Morality*, trans. David Walford and Ralf Meerbote, in *Theoretical Philosophy, 1755–1770*, ed. David Walford and Ralf Meerbote (New York: Cambridge University Press, 1992), 251 (II:279).

39. See, for example, Giorgio Tonelli, "Der Streit über die mathematische Methode in der Philosophie in der ersten Hälfte des 18. Jahrhunderts und die Entstehung von Kants Schrift über die *Deutlichkeit*," *Archiv für Philosophie* 9 (1959): 51–84.

40. See Beiser, "Kant's Intellectual Development: 1746–1781," 40. Similar arguments are found in Herman-J. De Vleeschwuer, *The Development of Kantian Thought: The History of a Doctrine*, trans. A. R. C. Duncan (London: Thomas Nelson and Son, 1962), 33–35.

41. Kant, *Inquiry*, 247 (II:275).

42. Kant, *Inquiry*, 255 (II:283).

43. Kant, *Inquiry*, 255 (II:283).

44. Kant, *Inquiry*, 247 (II:275).

45. Kant, *Inquiry*, 247 (II:275).

46. Kant, *Inquiry*, 247 (II:275).

47. Kant, *Inquiry*, 256 (II.283).

48. Kant, *Inquiry*, 248 (II:276).

49. Christian Wolff, *Vollständiges Mathematisches Lexikon* (Leipzig, 1747), 302.

50. Kant, *Inquiry*, 248 (II:276).

51. Kant, *Inquiry*, 249 (II:277).

52. Kant, *Inquiry*, 248 (II:276).

53. Kant, *Inquiry*, 249 (II:277).

54. Kant, *Inquiry*, 249, 269 (II:277, 296).

55. Kant, *Inquiry*, 252 (II:280).

56. Kant, *Inquiry*, 252 (II:280).

57. Kant, *Inquiry*, 252–53 (II: 280).

58. Kant, *Inquiry*, 254 (II:281).

59. Kant, *Inquiry*, 252 (II:280).

60. Kant, *Inquiry*, 258 (II:285–86).

61. Ernst Cassirer, *Kant's Life and Thought*, trans. James Haden (New Haven, Conn.: Yale University Press, 1981), 77.

62. Rudolf Malter, *Immanuel Kant in Rede und Gespräch* (Hamburg: Felix Meiner Verlag, 1990), 342 (423).

63. The editors of Mendelssohn's *Gesammelte Schriften* question the scholarship of many prominent Kantians (Fischer, Adickes, Vörlander, Cassirer, etc.) who claim that Mendelssohn was the author of the reviews of Kant's works in the *Litteraturbriefe*. Still, they think it is likely that Mendelssohn wrote or rewrote ex-

tended sections of the reviews in his capacity as editor of the *Litteraturbriefe*. They have therefore included the reviews in their edition of Mendelssohn's writings. See Moses Mendelssohn, "Briefe, die neueste Litteratur betreffend (4. Januar 1759–4. Juli 1765)," in *Moses Mendelssohn: Gesammelte Schriften, Jubiläumsausgabe*, vol. 5,1–5,4, ed. Eva J. Engel et al. (Stuttgart-Bad Cannstatt: Frommann-Holzboog Verlag, 2004), 602–16, 657–69 (5,1), 414–23, 505–6 (5,3a), 817–19 (5,3b).

64. At the end of the review of Kant's essay on *Negative Magnitudes*, Resewitz/Mendelssohn notes that he has spent many pages reviewing a very short article. He justifies the attention he has devoted to Kant's essay by saying "my spirit has found more nourishment there than in many large systems" (*Mein Geist hat mehr Nahrung darin gefunden, als in manchen großen Systemen*). See Moses Mendelssohn, *Litteraturbriefe* 324 (September 5, 1765): 669.

65. See Kuehn, *Kant: A Biography*, 142. While Manfred Kuehn is right to emphasize the role the controversy over *The Only Possible Argument* played in establishing Kant's public reputation in his biography, he fails to appreciate the connection between the Resewitz-Mendelssohn review and the success of Kant's *Inquiry* in the 1763 prize-essay competition.

66. Johann Caspar Lavater, *Reisetagebücher*, part 1: *Tagbuch von der Studien- und Bildungsreise nach Deutschland 1763 und 1764*, ed. Horst Weigelt (Göttingen: Vandenhoeck & Ruprecht, 1997), 797.

67. Kant, *Correspondence* (Lavater to Kant, April 8, 1774), 150–51 (X:165–66). Lavater asks Kant whether he will maintain (1) "That our critique could hardly be more remote from pure reason than it is," (2) "That until we fix our *observations* more on *human beings*, all our wisdom is folly," (3) "That the reason we always fall so horribly into error is that we seek to find outside of us what is only within us," (4) "That we cannot and may not have any knowledge whatsoever of the inner nature of things but only of their *relations* to our needs," (5) That any and every occupation, writing, meditation, reading is childishness and foolishness unless it be a means of sedation and a means of satisfying human needs," and (6) "That manifestly out of a thousand books and ten thousand bookish judgments there is hardly one that is not a would-be sedative of its author's needs—though this is by no means noticed by particular readers."

68. Kant, *Correspondence* (Lambert to Kant, November 13, 1765), 77 (X:51).

69. Kant, *Correspondence* (Lambert to Kant, November 13, 1765), 77 (X:51).

70. Lambert's *On the Method of More Correctly Proving Metaphysics, Theology, and Morals* was not published until 1918, when the manuscript was edited and published as a special volume of *Kant-Studien*. See Johann Heinrich Lambert, *Über die methode die Metaphysik, Theologie, und Moral richtiger zu beweisen, Kant-Studien, Erganzungshefte*, no. 42, ed. K. Bopp (Berlin: Verlag von Reuther & Reichard, 1918).

71. Kant, *Correspondence* (Lambert to Kant, November 13, 1765), 77 (10:51).

72. Kant, *Correspondence* (Lambert to Kant, November 13, 1765), 77 (10:51).

73. Lambert certainly had many purely intellectual reasons for writing to Kant, but he also had some practical matters in mind. He thought Kant might help him find a publisher for his *Anlage zur Architektonic oder Theorie des Einfachen und des Ersten in der philosophischen und mathematischen Erkenntniss*. Lambert expresses considerable frustration with the readers and booksellers in Berlin, who, he says,

"corrupt each other, both of them wanting to avoid any thorough thinking." Because they "philosophize exclusively about so-called *belles-lettres*," he could not find anyone willing to print a serious work on metaphysics, leaving his *Architektonic* to languish for want of a publisher. Lambert enclosed a number of pages from the work with his first letter to Kant, so that he would be able to inquire whether the publisher who had announced *The Proper Method of Metaphysics* might also be interested in Lambert's work. Kant showed the pages to his publisher, Kanter, who then wrote to Lambert himself and arranged a meeting in Berlin. While Kanter declined to publish the work himself, it was eventually brought forward by his partner and former apprentice Johann Friedrich Hartknoch. Hartknoch was the same publisher who would bring the *Critique of Pure Reason* to the public in 1781. See Kant, *Correspondence* (Lambert to Kant, November 13, 1765), 78 (X:53). See also Kant, *Correspondence* (Kant to Lambert, December 31,1765), 81 (X:54–55).

74. Kant, *Correspondence* (Lambert to Kant, November 13, 1765), 77 (X:51).

75. Kant, *Correspondence* (Lambert to Kant, November 13, 1765), 77–78 (X:52).

76. Kant, *Correspondence* (Lambert to Kant, November 13, 1765), 77–78 (X:52).

77. Kant, *Inquiry*, 268 (II:295).

78. Kant, *Correspondence* (Lambert to Kant, November 13, 1765), 77–78 (X:52).

79. Kant, *Correspondence* (Lambert to Kant, November 13, 1765), 77 (X:51).

80. Lambert, *Über die methode die Metaphysik, Theologie, und Moral richtiger zu beweisen*, 20 (§45).

81. Kant, *Correspondence* (Kant to Lambert, December 31, 1765), 81 (X:55).

82. Kant, *Correspondence* (Kant to Lambert, December 31, 1765), 81–82 (X:55–56).

83. Kant, *Correspondence* (Kant to Lambert, December 31, 1765), 82 (X:56).

84. Kant, *Correspondence* (Kant to Lambert, December 31, 1765), 82 (X:56).

85. See, for example, Eckart Förster, "Kant's Notion of Philosophy," *The Monist* 72 (1989): 285–86.

86. Kant, "Announcement," 294 (II:308). See also Förster, "Kant's Notion of Philosophy," 287.

87. Kant, "Announcement," 294 (II:308). See also Förster, "Kant's Notion of Philosophy," 287.

88. Kant, "Announcement," 294 (II:308). See also Förster, "Kant's Notion of Philosophy," 287.

89. Kant, "Announcement," 294–95 (II:308). See also Förster, "Kant's Notion of Philosophy," 287.

90. Kant, "Announcement," 295 (II:308–9). See also Förster, "Kant's Notion of Philosophy," 287–88.

91. Förster, "Kant's Notion of Philosophy," 288.

92. Kant, "Announcement," 295 (II:309).

93. See, for example, Christian Wolff, *Vernünftige Gedancken von Gott, der Welt, und der Seele des Menschen, auch allen Dingen überhaupt (German Metaphysics)*, in *Christian Wolff: Gesammelte Werke*, pt. 1, vol. 2.1, ed. Jean École et al. (Hildesheim: Georg Olms Verlag, 2009), §191. See also Baumgarten, *Metaphysics,*§503.

94. Kant, *Correspondence* (Kant to Lambert, December 31, 1765), 82 (X:54–57).

95. Kant, *Correspondence* (Kant to Lambert, December 31, 1765), 82 (X:56). Dieter Henrich has suggested that the title Kant mentions in his letter is, in fact, the first part of the work he would publish twenty years later as *The Groundwork of the Metaphysics of Morals* (1785). See Dieter Henrich, "Über Kants früheste Ethik," *Kant-Studien* 54 (1963): 404. Arnulf Zweig makes a similar claim in his notes on Kant's correspondence, suggesting that "Kant's *Metaphysische Anfangsgründe der Naturwissenschaft* did not in fact appear until 20 years later, in 1786." See *Immanuel Kant: Correspondence*, 83. It is certainly possible that the essays Kant mentioned in his letter to Lambert were early drafts or sketches for the works Kant published much later; however, I think Henrich and Zweig have failed to show that there is any material connection between the essays Kant proposes in his letter to Lambert and the works he published in the late 1780s. The similarities of their titles is simply not sufficient evidence that there is any real connection between them.

96. Moses Mendelsshon, *Kant: Träume eines Geistersehers*, AdB, 1767, 4.2, in *Moses Mendelssohn: Gesammelte Schriften, Jubiläumsausgabe*, vol. 5,2, ed. Eva J. Engel et al. (Stuttgart-Bad Cannstatt: Frommann-Holzboog Verlag, 2004), 73. Two earlier reviews—by Herder and Feder—did not identify Kant as the author of *Dreams of a Spirit-Seer*, though Herder was probably aware that Kant had written the book. See Gregory R. Johnson, *Kant on Swedenborg: Dreams of a Spirit-Seer and Other Writings* (West Chester, Pa.: Swedenborg Foundation, 2002), 114–18, 120–21.

97. Kant, *Correspondence* (Kant to Mendelssohn, April 8, 1766), 90 (X:70). Kant sent a copy of *Dreams of a Spirit-Seer* to Mendelssohn on February 7, 1766, along with copies for Lambert, Sulzer, Formey, Sack, Spalding, and Süsmilch. The number of copies Kant sent and their recipients show that Kant was eager to solidify his relations with the philosophers in Berlin. See Kant, *Correspondence* (Kant to Mendelssohn, February 7, 1766), 88 (X:67–68).

98. Alison Laywine associates this position with Kuno Fischer and Ernst Cassirer in her account of the reception of *Dreams of a Spirit-Seer*. See Alison Laywine, *Kant's Early Metaphysics and the Origins of the Critical Philosophy* (Atascadero, Calif.: Ridgeview, 1993), 15–24.

99. Alison Laywine defends this position, arguing that "the satire directed against Swedenborg in this work is equally directed against Kant himself—and this for the following reason: Kant and the Swedish spirit-seer both treat immaterial things as thought they could be objects of human sensibility. Swedenborg stands in for Kant here." See Laywine, *Kant's Early Metaphysics*, 8. Similar readings have been proposed by Frederick Beiser and Martin Schönfeld. See especially Schönfeld, *The Philosophy of the Young Kant*, 229–44.

100. Forster, *Kant and Skepticism*, 16–20.

101. Beiser, "Kant's Intellectual Development: 1746–1781," 45.

102. Zammito, *Kant, Herder, and the Birth of Anthropology*, 211, 215.

103. Kant, *Correspondence* (Kant to Lambert, December 31, 1765), 82 (X:56).

104. Kant, *Correspondence* (Kant to Mendelssohn, April 8, 1766), 90 (X:70).

105. Kant, *Correspondence* (Kant to Mendelssohn, April 8, 1766), 91 (X:71).

106. Kant, *Correspondence* (Kant to Mendelssohn, April 8, 1766), 91 (X:71).

107. Kant, *Correspondence* (Kant to Mendelssohn, April 8, 1766), 90 (X:70).

108. Kant, *Correspondence* (Kant to Mendelssohn, April 8, 1766), 90 (X:70). For similar claims about the value of metaphysics, see Kant, *Critique of Pure Reason*, 100–101, 118–19 (Ax-Axi, Bxxxii–Bxxxiii).

109. Kant, *Correspondence* (Kant to Mendelssohn, April 8, 1766), 90 (X:70).

110. Kant, *Correspondence* (Kant to Mendelssohn, April 8, 1766), 90 (X:70).

111. Kant, *Inquiry*, 255 (II:283). See also Kant, *Correspondence* (Kant to Lambert, December 31, 1765), 82 (X:57).

112. Kant, *Correspondence* (Kant to Mendelssohn, April 8, 1766), 90 (X:70).

113. Kant, *Correspondence* (Kant to Mendelssohn, April 8, 1766), 91 (X:71).

114. Kant, *Correspondence* (Kant to Mendelssohn, April 8, 1766), 91 (X:71). See also Kant, *Correspondence* (Kant to Lambert, December 31, 1765), 82 (X:56–57).

115. Kant, *Correspondence* (Kant to Lambert, December 31, 1765), 82 (X:56–57).

116. Kant, *Correspondence* (Kant to Mendelssohn, April 8, 1766), 91 (X:71). On the relationship between "catharticon" and "organon" in Kant's critical philosophy, see Tonelli, *Kant's "Critique of Pure Reason" within the Tradition of Modern Logic*, 39–40.

117. Kant, *Correspondence* (Kant to Charlotte von Knobloch, August 10, 1762/1763), 71 (X:44).

118. Immanuel Kant, *Dreams of a Spirit-Seer Elucidated by the Dreams of Metaphysics*, trans. David Walford and Ralf Meerbote, in *Theoretical Philosophy, 1755–1770*, ed. David Walford and Ralf Meerbote (New York: Cambridge University Press, 1992), 307–8 (II:320).

119. Kant, *Dreams of a Spirit-Seer*, 308 (II:320).

120. Kant, *Dreams of a Spirit-Seer*, 305 (II:317).

121. Kant, *Dreams of a Spirit-Seer*, 308 (II:320).

122. Kant, *Dreams of a Spirit-Seer*, 308 (II:320).

123. Kant, *Dreams of a Spirit-Seer*, 308 (II:320).

124. Kant, *Dreams of a Spirit-Seer*, 308 (II:320).

125. Kant, *Dreams of a Spirit-Seer*, 311 (II:323).

126. Kant, *Dreams of a Spirit-Seer*, 330–31 (II:343).

127. Kant, *Dreams of a Spirit-Seer*, 330–31 (II:343).

128. Kant, *Dreams of a Spirit-Seer*, 329 (II:342).

129. Kant, *Dreams of a Spirit-Seer*, 335 (II:348).

130. Kant, *Dreams of a Spirit-Seer*, 336 (II:349).

131. Kant, *Correspondence* (Kant to Mendelssohn, April 8, 1766), 66 (X:70).

132. Kant, *Dreams of a Spirit-Seer*, 336 (II:349).

133. Kant, *Dreams of a Spirit-Seer*, 336 (II:349).

134. Kant, *Dreams of a Spirit-Seer*, 336 (II:349).

135. Kant, *Inquiry*, 247 (II:275).

136. Kant, *Dreams of a Spirit-Seer*, 354–59 (II:368–73).

137. Beiser, "Kant's Intellectual Development: 1746–1781," 45.

138. Kant, *Dreams of a Spirit-Seer*, 354 (II:368).

139. Kant, *Notes and Fragments*, 24 (XX:181).

140. Beiser, "Kant's Intellectual Development: 1746–1781," 43. See also Schönfeld, *The Philosophy of the Young Kant,* 231.

141. There are ways of approximating the referential context of Kant's remarks, using the system of notation introduced by Marie Rischmüller in her edition of Kant's *Remarks.* See Marie Rischmüller, *Immanuel Kant: Bemerkungen in den Beobachtungen über das Gefühl des Schönen und Erhabenen* (Hamburg: Meiner, 1991). Paul Guyer has reproduced Rischmüller's notation in the Cambridge edition of Kant's *Notes and Fragments.* See Kant, *Notes and Fragments,* 2. Concordances indicating the context and reference of other *Reflexionen* have been developed by Norbert Hinske, Ricardo Pozzo, Günther Gawlich, and Lothar Kreimendahl.

142. Kant, *Notes and Fragments,* 24 (XX:180).

143. Kant, *Notes and Fragments,* 24 (XX:180).

144. Kant, *Dreams of a Spirit-Seer,* 354 (II:367).

145. Kant, *Dreams of a Spirit-Seer,* 354 (II:367).

146. Kant, *Dreams of a Spirit-Seer,* 354 (II:367).

147. Kant, *Dreams of a Spirit-Seer,* 354 (II:368).

148. Kant, *Dreams of a Spirit-Seer,* 354 (II:368).

149. Kant, *Correspondence* (Kant to Mendelssohn, April 8, 1766), 90 (X:70).

150. Kant, *Correspondence* (Kant to Lambert, December 31, 1765), 82 (X:56).

151. Kant, *Correspondence* (Kant to Lambert, December 31, 1765), 82 (X:56).

152. Beiser, "Kant's Intellectual Development: 1746–1781," 42.


## Chapter 3

1. Kant, *Correspondence* (Kant to Herz, February 21, 1772), 132 (X:129). Arnulf Zweig translates "Die Grenzen der Sinnlichkeit und der Vernunft" (X:129) as "The Limits of Sensibility and Reason" in the translation of Kant's letter included in the Cambridge edition. Yet when Kant mentions the same title in a previous letter to Herz, Zweig renders it "The Bounds of Sensibility and of Reason." See Kant, *Correspondence* (Kant to Herz, June 7, 1771), 127 (X:122–23). This inconsistency is problematic, not only because it renders the same title differently, but also because Kant makes a technical distinction between limits (*Schranken*) and bounds (*Grenzen*) in Kant, *Prolegomena,* 142 (IV:352). I have emended Zweig's translation and other translations which render *Die Grenzen der Sinnlichkeit und der Vernunft* as "The Limits of Sensibility and Reason," replacing them with "The Bounds of Sensibility and Reason" throughout this chapter. The latter translation follows the lexicon established for the *Cambridge Edition of the Works of Immanuel Kant.*

2. Kant, *Correspondence* (Kant to Herz, February 21, 1772), 133 (X:130).

3. Kant, *Correspondence* (Kant to Herz, February 21, 1772), 133 (X:130). Zweig translates the question "auf welchem Grunde beruhet die Beziehung deienigen was man in uns Vorstellung nennt, auf den Gegenstand?" as "What is the ground of the relation of that which in us is called representation to the object." Throughout this chapter, I refer to this question as "the question concerning the ground of the relation . . ." in order to avoid awkward repetition.

4. On this debate, see the exchange between Wolfgang Carl and Lewis White Beck in Eckart Förster, *Kant's Transcendental Deductions: The Three Critiques and the "Opus Postumum"* (Stanford, Calif.: Stanford University Press, 1989), 3–26.

5. *Reflexionen* referring to a critique of pure reason have been dated prior to Kant's letter to Herz, though the dates are unreliable. *Reflexion* 3964 (c. 1769) says metaphysics is "a critique of pure reason and not a doctrine," while *Reflexion* 3970 (c. 1769) calls metaphysics "the critique of human reason." See Kant, *Notes and Fragments*, 106–7 (XVII:368–69). See also Mohr, *Kant's Theoretische Philosophie*, 40.

6. Kant, *Correspondence* (Kant to Herz, February 21, 1772), 135 (X:132).

7. In the "Introduction" to their translation of the *Critique of Pure Reason*, Paul Guyer and Allen W. Wood say the work Kant was preparing was "for the first time entitled a Critique of Pure Reason" in Kant's 1772 letter to Herz. See Kant, *Critique of Pure Reason*, 47–48. Given the text of Kant's letter in the *Akademie* edition, it is not clear that this statement is correct. It is probable that Guyer and Wood were relying on Immanuel Kant, *Philosophical Correspondence, 1759–1799*, ed. and trans. Arnulf Zweig (Chicago: University of Chicago Press, 1967), 73, where Zweig renders the key passage in Kant's February 21, 1772, letter to Herz as "now I am in a position to bring out a 'Critique of Pure Reason' that will deal with the nature of practical as well as theoretical knowledge." In the more recent Cambridge edition of Kant's correspondence, Zweig does not capitalize the phrase or mark it off with quotation marks.

8. The other title Kant refers to in his 1772 letter to Herz, "The Bounds of Sensibility and Reason," is clearly marked as a title, appearing as "D i e  G r e n t z e n  d e r  S i n n l i c h k e i t  u n d  d e r  V e r n u n f t" in the *Akademie* edition (X:129) and "The Limits of Sensibility and Reason" in the Cambridge edition (132).

9. Werner Stark lists Kant's letter in a list of "missing pieces" (*verschollenen Stücke*) from the collection of the Staatsbibliothek in Berlin. See Werner Stark, *Nachforschungen zu Briefen und Handschriften Immanuel Kants* (Berlin: Akademie Verlag, 1993), 277. Thankfully, the typographical setting of the passage in question does not vary in German editions of Kant's correspondence from the nineteenth and twentieth centuries. Kant's reference to a "Critic der reinen Vernunft" in his 1772 letter to Herz is not spaced or marked as a title in any way in the *Akademie* edition, the Cassirer edition, the Fischer edition, or the Schöndörfer-Malter editions of Kant's correspondence. English editions have been less consistent, but the Cambridge edition agrees with the German editions on this point.

10. Lewis White Beck, "Kant's Letter to Marcus Herz February 21, 1772," in *Studies in the Philosophy of Kant* (New York: Bobbs-Merrill, 1965), 58. See also Kant, *Correspondence*, 138, note 7, where Zweig assumes that "*eine Critick der reinen Vernunft* is a description, since Kant has already announced another intended name for the work."

11. Kant, *Correspondence* (Kant to Herz, February 21, 1772), 132 (X: 130).

12. Kant, *Correspondence* (Kant to Herz, February 21, 1772), 133 (X:130).

13. Kant, *Correspondence* (Kant to Suckow, December 15, 1769), 101 (X:83).

14. Kant, *Correspondence* (Kant to Freiherr von Fürst und Kupfenberg, March 16, 1770), (X:90).

15. Kant, *Correspondence* (Kant to Freiherr von Fürst und Kupfenberg,

March 16, 1770), (X:91). See also Kant, *Correspondence* (Kant to King Frederick II, March 19, 1770), (X:92–93).

16. Kant, *Correspondence* (Kant to Freiherr von Fürst und Kupfenberg, March 16, 1770), (X:90).

17. Herz is referred to as "*berolinensis, gente iudaeus, medicinae et philosophiae cultor*" on the title page of Kant's dissertation, meaning that he is "from Berlin, of Jewish descent, a student of medicine and philosophy." The fact that Herz defended Kant's dissertation is a testament to Herz's character and his philosophical acumen, but also Kant's liberalism. German universities had only recently begun accepting Jewish students and many still denied them advanced degrees at the time of Kant's defense. Of course, this does not excuse the anti-Semitic comments in Kant's *Anthropology* or the anti-Judaism of his account of rational religion in *Religion within the Boundaries of Mere Reason.* See, for example, Immanuel Kant, "Anthropology from a Pragmatic Point of View," trans. Robert B. Louden, in *Anthropology, History, and Education,* ed. Robert B. Louden and Günter Zöller (Cambridge: Cambridge University Press, 2007), 312 (VII:205–6). See also Immanuel Kant, "Religion within the Boundaries of Mere Reason," trans. George di Giovanni, in *Religion and Rational Theology,* ed. Allen W. Wood and George di Giovanni (New York: Cambridge University Press, 1996), 146–63 (VI:115–37).

18. Immanuel Kant, *On the Form and Principles of the Sensible and the Intelligible World (Inaugural Dissertation),* trans. G. B. Kerferd and D. E. Walford, in *Theoretical Philosophy, 1755–1770,* ed. David Walford and Ralf Meerbote (New York: Cambridge University Press, 1992), 377 (II:387).

19. Kant, *Inaugural Dissertation,* 377 (II:387).

20. Kant, *Inaugural Dissertation,* 382–83 (II:392).

21. Kant, *Inaugural Dissertation,* 391 (II:398).

22. Kant, *Inaugural Dissertation,* 401–5 (II:406–10).

23. I have used the words "intellect" and "intelligence" to translate Kant's *intelligentia,* in order to preserve the etymological connection between *intelligibile* and "intellectual." However, it should be noted that the German translation of Baumgarten's *Metaphysica* uses *Verstand* to translate *intellectus,* a Latin cognate of *intelligentia.* Wolff also used the word *Verstand* for the intellectual faculty of the human soul in his *Rational Thoughts on God, the World, and the Soul of Human Beings* (1720). Later, in the Latin *Psychologica Empirica,* he called the same faculty *intellectus.* Following these conventions, the faculty of intellectual cognition that Kant describes in his dissertation could also be called "understanding."

24. Kant, *Inaugural Dissertation,* 384 (II:392).

25. Kant, *Inaugural Dissertation,* 384 (II:392).

26. Kant, *Inaugural Dissertation,* 384 (II:392).

27. Kant, *Inaugural Dissertation,* 384 (II:392).

28. Kant, *Inaugural Dissertation,* 384 (II:392). I have modified Kerferd and Walford's translation to reflect the fact that Kant refers to sensible and intellectual "representations" rather than sensible and intellectual "things" when he writes "*patet, sensitive cogitata esse rerum repraesentationes, uti apparent, intellectualia autem sicuti sunt.*"

29. Kant, *Inaugural Dissertation,* 389 (II:396).

30. Kant, *Inaugural Dissertation*, 387–88 (II:395).
31. Kant, *Inaugural Dissertation*, 387–88 (II:395).
32. Kant, *Inaugural Dissertation*, 387–88 (II:395).
33. Kant, *Inaugural Dissertation*, 386 (II:394).
34. Kant, *Inaugural Dissertation*, 387 (II:395).
35. Kant, *Inaugural Dissertation*, 387 (II:395).
36. Kant, *Inaugural Dissertation*, 386 (II:394).
37. Kant, *Inaugural Dissertation*, 390 (II: 397–398).
38. Kant, *Inaugural Dissertation*, 407 (II:411).
39. Kant, *Inaugural Dissertation*, 408 (II:412). Kant's discussion of subreptive fallacies should be compared to the discussion of surreptitious concepts in Kant, *Dreams of a Spirit-Seer*, 308 (II:320).
40. Kant, *Inaugural Dissertation*, 408–10 (II:412–15).
41. Kant, *Inaugural Dissertation*, 412–13 (II:416–17).
42. Kant, *Inaugural Dissertation*, 415 (II:419).
43. Kant, *Correspondence* (Kant to Lambert, September 2, 1770), 107 (X:97).
44. Kant, *Correspondence* (Kant to Lambert, September 2, 1770), 109 (X:98).
45. Kant, *Correspondence* (Kant to Lambert, September 2, 1770), 109 (X:98)
46. Lewis White Beck and Alison Laywine have argued that Lambert's response to Kant's dissertation was, along with the influence of Hume, decisive for Kant's response to the question concerning "the ground of the relation . . ." See Lewis White Beck, "Lambert and Hume in Kant's Development from 1769 to 1772," in *Essays on Kant and Hume* (New Haven, Conn.: Yale University Press, 1978), 106–10. See also Alison Laywine, "Kant in Reply to Lambert on the Ancestry of Metaphysical Concepts," *Kantian Review* 5 (2001): 1–48. Howeve, I suspect that Kant generally ignored the content of the letters he received from Lambert and Mendelssohn, focusing instead on the fact that he had not convinced them, and attempting to find a more convincing way to present the approach he employed in his inaugural dissertation. Following a suggestion by Eric Watkins, I am inclined to think it was the debate with Herz, rather than Lambert or the influence of Hume, that led Kant to the question concerning "the ground of the relation . . ." See Eric Watkins, "The Critical Turn: Kant and Herz from 1770 to 1772," in *Kant und die Berliner Aufklärung: Akten des IX. Internationalen Kant-Kongress*, vol. 2, ed. Volker Gerhardt, Rolf-Peter Horstmann, and Ralph Schumacher (Berlin: Walter de Gruyter, 2001), 69–77.
47. Kant, *Correspondence* (Lambert to Kant, October 13, 1770), 114–15 (X:105).
48. Kant, *Correspondence* (Lambert to Kant, October 13, 1770), 115 (X:105).
49. Kant, *Correspondence* (Sulzer to Kant, December 8, 1770), 121 (X:112).
50. Kant, *Correspondence* (Herz to Kant, September 11, 1770), 110 (X:100). See also Kant, *Correspondence* (Mendelssohn to Kant, December 25, 1770), 122–24 (X:113–16).
51. Kant, *Correspondence* (Mendelssohn to Kant, December 25, 1770), 123 (X:114). Whether Mendelssohn's letter really concerns only "peripheral matters" or represents a more substantial engagement with Kant's work is debatable. Corey Dyck has shown that Mendelssohn's objections to Kant's claims about

time certainly constitute a forceful criticism in Corey Dyck, "Turning the Game against the Idealist: Mendelssohn's Refutation of Idealism in the *Morgenstunden* and Kant's Replies," in *Moses Mendelssohn's Metaphysics and Aesthetics*, ed. Reinier Munk (Dordrecht: Springer, 2011), 159–82. However, because Mendelssohn does not comment on Kant's claims about the distinction between sensible and intellectual cognition, I take him at his word. Unlike Lambert and Sulzer, who recognized that this distinction was central to Kant's dissertation, Mendelssohn has nothing to say on this subject.

52. Kant, *Correspondence* (Kant to Herz, June 7, 1771), 126 (X:122). That Kant mentions Mendelssohn's more superficial criticism along with Lambert's more substantive criticism is perhaps not surprising. Herz was close to Mendelssohn, so he would have been interested to know about Kant's response to Mendelssohn's letter.

53. Kant, *Correspondence* (Kant to Herz, June 7, 1771), 127 (X:122).

54. Kant, *Correspondence* (Kant to Herz, June 7, 1771), 126 (X:122).

55. Kant, *Correspondence* (Kant to Herz, June 7, 1771), 127 (X:123). Kuno Fischer and Hans Vaihinger claim that Kant derived the title *The Bounds of Sensibility and Reason* (*Die Grentzen der Sinnlichkeit und der Vernunft*) from the subtitle of Lessing's *Laokoon*, "On the Limits of Painting and Poetry" ("Über die Grenzen der Malerei und Poesie"). They argue that Herz would have recognized the reference, because Herz compares Kant to Lessing in his *Inquiry Concerning Taste and the Causes of Its Difference* (1776) and Kant was familiar with this work. While Vaihinger seems to be unaware of the anachronism of this account, Fischer recognizes that the letter in which Kant describes *The Bounds of Sensibility and Reason* predates the publication of Herz's book and his comparison of Kant and Lessing by five years. Unfortunately, he does not seem to recognize that this makes his explanation of Kant's title highly implausible. See Kuno Fischer, *Geschichte der neueren Philosophie*, 4th ed., vol. 5: *Kant und seine Lehre* (Heidelberg: Carl Winter, 1899), 376. See also Hans Vaihinger, *Commentar zu Kants Kritik der reinen Vernunft*, vol. 1, 153. See also Mohr, *Kant's Theoretische Philosophie*, 39–40.

56. Kant, *Correspondence* (Kant to Herz, June 7, 1771), 126 (X:122).

57. Kant, *Inaugural Dissertation*, 387 (II:395).

58. Kant, *Correspondence* (Kant to Herz, June 7, 1771), 127 (X:123).

59. Kant, *Correspondence* (Kant to Herz, June 7, 1771), 127 (X:122).

60. Kant, *Correspondence* (Kant to Herz, February 21, 1772), 132 (X:129).

61. Kant, *Correspondence* (Kant to Herz, February 21, 1772), 132 (X:129).

62. Kant, *Correspondence* (Kant to Herz, February 21, 1772), 132 (X:129). Kant writes "Ich dachte mir darinn zwey Theile, einen theoretischen und practischen." In this passage, the verb *denken* is in the imperfect tense (*Präteritum*). The conjugation of the verb in this form indicates that at some point in the past, Kant "thought" of dividing *The Bounds of Sensibility and Reason* into two parts.

63. Kant, *Correspondence* (Kant to Herz, February 21, 1772), 132 (X:129).

64. Kant, *Correspondence* (Kant to Herz, February 21, 1772), 132 (X:129).

65. *Anmerkungen* (IV:572).

66. See Tonelli, *The Critique of Pure Reason within the Tradition of Modern Logic*, 225–341.

67. While *nun* generally means "now," the appropriateness of Zweig's translation ("then") is confirmed by the tense of Kant's description of his plans for *The Bounds of Sensibility and Reason*. Kant writes "nun machte ich mir den Plan zu einem Werke welches etwa den Titel haben könte: Die Grentzen der Sinnlichkeit und der Vernunft." The fact that Kant uses the verb *machen* in the imperfect tense (*machte*) indicates that he was referring to the past (*Vergangenheit*). A more literal translation might read "And now I made the plan for a work which might perhaps have the title: *The Bounds of Sensibility and Reason*." Like Zweig's translation, this more literal translation also reflects the retrospective character of Kant's comments.

68. Kant, *Correspondence* (Kant to Herz, February 21, 1772), 132 (X:129).

69. Kant, *Correspondence* (Kant to Herz, February 21, 1772), 132 (X:129). Kant's German reads "sahe ich in denen Zwischenzeiten der Geschäfte und der Erholungen, die ich so nöthig habe, den Plan der Betrachtungen, über die wir disputirt hatten, noch einmal an, um ihn an die gesammte Philosophie und übrige Erkenntnis zu passen und dessen Ausdehnung und Schranken zu begreifen."

70. Kant, *Correspondence* (Kant to Herz, February 21, 1772), 133 (X:130). Kant's German reads "Indem ich den theoretischen Theil in seinem gantzen Umfange und mit den wechselseitigen Beziehungen aller Theile durchdachte, so bemerkte ich: daß mir noch etwas wesentliches mangele, welches ich bey meinen langen metaphysischen Untersuchungen, sowie andre, aus der Acht gelassen hatte und welches in der That den Schlüßel zu dem gantzen Geheimnisse, der bis dahin sich selbst noch verborgenen Metaphys:, ausmacht."

71. Kant, *Correspondence* (Kant to Herz, February 21, 1772), 133 (X:130).

72. At this point, my account of Kant's letter diverges significantly from the readings proposed by Vleeschauwer, Beck, and Laywine, who regard Kant's 1772 letter to Herz as a thoroughly retrospective, backward-looking document. See Vleeschauwer, *The Development of Kantian Thought*, 59–60; See also White Beck, "Kant's Letter to Marcus Herz February 21, 1772," 23. I agree with Jennifer Mensch that this reading of Kant's letter is mistaken. See Jennifer Mensch, "The Key to All Metaphysics: Kant's Letter to Herz, 1772," in *Kantian Review* 12, no. 2 (2007): 126.

73. Kant, *Correspondence* (Kant to Herz, February 21, 1772), 132 (X:129).

74. Marcus Herz, *Observations from Speculative Philosophy. Kant's "Critique of Pure Reason": Background Source Materials*, ed. and trans. Eric Watkins (New York: Cambridge University Press, 2009), 283 (18–20).

75. Herz, *Observations from Speculative Philosophy*, 286 (27). Kant had argued that "sensibility" concerned "the receptivity of a subject in virtue of which it is possible for the subject's own representative state to be affected in a definite way by the presence of some object," producing "sensible representations" or "phenomena." "Intellect," on the other hand, was "the faculty of a subject in virtue of which it has the power to represent things which cannot by their own quality come before the senses of that subject," producing "intellectual representations" or "noumena." See Kant, *Inaugural Dissertation*, 384 (I:392).

76. Herz, *Observations from Speculative Philosophy*, 299 (88). See also Kant, *Inaugural Dissertation*, 384 (II:392).

77. Herz is particularly concerned to prove the existence of God and the immortality of the soul. See Herz, *Observations from Speculative Philosophy*, 299 (88); and Watkins, "The Critical Turn: Kant and Herz from 1770 to 1772," 72.

78. Watkins, "The Critical Turn: Kant and Herz from 1770 to 1772," 72–73.

79. Watkins, "The Critical Turn: Kant and Herz from 1770 to 1772," 72–73.

80. Kant, *Inaugural Dissertation*, 389 (II:396).

81. Kant, *Correspondence* (Kant to Lambert, December 31, 1765), 82 (X:56).

82. Kant, *Correspondence* (Kant to Herz, February 21, 1772), 133 (X:130).

83. Kant, *Inaugural Dissertation*, 387 (II:395).

84. Kant, *Correspondence* (Kant to Herz, June 7, 1771), 127 (X:122).

85. Kant, *Correspondence* (Kant to Herz, June 7, 1771), 127 (X:123).

86. Kant, *Correspondence* (Kant to Herz, February 21, 1772), 133 (X:130).

87. Kant, *Correspondence* (Kant to Herz, February 21, 1772), 133 (X:130).

88. Kant, *Correspondence* (Kant to Herz, February 21, 1772), 133 (X:130).

89. Kant, *Inaugural Dissertation*, 384 (II:392).

90. Kant, *Correspondence* (Kant to Herz, February 21, 1772), 133 (X:131).

91. Kant, *Correspondence* (Kant to Herz, February 21, 1772), 133 (X:130).

92. Kant, *Correspondence* (Kant to Herz, February 21, 1772), 133 (X:130–31).

93. Later correspondence with Herz documents the difficulties Kant experienced while formulating the arguments of the first *Critique*. See Kant, *Correspondence* (Kant to Herz, late 1773; August 20, 1777; early April, 1778), 140, 164, 167 (X:144, 213, 232).

94. See Förster, *Kant's Transcendental Deductions*, 3–20.

95. Kant, *Correspondence* (Kant to Herz, February 21, 1772), 133 (X:130).

96. Kant, *Correspondence* (Kant to Herz, February 21, 1772), 133 (X:130).

97. Kant, *Critique of Pure Reason*, 253 (B145).

98. Kant, *Critique of Pure Reason*, 250 (B139).

99. Kant, *Correspondence* (Kant to Herz, February 21, 1772), 134 (X:131).

100. Kant, *Correspondence* (Kant to Herz, February 21, 1772), 134 (X:131).

101. Kant, *Inaugural Dissertation*, 390 (II:397).

102. Kant, *Correspondence* (Kant to Herz, February 21, 1772), 134 (X:131).

103. It could be argued that Kant's example is confused, since he is trying to demonstrate the validity of the relation between intellectual representations and their objects, and the accounts of mathematics Kant provides in both his inaugural dissertation and the *Critique of Pure Reason* involve pure sensible intuition.

104. Kant, *Correspondence* (Kant to Herz, February 21, 1772), 134 (X:131).

105. Kant, *Correspondence* (Kant to Herz, February 21, 1772), 134 (X:131).

106. Kant, *Correspondence* (Kant to Herz, February 21, 1772), 134 (X:132).

107. Kant, *Correspondence* (Kant to Herz, February 21, 1772), 135 (X:132).

108. Kant, *Correspondence* (Kant to Herz, June 7, 1771), 127 (X:123).

109. Kant, *Correspondence* (Kant to Herz, February 21, 1772), 134 (X:132).

110. Kant, *Correspondence* (Kant to Herz, February 21, 1772), 134 (X:132).

111. Kant, *Correspondence* (Kant to Herz, February 21, 1772), 134 (X:131).

112. Kant, *Correspondence* (Kant to Herz, February 21, 1772), 133 (X:130).

113. Kant, *Correspondence* (Kant to Herz, Late 1773), 140 (X:144).

114. Kant, *Correspondence* (Kant to Herz, November 24, 1776), 160 (X:199).

115. See Förster, *Kant's Transcendental Deductions,* 3–20. See also Wolfgang Carl, *Der schweigende Kant: Die Entwürfe zu einer Deduktion der Kategorien vor 1781* (Göttingen: Vandenhoeck & Ruprecht, 1989), 74–102. Paul Guyer and Alison Laywine have also examined the development of Kant's *Critique* using the *Duisburg Nachlaß.* See Paul Guyer, *Kant and the Claims of Knowledge* (Cambridge: Cambridge University Press, 1987), 25–70; and Alison Laywine, "Kant on Sensibility and the Understanding in the 1770s," *Canadian Journal of Philosophy* 33, no. 4 (2003): 443–82. On Kant's notes and fragments from the 1770s, see W. H. Werkmeister, *Kant's Silent Decade: A Decade of Philosophical Development,* (Tallahassee: University Presses of Florida, 1979).

116. Kant, *Critique of Pure Reason,* 704 (A855/B883).

## Chapter 4

1. Kant, *Correspondence* (Kant to Herz, After May 11, 1781), 181 (X:269).

2. Johann Georg Hamann, *Briefwechsel,* vol. 4 (Hamann to Herder, April 20, 1781), ed. Arthur Henkel (Frankfurt am Main: Insel Verlag, 1959), 285.

3. Kant, *Correspondence* (Mendelssohn to Kant, April 10, 1783), 190 (X:308). Kant had written to beg Mendelssohn to read and promote the *Critique of Pure Reason* in 1786. See Kant, *Correspondence* (Kant to Mendelssohn, August 16, 1783), 202–3 (X:345).

4. Christian Garve and Johann Georg Heinrich Feder, "The Göttingen Review," in *Kant's Early Critics: The Empiricist Critique of the Theoretical Philosophy,* ed. Brigitte Sassen (New York: Cambridge University Press, 2000), 53–58. Kant had fewer objections to Garve's original review when it appeared in the *Allgemeine deutsche Bibliothek* in 1783. He still accused Garve of "frequently mistaking my meaning," but he acknowledged this was "hardly avoidable." See Kant, *Correspondence* (Kant to Schultz, August 22, 1783), 206 (X:349).

5. Kant, *Critique of Pure Reason,* 120 (Bxxxvii).

6. On the differences between the two editions of the first *Critique,* see Erdmann, Benno. *Kants Kriticismus in der ersten und in der zweiten Auflage der "Kritik der reinen Vernunft"* (Leipzig: Voss, 1878).

7. Kant, *Critique of Pure Reason,* 103 (Axvi).

8. Kant, *Critique of Pure Reason,* 120–21 (Bxxxviii).

9. Kant, *Critique of Pure Reason,* 439, 508, 590, 647 (A395, A486/B514, A642/B671, A747/B775).

10. Kant, *Critique of Pure Reason,* 101–3, 113–14 (Axiii–xvi, Bxxii–xxiv).

11. Kant, *Critique of Pure Reason,* 101 (Axi–xii).

12. Kant, *Critique of Pure Reason,* 101 (Axii).

13. Kant, *Critique of Pure Reason,* 113 (Bxxii).

14. Kant, *Critique of Pure Reason,* 133 (A11/B25).

15. Kant, *Critique of Pure Reason,* 99 (Avii–Aviii).

16. Kant, *Critique of Pure Reason,* 99 (Aviii–Axi).

17. Kant, *Critique of Pure Reason,* 101 (Axiii)

18. Kant, *Critique of Pure Reason,* 99 (Avii).

19. Kant, *Critique of Pure Reason*, 99 (Aviii).
20. Kant, *Critique of Pure Reason*, 99 (Aviii).
21. Kant, *Critique of Pure Reason*, 99 (Aviii).
22. Kant, *Critique of Pure Reason*, 99 (Aviii).
23. Kant, *Critique of Pure Reason*, 99 (Aviii).
24. Kant, *Critique of Pure Reason*, 99 (Aviii).
25. Kant, *Critique of Pure Reason*, 99 (Aviii).
26. Kant, *Critique of Pure Reason*, 117, 139, 407 (Bxxx, B7, B395).
27. Kant, *Critique of Pure Reason*, 127 (A2).
28. Kant, *Critique of Pure Reason*, 127 (A2).
29. Kant, *Critique of Pure Reason*, 99 (Aviii–ix).
30. Kant, *Critique of Pure Reason*, 99 (Aviii–ix).
31. Kant, *Critique of Pure Reason*, 99 (Aviii–ix).
32. Kant, *Critique of Pure Reason*, 99 (Aix). The fact that Kant calls the administration of the dogmatists "despotic" is significant. In remarks on Achenwall's *Ius Naturalis* (1763), Kant says public administration depends on conformity to laws, because rules are necessary for the execution of public business. These rules must be stable for society to function, but they also have to be just, which means they must "derive from the equality of the rights of all, and, likewise, the equal distribution of burdens has to derive from the fact that everyone who is especially burdened can seek their right." Despotism makes this impossible, because it "interferes with public administration," breaking the rules that govern public affairs and privileging the rights of the sovereign over the rights of everyone else. See Kant, *Reflexion* 7764 (1770s, XIX:510). See also Kant, *Reflexion* 6188, where Kant says, "Despot is he who regards his subjects as his property. Now, he can be kind, but without consulting the will of the people, in what way they can want it to be. He thus does not see them (a tyrant is a cruel despot) as ends in themselves, from whose will he alone is allowed to derive laws, but only as means to his ends" (1785–89, XVIII:430).
33. Kant, *Critique of Pure Reason*, 99–100 (Aix). Kant is generally dismissive of skepticism in his accounts of the history of philosophy. In the "History of Pure Reason" with which he concludes the *Critique of Pure Reason*, he includes skeptics like David Hume among the "observers of a scientific method" in philosophy and credits them with "proceeding systematically," even though skepticism is unable to "bring human reason to full satisfaction." See Kant, *Critique of Pure Reason*, 704 (A855/B883). Later, in the drafts for his essay on the progress of metaphysics, Kant says that skepticism is not "a serious view that has been current in any period of philosophy." See Immanuel Kant, *What Real Progress Has Metaphysics Made in Germany since the Time of Leibniz and Wolff*, trans. Henry Allison, in *Theoretical Philosophy after 1781*, ed. Henry Allison and Peter Heath (New York: Cambridge University Press, 2002), 356 (XX:263). These remarks suggest that Kant thought there was no reason to try to refute skepticism.
34. Kant, *Critique of Pure Reason*, 100 (Aix).
35. Kant, *Critique of Pure Reason*, 100 (Aix).
36. Kant, *Critique of Pure Reason*, 100 (Ax).
37. Kant, *Critique of Pure Reason*, 100 (Ax).

38. Kant, *Critique of Pure Reason,* 100 (Ax).

39. Kant, *Critique of Pure Reason,* 100–101 (Axi).

40. Kant, *Critique of Pure Reason,* 100 (Ax).

41. Kant, *Critique of Pure Reason,* 100 (Ax).

42. Etienne Gilson, *The Unity of Philosophical Experience* (San Francisco: Ignatius, 1999), 246. It should also be noted that Gilson makes this remark in the context of a discussion of the breakdown of Kant's "philosophical restoration" of metaphysics and its ultimate degeneration "into the various forms of contemporary agnosticism, with all sorts of moralisms and would-be mysticisms as ready shelters against philosophical despair." Gilson thinks these moralisms and mysticisms are proof that "the so-called death of philosophy" is "regularly attended by its revival."

43. Kant, *Critique of Pure Reason,* 100 (Ax).

44. On the natural predisposition of human beings to metaphysics, see Kant, *Critique of Pure Reason,* 147–48 (B21–B22).

45. Kant, *Critique of Pure Reason,* 100 (Ax).

46. Kant, *Critique of Pure Reason,* 101 (Axi).

47. Thomas Hobbes, *On the Citizen,* ed. and trans. Richard Tuck and Michael Silverthorne (Cambridge: Cambridge University Press, 1998), 54 (I.3.27); René Descartes, "Author's Replies to the Fourth Set of Objections," in *The Philosophical Writings of Descartes,* vol. 2, ed. and trans. John Cottingham (Cambridge: Cambridge University Press, 1985–91), 178 (256); Baruch Spinoza, *Ethics,* trans. Samuel Shirley (Indianapolis, Ind.: Hackett, 1992), 57; Gottfried Wilhelm Leibniz, *Theodicy,* trans. E. M. Huggard (Eugene, Ore.: Wipf and Stock), 91 (§29).

48. Kant, *Critique of Pure Reason,* 101 (Axii). Otfried Höffe has connected Kant's judicial metaphor to the entry on "critique" in the *Encyclopédie.* See Otfried Höffe, *Kant's "Critique of Pure Reason": The Foundation of Modern Philosophy* (Dordrecht: Springer, 2010), 29.

49. Kant, *Critique of Pure Reason,* 101 (Axii). Guyer and Wood's decision to translate *Machtsprüche* as "mere decrees" neglects what is perhaps the most important aspect of Kant's comment, which implies that "mere decrees" are asserted through force *(Macht)* rather than right *(Recht).* Kemp Smith's translation of *Machtsprüche* as "despotic decrees" is also misleading, since Kant makes no reference to despotism in this passage, but at least it does not neutralize Kant's reference to *Macht* the way that Guyer and Wood's translation does.

50. Kant, *Critique of Pure Reason,* 649 (A751/B779). Kant presents a different view of the state of nature at the beginning of the chapter on "Public Right" in the *Rechtslehre,* where he says that the state of nature is not necessarily a state of injustice, but rather "a state *devoid of justice (status iustitia vacuus)* in which when rights are *in dispute (ius controversum)*" "there would be no judge competent to render a verdict having rightful force." See Immanuel Kant, *The Metaphysics of Morals,* trans. Mary Gregor, in *Practical Philosophy,* ed. Mary Gregor (New York: Cambridge University Press, 1996), 456 (VI:312).

51. Kant, *Critique of Pure Reason,* 649 (A751/B779).

52. Kant, *Critique of Pure Reason,* 101 (Axii).

53. Kant, *Critique of Pure Reason,* 649–650 (A751/B779).

54. Kant, *Critique of Pure Reason*, 650 (A752/B780).

55. This, at least, is the view of monarchy Kant presents in his lectures on Achenwall's *Ius Naturalis* (1763) from the 1780s. See Kant, *Reflexionen* 8009–8022 (XIX:581–85); See also Kant, *Lectures on Anthropology*, 332 (XXV:1202); On republicanism and the rule of law, see Immanuel Kant, *Toward Perpetual Peace*, trans. Mary Gregor, in *Practical Philosophy*, ed. Mary Gregor (New York: Cambridge University Press, 1996), 322 (VIII:349–50).

56. Kant, *Critique of Pure Reason*, 649–50 (A751/B779-A752/B780).

57. Kant, *Toward Perpetual Peace*, 322 (VIII:349).

58. The significance of Kant's use of political metaphors in his theoretical philosophy has been discussed by Hans Saner, Hannah Arendt, Nora O'Neill, Susan Meld Shell, and many others. For a helpful survey of this literature, see Kimberly Hutchings, *Kant, Critique and Politics* (New York: Routledge, 1996), 27–36.

59. Kant, *Critique of Pure Reason*, 101 (Axii).

60. See, for example, Kant's correspondence with Lavater, who asked whether Kant's critique would maintain that "out of a thousand books and ten thousand bookish judgments, there is hardly one that is not a would-be sedative of the author's needs—though this is by no means noticed by particular readers." See Kant, *Correspondence* (Lavater to Kant, April 18, 1774), 150 (X:166).

61. Kant, *Critique of Pure Reason*, 150 (B27).

62. Kant, *Critique of Pure Reason*, 150 (B27).

63. Kant, *Critique of Pure Reason*, 150 (B27). Kant includes the claim that judgments about the books and systems of other philosophers are groundless, unless they have a critique of pure reason for their touchstone, in one of the marginal notes written in his copy of the first (A) edition of the *Critique of Pure Reason*. See Kant, *Nachträge zur Kritik der reinen Vernunft* (XXIII:44).

64. Immanuel Kant, *Lectures on Metaphysics*, ed. and trans. Karl Ameriks and Steve Naragon (New York: Cambridge University Press, 1997), 301 (XXVIII:534). The distinction between historical and philosophical cognition can be traced back to the first chapter Wolff's *Preliminary Discourse*, which distinguishes between historical, philosophical, and mathematical cognition. See Christian Wolff, *Preliminary Discourse on Philosophy in General*, trans. Richard J. Blackwell (Indianapolis, Ind.: Bobbs-Merrill, 1963), 3–16. Kant also refers to Wolff's distinction between historical and philosophical cognition, and the necessity of philosophizing, in his logic lectures. See Kant, *Lectures on Logic*, 35–36, 257–58 (XXIV:49–50, 797–98).

65. Kant, *Lectures on Logic*, 35 (XXIV:49–50).

66. Kant, *Lectures on Logic*, 37, 538 (IX:25; XXIV:52).

67. Kant, *Critique of Pure Reason*, 101, 150 (Axii, AB27). In the second "Introduction," Kant refers to a critique of "the pure faculty of reason itself" (*das reinen Vernunftvermögen selbst*) rather than a critique of "the faculty of reason in general" (*das Vernunftvermögen überhaupt*). I take the two expressions to be equivalent, since Kant goes on to say that the faculty of reason in general concerns "all the cognitions after which reason might strive independently of all experience" and calls cognition sought independently of experience "pure."

68. Kant, *Critique of Pure Reason*, 389 (A302/B358).

69. Kant, *Critique of Pure Reason*, 407 (B395).

70. The broader interpretation of the faculty of reason proposed here is also endorsed by Vaihinger and Kemp Smith. Vaihinger proposes interpreting the reference to "pure reason" (*reinen Vernunft*) in the title, as well as Kant's reference to a critique of "the faculty of reason in general" as a critique of "the entire human faculty of cognition: sensibility, understanding, and itself" (*das ganze menschliche Erkenntnisvermögen: Sinnlichkeit, Verstand, zugleich Vernunft selbst*). See Vaihinger, *Commentar I*, 117. Kemp Smith also suggests that Kant employs the term in three different senses, the most general of which includes everything a priori in sensibility as well as understanding. See Kemp Smith, *Commentary*, 2, 9.

71. Kant, *Critique of Pure Reason*, 149 (A11/B24).

72. Kant, *Critique of Pure Reason*, 696 (A841/B869).

73. Kant, *Critique of Pure Reason*, 101 (Axii).

74. Kant, *Critique of Pure Reason*, 127 (A1).

75. Kant, *Critique of Pure Reason*, 127 (A1–A2).

76. Kant, *Critique of Pure Reason*, 128 (A2).

77. Kant, *Critique of Pure Reason*, 128 (A2).

78. Kant, *Critique of Pure Reason*, 128 (A2/B6–A3/B7).

79. Kant, *Critique of Pure Reason*, 128 (A2/B6–A3/B7).

80. Kant, *Critique of Pure Reason*, 128 (A2/B6–A3/B7).

81. Kant, *Critique of Pure Reason*, 128 (A2/B6–A3/B7).

82. Kant, *Critique of Pure Reason*, 99 (Aviii).

83. Immanuel Kant, *New Elucidation of the First Principles of Metaphysical Cognition*, trans. David Walford and Ralf Meerbote, in *Theoretical Philosophy, 1755–1770*, ed. David Walford and Ralf Meerbote (New York: Cambridge University Press, 1992), 5 (I:387).

84. Kant, *Inquiry*, 256 (II:283).

85. Kant, *Inaugural Dissertation*, 387 (II:395).

86. Kant, *Inaugural Dissertation*, 387–388 (II:395).

87. Kant, *Inaugural Dissertation*, 384 (II:392). Kant does not distinguish intelligence (*intelligentia*), reason (*rationalitas*), and understanding (*intellectus*) in his inaugural dissertation. The three terms are used synonymously.

88. Kant, *Critique of Pure Reason*, 128 (A2).

89. Kant, *Critique of Pure Reason*, 156 (A20/B34–A20/B35).

90. Kant, *Critique of Pure Reason*, 194 (A51/B75–A51/B76).

91. See, for example, Kant, *Critique of Pure Reason*, 155–56, 195–97 (A20/B34, A55/B79–A57/B82).

92. Kant, *Critique of Pure Reason*, 101 (Axii).

93. Kant, *Critique of Pure Reason*, 101 (Axii).

94. Kant, *Prolegomena to Any Future Metaphysics*, 119 (IV:327).

95. Kant, *Prolegomena to Any Future Metaphysics*, 119 (IV:327).

96. Kant, *Prolegomena to Any Future Metaphysis*, 122–40 (IV:331–50).

97. Kant, *Prolegomena to Any Future Metaphysics*, 153 (IV:365).

98. Kant, *Prolegomena to Any Future Metaphysics*, 152 (IV:364).

99. Kant, *Critique of Pure Reason*, 101 (Axii).

100. Kant, *Critique of Pure Reason*, 156, 193, 204–18 (A20/B34, A50/B74–A51/B75, A66/B91–A83/B116 ). See also the masterful study by Béatrice

Longuenesse, which has inspired much of the debate about the *Leitfaden* chapter in recent years. Béatrice Longuenesse, *Kant and the Capacity to Judge: Sensibility and Discursivity in the Transcendental Analytic of the "Critique of Pure Reason,"* trans. Charles T. Wolfe (Princeton, N.J.: Princeton University Press, 1998).

101. Kant, *Critique of Pure Reason*, 399, 402. (A320/B377, A327/B383–A327/B384).

102. Kant, *Critique of Pure Reason*, 385 (A295/B352).

103. Kant, *Critique of Pure Reason*, 386–87, 399–405 (A298/B354–A298/B355, A321/B377–A332/B389). See also Michelle Grier, *Kant's Doctrine of Transcendental Illusion* (Cambridge: Cambridge University Press, 2001), 101–39.

104. Kant, *Critique of Pure Reason*, 385, 459, 460 (A296/B352, A406/B433, A407/B434).

105. It should be noted that analytic and Continental hostility to metaphysics has declined to some degree in the last few decades. Although empiricism, pragmatism, and naturalism remain central commitments for many analytic philosophers, modal metaphysics has shown itself to be a viable alternative. Heideggerean accounts of the history of metaphysics as "the forgetting of being" are still common in Continental philosophy, as are post-structuralist suspicions of metaphysical claims of universality and necessity; however, the influence of figures like Gilles Deleuze and Alain Badiou has led to greater interest in mathematics, science, and metaphysics in Continental philosophy.

106. On the "elimination" and "overcoming" of metaphysics, see A. J. Ayer, *Language, Truth, and Logic* (New York: Dover, 1952), 34–35; and Martin Heidegger, "Overcoming Metaphysics," in *The End of Philosophy*, ed. and trans. Joan Stambaugh (Chicago: University of Chicago Press, 2003), 88–89, 92. The attempt to save Kant's critique by focusing on what is useful for "truly empirical philosophy" and excluding everything that might be construed as "transcendental metaphysics" should also be noted in P. F. Strawson, *The Bounds of Sense: An Essay on Kant's "Critique of Pure Reason"* (London: Routledge, 2004), 19, 32, 38–39. A similar gesture is found in the work of Michel Foucault, who contrasts the "critical attitude" of Kant's conception of enlightenment with the search for "formal structures with universal value" in Kant's *Critique of Pure Reason*. See Michel Foucault, "What Is Enlightenment?" trans. Catherine Porter, in *The Essential Foucault*, ed. Paul Rabinow and Nikolas Rose (New York: New, 2003), 53.

107. Kant, *Critique of Pure Reason*, 112–14 (Bxxi–Bxxv).

108. Kant, *Critique of Pure Reason*, 101 (Axii).

109. Kant, *Critique of Pure Reason*, 387 (A299/B356).

110. Kant, *Critique of Pure Reason*, 101 (Axi-Axii).

111. Kant, *Critique of Pure Reason*, 101 (Axiii).

112. The image of the critique of pure reason as a "court of justice" remains in the "Discipline of Pure Reason," which Kant did not alter in the second (B) edition. There is also a reference to an "appointed judge" at Kant, *Critique of Pure Reason*, 109 (Bxiii), though the context differs considerably from the "Preface" to the first (A) edition.

113. Kant, *Critique of Pure Reason*, 113 (Bxxii).

114. Kant, *Prolegomena to Any Future Metaphysics*, 53 (IV:255).

115. Kant, *Prolegomena to Any Future Metaphysics*, 70–71, 77–82, 89–90 (IV:275, 280–86, 294–96). A similar argument is to be found in the "Introduction" to the second (B) edition of the Kant, *Critique of Pure Reason*, 147 (B20-B21).

116. Kant, *Prolegomena to Any Future Metaphysics*, 70, 154–160 (IV:274–75, 365–72).

117. Kant, *Critique of Pure Reason*, 106–100 (Bviii–Bxvi).

118. Kant, *Critique of Pure Reason*, 110 (Bxv).

119. Kant, *Critique of Pure Reason*, 106 (Bviii).

120. Kant, *Critique of Pure Reason*, 106 (Bviii).

121. Kant, *Critique of Pure Reason*, 106–7 (Bix).

122. Kant, *Critique of Pure Reason*, 107 (Bix).

123. Kant uses the material conditions of the cognition of objects to distinguish transcendental logic from general logic in Kant, *Critique of Pure Reason*, 195–99 (A55/B79–A62/B86).

124. Kant, *Critique of Pure Reason*, 108, 631 (Bxii, A715/B743–A716/B744). See also *Prolegomena to Any Future Metaphysics*, 77–80 (IV:280–84). Philip Kitcher presents a very helpful summary of Kant's approach to mathematics in Philip Kitcher, "Kant on the Foundations of Mathematics," *The Philosophical Review* 84, no. 1 (1975): 23–50.

125. Kant, *Critique of Pure Reason*, 630 (A713/B741).

126. Kant, *Critique of Pure Reason*, 107–8 (Bxi).

127. Kant, *Critique of Pure Reason*, 109 (Bxiii).

128. Kant, *Critique of Pure Reason*, 109 (Bxiii).

129. See Kant's discussion of the scientific inadequacy of empiricism at Kant, *Critique of Pure Reason*, 225–26 (AA95/B127–A95/B129).

130. Kant, *Critique of Pure Reason*, 109–10 (Bxiv–xvi).

131. Kant, *Critique of Pure Reason*, 111 (Bxviii–xix).

132. Kant, *Critique of Pure Reason*, 111 (Bxviii–xix).

133. Kant, *Critique of Pure Reason*, 101, 108 (Axii, Bxii). Despite the rationalism of his understanding of the revolution in the natural sciences, Kant says he will consider natural science "only as it is grounded on empirical principles" in the second "Preface." This is surprising, because he had already rejected the idea that natural science is founded on empirical principles in Immanuel Kant, *Metaphysical Foundations of Natural Science*, trans. Michael Friedman, in *Theoretical Philosophy after 1781*, ed. Henry Allison and Peter Heath (New York: Cambridge University Press, 2002), 183–86 (IV:467–70).

134. This point was made by N. R. Hanson, "Copernicus' Role in Kant's Revolution," *Journal of the History of Ideas* 20, no. 2 (1959): 274–81. See also Murray Miles, "Kant's Copernican Revolution," *Kant-Studien* 97, no. 1 (2006): 1–32.

135. Kant, *Critique of Pure Reason*, 110 (Bxvi).

136. Kant, *Critique of Pure Reason*, 113 (Bxxii).

137. Kant, *Critique of Pure Reason*, 113 (Bxxii). One of the most significant differences between the "Preface" to the first (A) edition of the *Critique of Pure Reason* and the "Preface" to the second (B) edition is Kant's rehabilitation of the role hypotheses play in science in the "Preface" to the second (B) edition. In the "Preface" to the first (A) edition, Kant calls the hypothesis "a forbidden com-

modity, which should not be put up for sale even at the lowest price, but must be confiscated as soon as it is discovered," while he describes his new approach to metaphysics as a hypothesis in the "Preface" to the second (B) edition. See Kant, *Critique of Pure Reason*, 102, 110, 113 (Axv, Bxvi, Bxxii).

138. Kant, *Critique of Pure Reason*, 102 (Axv).

139. Kant, *Critique of Pure Reason*, 113 (Bxxii). See also Hanson, "Copernicus' Role in Kant's Revolution," 277–78.

140. Kant, *Critique of Pure Reason*, 123 (Bxliii).

141. Kant, *Critique of Pure Reason*, 110 (Bxvi).

142. Kant, *Critique of Pure Reason*, 110 (Bxvi).

143. Kant even considered changing the name of his transcendental idealism to critical idealism to avoid some of these misunderstandings. See Kant, *Prolegomena to Any Future Metaphysics*, 87–88 (IV:292–94).

144. Kant, *Critique of Pure Reason*, 110 (Bxvi).

145. Kant, *Critique of Pure Reason*, 110 (Bxvii).

146. Kant, *Critique of Pure Reason*, 110 (Bxvii).

147. The use of the word "faculty" to translate the German *Vermögen* has been the source of a number of confusions regarding Kant's epistemology. A "faculty" is often thought to be a "part" of the mind, because this is how the term is supposed to have been used in "faculty" psychology. In Kant, however, the idea of a "faculty" (*Vermögen*) should be understood etymologically. Just as the English word "faculty" is derived from the French *faculté* (power, ability), which is, in turn derived from the Latin *facultas* (power, ability), the German *Vermögen* is derived from the word for "possibility" *(Möglichkeit)*. A more appropriate translation of Kant's *Vermögen* might be "capacity," because this would at least preserve the equivalence of the German terms *Vermögen* and *Fähigkeit*, which best preserves the role that *Vermögen* plays in Kant's epistemology. I would suggest similar translations for Wolff and Baumgarten, who have a more "capacity"-oriented psychology than is usually acknowledged, but that is beyond the scope of the present work.

148. Kant, *Critique of Pure Reason*, 155–57, 172–74 (A19/B33–A22/B36).

149. Kant, *Critique of Pure Reason*, 110–11 (Bxvii).

150. Kant, *Critique of Pure Reason*, 111 (Bxvii).

151. Kant rejected this approach in his 1772 letter to Herz. See Kant, *Correspondence* (Kant to Herz, February 21, 1772), 133 (X:130).

152. Kant, *Critique of Pure Reason*, 111 (Bxvii).

153. Kant, *Critique of Pure Reason*, 111 (Bxvii).

154. Kant, *Critique of Pure Reason*, 227–28, 230–32, 256–57 (A96–A97, A103–A106, B150–B152).

155. Kant, *Critique of Pure Reason*, 111–12 (Bxvii–Bxix).

156. Kant, *Critique of Pure Reason*, 111 (Bxviii).

157. Kant, *Critique of Pure Reason*, 111 (Bxviii–Bxix).

158. Kant, *Critique of Pure Reason*, 111 (Bxix).

159. Kant, *Critique of Pure Reason*, 111–113 (Bxviii–Bxxii).

160. Immanuel Kant, *Groundwork of the Metaphysics of Morals*, trans. Mary Gregor, in *Practical Philosophy*, ed. Mary Gregor (New York: Cambridge University Press, 1996), 66 (IV:412–13).

161. Kant, *Critique of Pure Reason*, 533–46 (A533/B561–A558/B586).

162. Kant, *Critique of Pure Reason*, 112–13 (Bxxi).

163. Kant, *Critique of Pure Reason*, 112 (Bxxi).

164. Kant, *Critique of Pure Reason*, 112 (Bxx).

165. It could be argued that things in themselves are not really "in them-selves" if they are "beings of reason," even though Kant identifies "a concept with-out an object, like the *noumena*, which cannot be counted among the possibilities, although they must not on that ground be asserted to be impossible" with an "*ens rationis*" at Kant, *Critique of Pure Reason*, 382 (AA290/B347).

166. Kant, *Critique of Pure Reason*, 112 (Bxx).

167. Kant, *Critique of Pure Reason*, 111 (Bxviii–xix).

168. Kant, *Critique of Pure Reason*, 111 (Bxvii).

169. Kant, *Critique of Pure Reason*, 114 (Bxxiii–xxiv).

170. A number of different definitions of a critique of pure reason can be found in Kant's later works, as well as his lectures and notes. Most of them are variations on one of the four definitions considered in this chapter, though they are often modified to specify the contributions of Kant's to moral philosophy, aesthetics, and teleology. See, for example, Immanuel Kant, *Critique of Practical Reason*, trans. Mary Gregor, in *Practical Philosophy*, ed. Mary Gregor (New York: Cambridge University Press, 1996), 182–86 (V:52–57); and Immanuel Kant, *Critique of the Power of Judgment*, ed. Paul Guyer, trans. Paul Guyer and Eric Matthews (New York: Cambridge University Press, 2000), 61–66 (V:174–79).

171. Kant, *Critique of Pure Reason*, 132–33 (A11/B24–A11/B25).

172. Kant, *Critique of Pure Reason*, 133 (A11/B25).

173. Kant, *Critique of Pure Reason*, 101 (Axii).

174. Kant, *Critique of Pure Reason*, 213 (A81/B107).

175. Kant, *Critique of Pure Reason*, 213–214 (A82/B108).

176. Kant, *Critique of Pure Reason*, 214 (A82/B108–A83/B109).

177. Kant, *Critique of Pure Reason*, 213, 134 (A82/B107, A13/B27).

178. Kant, *Critique of Pure Reason*, 133 (A11/B25).

179. Kant, *Critique of Pure Reason*, 133 (A12/B25).

180. Kant, *Critique of Pure Reason*, 133 (A12/B25).

181. Kant, *Critique of Pure Reason*, 134 (A14/B28).

182. Kant, *Critique of Pure Reason*, 104–5, 123, 127 (Axxi, Bxliii, XXIII:20). The aims of the *Metaphysics of Nature* must be distinguished from the objectives of Kant's *Metaphysical Foundations of Natural Science* (1786), which presupposes certain principles of the metaphysics of nature, but only those that are relevant to the particular problems related to the doctrine of "body" with which Kant is concerned in the *Metaphysical Foundations*. See Kant, *Metaphysical Foundations of Natural Science*, 184–85 (IV:469–70). See also Kant, *Correspondence* (Kant to Schütz, September 13, 1785), 229 (X:406). See also Eckart Förster, *The Twenty-Five Years of Philosophy: A Systematic Reconstruction*, trans. Brady Bowman (Cambridge, Mass.: Harvard University Press, 2012), 46. The aims of Kant's *Metaphysics of Nature* should also be distinguished from the writings contained in the *Opus Postumum* (c. 1790–1801), which were supposed to provide a transition from the metaphysical foundations of natural science to physics. See Eckart Förster, *Kant's*

*Final Synthesis: An Essay on the "Opus Postumum"* (Cambridge, Mass.: Harvard University Press, 2000), 1–23.

183. Kant, *Critique of Pure Reason*, 105 (Axxi).

184. Karl Leonhard Reinhold, "The Foundations of Philosophical Knowledge," trans. George di Giovanni, in *Between Kant and Hegel: Texts in the Development of Post-Kantian Idealism*, ed. George di Giovanni and H. S. Harris (Indianapolis, Ind.: Hackett, 2000), 64 (63).

185. Reinhold, *The Foundations of Philosophical Knowledge*, 66–67 (69–70).

186. Johann Gottlieb Fichte, "Second Introduction to the *Wissenschaftslehre*," in *Introductions to the Wissenschaftslehre and Other Writings*, ed. and trans. Daniel Breazeale (Indianapolis, Ind.: Hackett, 1994), 62–63 (478–79). See also Günter Zöller, "From Critique to Metacritique: Fichte's Transformation of Kant's Transcendental Idealism," in *The Reception of Kant's Critical Philosophy: Fichte, Schelling, & Hegel*, ed. Sally Sedgwick (Cambridge: Cambridge University Press, 2000), 128–46.

187. Kant, *Correspondence* ("Declaration concerning Fichte's *Wissenschaftslehre*"), 559 (XII:370–71). I would like to thank Karin de Boer for calling to my attention to an important error in translation of Kant's "Declaration" contained in the Cambridge edition of Kant's *Correspondence*. Kant writes "Hierbey muß ich noch bemerken, daß die Anmaßung, mir die Absicht unterzuschieben: ich habe bloß eine Proprädevtik zur Transscendental-Philosophie, nicht das System dieser Philosophie selbst, liefern wollen, mir unbegreiflich ist. Es hat mir eine solche Absicht nie in Gedanken kommen können, da ich selbst das vollendete Ganze der reinen Philosophie in der Critic der reinen Vernunft für das beste Merkmal der Wahrheit derselben gepriesen habe," which Zweig renders as "I must remark here the assumption that I have intended to publish only a propaedeutic to transcendental philosophy and not the actual system of this philosophy is incomprehensible to me. Such an intention could never have occurred to me, since I took the completeness of pure philosophy within the Critique of Pure Reason to be the best indication of the truth of that work." A more accurate translation of the second sentence would be "Such an intention could never have occurred to me, since I have praised the completed whole of pure philosophy in the Critique of Pure Reason as the best indication of its truth." This more accurate translation shows that Kant recognized that the *Critique of Pure Reason* was not the complete system of pure philosophy and confirms his attention to complete the system he had described.

## Chapter 5

1. See the reviews by Feder, Garve, Tiedeman, Schaumann, Selle, and Tittel in Sassen, *Kant's Early Critics*, 53–54, 75, 81–92, 139–68, 193–209.

2. Kant, *Prolegomena to Any Future Metaphysics*, 85–88, 111–14, 160–66 (IV:290–94, 318–22, 372–80). See also Kant, *Critique of Pure Reason*, 143–46, 187–88, 245–66, 326 (B14-B19, A46/B63–A49/B66, B129–B168, B274–B75).

3. Kant, *Prolegomena to Any Future Metaphysics*, 163 (IV:375).

4. Kant, *Critique of Pure Reason*, 123 (Bxliii).

5. Kant, *Critique of the Power of Judgment*, 58 (V:170).

6. Kant, *Groundwork of the Metaphysics of Morals*, 47 (IV:391). While Kant regards both the *Groundwork* and the second *Critique* as propaedeutics to the *Metaphysics of Morals*, he denies the necessity of a critique of pure practical reason in the "Preface" to the *Groundwork*. He affirms the necessity of that critique in Kant, *Critique of Practical Reason*, 139, 143 (V:3, 8).

7. Kant, *Correspondence* (Kant to Garve, September 21, 1798), 551 (XII:257).

8. In the same passage, Kant adds that the *Metaphysical Foundations of Natural Science* "presupposes an empirical concept," in addition to being a "mere application" of the principles of the *Metaphysics of Nature*. See Kant, *Correspondence* (Kant to Schütz, September 13, 1785), 229 (X:406).

9. Kant, *Correspondence* ("Declaration Concerning Fichte's *Wissenschafts-lehre*"), 559–60 (XII:371). Kant notes that his work on the *Transition from the Metaphysical Foundations of Natural Science to Physics* (later known as the *Opus Postumum*) was extremely difficult, because he was suffering from a kind of mental paralysis, which left him feeling like an intellectual invalid. See Kant, *Correspondence* (Kant to Garve, September 21, 1798), 551 (XII:257); and Kant, *Correspondence* (Kant to Kiesewetter, October 19, 1798), 553 (XII:259).

10. Henry Allison provides a very helpful account of the origin and purpose of Kant's abstract, which was originally called *Prolegomena to a Metaphysics Yet to Be Written* (*Prolegomena einer noch zu schreibenden Metaphysik*), apparently in reference to Kant's *Metaphysics of Nature*. See Kant, *Theoretical Philosophy after 1781*, 31–35.

11. Kant, *Theoretical Philosophy after 1781*, 33.

12. Kant, *Prolegomena to Any Future Metaphysics*, 53 (IV:255).

13. Kant, *Prolegomena to Any Future Metaphysics*, 161 (IV:373).

14. Kant, *Critique of Pure Reason*, 101 (Axii).

15. Kant, *Prolegomena to Any Future Metaphysics*, 69 (IV:271).

16. Kant, *Prolegomena to Any Future Metaphysics*, 70 (IV:274).

17. Kant, *Prolegomena to Any Future Metaphysics*, 70 (IV:274).

18. Kant, *Prolegomena to Any Future Metaphysics*, 70 (IV:274–75).

19. Kant, *Prolegomena to Any Future Metaphysics*, 77 (IV:281).

20. Kant, *Prolegomena to Any Future Metaphysics*, 80 (IV:285).

21. Kant, *Prolegomena to Any Future Metaphysics*, 79 (IV:283).

22. Kant, *Prolegomena to Any Future Metaphysics*, 64, 79 (IV:268–69, 283).

23. Kant, *Prolegomena to Any Future Metaphysics*, 77–79 (IV:281–82).

24. Kant, *Prolegomena to Any Future Metaphysics*, 79 (IV:283).

25. Kant, *Prolegomena to Any Future Metaphysics*, 90 (IV:295).

26. See, for example, the distinction between intuitive and discursive judgments and principles in Kant, *Lectures on Logic*, 225, 309–10, 382, 537, 606 (IX:23, 110, XXIV:279–80, 857–58).

27. Kant, *Prolegomena to Any Future Metaphysics*, 90 (IV:295).

28. Kant, *Prolegomena to Any Future Metaphysics*, 92 (IV:298).

29. Kant, *Prolegomena to Any Future Metaphysics*, 92 (IV:298).

30. Kant, *Prolegomena to Any Future Metaphysics*, 97 (IV:303).

31. Kant, *Prolegomena to Any Future Metaphysics*, 119 (IV:327).

32. Kant, *Prolegomena to Any Future Metaphysics*, 121 (IV:329).
33. Kant, *Prolegomena to Any Future Metaphysics*, 121 (IV:329).
34. Kant, *Prolegomena to Any Future Metaphysics*, 120 (IV:328–29).
35. Kant, *Prolegomena to Any Future Metaphysics*, 143 (IV:353).
36. Kant, *Critique of Pure Reason*, 99 (Avii).
37. Kant, *Critique of Pure Reason*, 99 (Aviii).
38. Kant, *Prolegomena to Any Future Metaphysics*, 154 (IV:365).
39. Kant, *Prolegomena to Any Future Metaphysics*, 154 (IV:365).
40. Kant, *Prolegomena to Any Future Metaphysics*, 159 (IV:371–72).
41. Kant, *Prolegomena to Any Future Metaphysics*, 160 (IV:372).
42. Kant, *Prolegomena to Any Future Metaphysics*, 167 (IV:380).
43. Kant, *Prolegomena to Any Future Metaphysics*, 167 (IV:380).
44. Kant, *Critique of Pure Reason*, 114 (Bxxiv).
45. Kant, *Critique of Pure Reason*, 113 (Bxxii).
46. Kant, *Critique of Pure Reason*, 114 (Bxxiv).
47. Kant, *Critique of Pure Reason*, 133 (A22/B25). Kant also emphasizes the negative utility of his critique in the "Canon of Pure Reason." See Kant, *Critique of Pure Reason*, 672 (A795/B823).
48. Kant, *Critique of Pure Reason*, 149 (A11/B25).
49. Sassen, *Kant's Early Critics*, 57.
50. Sassen, *Kant's Early Critics*, 9.
51. Kant, *Critique of Pure Reason*, 114 (Bxxiv).
52. Kant, *Critique of Pure Reason*, 115 (Bxxv).
53. Kant also emphasizes the practical utility of his critique in the "Canon of Pure Reason," but there he treats the possibility of morality as an important effect of the critique of pure reason, rather than the cause motivating the enterprise. See *Critique of Pure Reason*, 672–90 (A795/B823–A831/B859). Whether the emphasis Kant places on the practical utility of his critique can be traced back to Reinhold's attempts to popularize the critical philosophy remains unclear. Reinhold's influence has been disputed by Manfred Kuehn, who thinks that Kant's early critics had more of an effect on the development of the critical philosophy than Reinhold. See Manfred Kuehn, "Kant's Critical Philosophy and Its Reception—the First Five years (1781–1786)," in *The Cambridge Companion to Kant and Modern Philosophy*, ed. Paul Guyer (New York: Cambridge University Press, 2006), 657–58.
54. Kant, *Critique of Pure Reason*, 115–16 (Bxxvi–xxix).
55. Kant, *Critique of Pure Reason*, 117 (Bxxx–xxxi).
56. Kant, *Critique of Pure Reason*, 117 (Bxxx).
57. Kant, *Critique of Pure Reason*, 114–15 (Bxxv).
58. Kant, *Critique of Pure Reason*, 117 (Bxxx).
59. Kant explains the relationship between practical philosophy and faith more extensively in "What Does It Mean to Orient Oneself in Thinking?" (1786), but it is worth noting that this conception of "faith" (*Glaube*) he defends in that essay does not depend on the "denial" or "suspension" (*Aufhebung*) of knowledge that Kant proposes in the second (B) "Preface." On the contrary, Kant says faith is to be regarded as a pure rational hypothesis in theoretical philosophy and a

postulate of reason in practical philosophy. See Immanuel Kant, "What Does It Mean to Orient Oneself in Thinking?" trans. Allen W. Wood, in *Religion and Rational Theology*, ed. Allen W. Wood and George di Giovanni (New York: Cambridge University Press, 1996), 13–16 (VIII:140–44).

60. Kant, *Critique of Pure Reason*, 117 (Bxxxii).

61. Kant, *Critique of Pure Reason*, 117 (Bxxx–xxxii).

62. Kant, *Critique of Pure Reason*, 117 (Bxxxi).

63. Kant, *Critique of Pure Reason*, 119 (Bxxxv).

64. Kant, *Critique of Pure Reason*, 119 (Bxxxv).

65. Kant, *Critique of Pure Reason*, 119 (Bxxxv).

66. Kant, *Critique of Pure Reason*, 119 (Bxxxiv).

67. Kant, *Critique of Pure Reason*, 704 (A855/B883). For an example of a text in which Kant identifies Wolff and dogmatism, see Kant, *What Real Progress Has Metaphysics Made in Germany*, 354–56 (XX:261–62).

68. Kant, *Critique of Pure Reason*, 117–19 (Bxxxi–Bxxxv).

69. Kant, *Critique of Pure Reason*, 119–20 (Bxxxvi).

70. Kant, *Critique of Pure Reason*, 120 (Bxxxvi).

71. Kant, *Critique of Pure Reason*, 120 (Bxxxvi).

72. Kant, *Critique of Pure Reason*, 120 (Bxxxvi).

73. Wolff writes that "in order to know whether our abilities are fitted for philosophical enquiries, it ought to be our first care, to learn what are the powers of the human understanding, together with their right use and application in the knowledge and search for truth." See Christian Wolff, *Logic, or Rational Thoughts on the Powers of the Human Understanding*, in *Christian Wolff: Gesammelte Werke*, pt. 3, vol. 77, ed. Jean École et al. (Hildesheim: Georg Olms Verlag, 2003), 5 (X).

74. Kant, *Critique of Pure Reason*, 117–18 (Bxxxii).

75. Kant, *Critique of Pure Reason*, 118 (Bxxxiii).

76. See, for example, René Descartes, *Discourse on Method*, in *The Philosophical Writings of Descartes*, vol. 1, trans. John Cottingham, Robert Stoothoff, and Dugald Murdoch (Cambridge: Cambridge University Press, 1985), 111–12 (VI.2–3). See also Thomas Hobbes, *Leviathan*, ed. Richard Tuck (Cambridge: Cambridge University Press, 1996), 86–87 (I.13).

77. Kant, *Notes and Fragments*, 7 (XX:44).

78. Kant, *Notes and Fragments*, 7 (XX:44).

79. Kant, *Notes and Fragments*, 7 (XX:44).

80. On the anti-metaphysical interpretation of this passage, see Beiser, "Kant's Intellectual Development: 1746–1781," 43–45. For an interpretation stressing the primacy of practical reason, see Richard Velkley, *Freedom and the End of Reason: On the Moral Foundations of Kant's Critical Philosophy* (Chicago: University of Chicago Press, 1989), 6–8, 61–88. See also Zammito, *Kant, Herder, and the Birth of Anthropology*, 91–99.

81. Kant, *Critique of Pure Reason*, 119 (Bxxiv).

82. Johann August Eberhard, "Das Gebiet des reinen Verstandes," in *Immanuel Kant: Der Streit mit Johann August Eberhard*, ed. Marion Lauschke and Manfred Zahn (Hamburg: Felix Meiner Verlag, 1998), 58–59 (III.2.289). See also Kant, *On a Discovery*, 283 (VIII:187).

83. Although Leibniz is famous for his rationalism, his most recent biographer has noted that "he was in fact well aware of the limits of the created intellect," especially the fact that "in everyday life, as well as in crucial fields such as medicine, jurisprudence, and religion, exact data on which to base his logical calculation were not (and often could not be) available." See Maria Rosa Antognazza, *Leibniz: An Intellectual Biography* (Cambridge: Cambridge University Press, 2009), 244–45.

84. Kant, *On a Discovery*, 283 (VIII:187).

85. Kant, *On a Discovery*, 283 (VIII:187). I have modified Henry Allison's translation, which renders Kant's exclaimation "allein wie viele für neu gehaltene Entdeckungen sehen jetzt nicht geschickte Ausleger ganz klar in den Alten, nachdem ihnen gezeigt worden, wornach sie sehen sollen!" as "yet how many discoveries regarded as new are not now seen with complete clarity in the ancients by skilled interpreters, once they have been shown what they should look for!" While Allison takes *nicht* (not) to modify *sehen* (to see), it actually modifies *geschickte Ausleger* (skilled interpreters), which I have translated as "unskilled interpreters." This revision helps us see that Kant is calling Eberhard's skill as an interpreter of Leibniz into question in this passage, instead of admitting there are new discoveries in the works of the ancients that even skilled interpreters have not yet found.

86. Kant, *On a Discovery*, 283 (VIII:187).

87. Kant, *On a Discovery*, 284 (VIII:189).

88. Johann August Eberhard, "Über die Schranken der menschlichen Erkenntnis," in *Immanuel Kant: Der Streit mit Johann August Eberhard*, ed. Marion Lauschke and Manfred Zahn (Hamburg: Felix Meiner Verlag, 1998), 3 (I.2.9).

89. Eberhard, "Über die Schranken der menschlichen Erkenntnis," 11 (I.2.22).

90. Eberhard, "Über die Schranken der menschlichen Erkenntnis," 4–13 (I.2.11–26).

91. Eberhard, "Über die Schranken der menschlichen Erkenntnis," 11 (I.2.23). Eberhard also refers to a *Leibnizische Vernunftkritik* ("Leibnizian critique of reason") in several places. At (I.2.25), for example, he remarks that "the Leibnizian critique of reason leads to different conclusions than the Kantian one." He also says, at (I.2.26), that "the determination of the boundaries of human knowledge in the Leibnizian critique of reason should not be given up."

92. Henry Allison includes translations of these tables in the appendix to his translation of *On a Discovery*. I have retranslated them here, because I think they are helpful for understanding the critique that Eberhard attributes to Leibniz, and also because the work in which Allison's translations appear is no longer widely available. See Henry E. Allison, *The Kant-Eberhard Controversy* (Baltimore: Johns Hopkins University Press, 1973), 178–82.

93. See Allison, *The Kant-Eberhard Controversy*, 45. See also Frederick C. Beiser, *The Fate of Reason: German Philosophy from Kant to Fichte* (Cambridge, Mass.: Harvard University Press, 1993), 217–224.

94. Kant, *Correspondence* (Reinhold to Kant, April 9, 1789), (XI:17).

95. Kant, *Correspondence* (Kant to Reinhold, May 12 and May19, 1789), 296–310 (XI:32–48).

96. Kant, *Correspondence* (Kant to Reinhold, September 21, 1789), (XI:89).

97. Kant, *On a Discovery*, 327–28 (VIII:239–40)

98. See, for example, Kant, *On a Discovery*, 283, 284–85, 303, 306, 310, 313, 315, 321, 326–27, 332, 336 (VIII:187, 189, 211, 214, 219 223, 225, 232–33, 238–39, 246, 251).

99. On Kant's objection to "merely logical" distinctions between phenomena and noumena in the inaugural dissertation and *Critique of Pure Reason*, see J. Colin McQuillan, "A Merely Logical Distinction? Kant's Objection to Leibniz and Wolff," *Epoché* 20, no.2 (2016): 387–405.

100. Kant, *On a Discovery*, 304–6 (VIII:212–15).

101. Kant, *On a Discovery*, 310 (VIII:219–20).

102. Kant, *On a Discovery*, 283 (VIII:187).

103. Kant, *On a Discovery*, 333 (VIII:247).

104. Kant, *Critique of Pure Reason*, 702–3 (A853/B881).

105. Kant, *Critique of Pure Reason*, 703 (A854/B882).

106. Kant, *Critique of Pure Reason*, 704 (A855/B883).

107. Kant argues that dogmatism and skepticism are self-refuting in the "Preface" to the first (A) edition of the first *Critique*. See Kant, *Critique of Pure Reason*, 99–100 (Aix–Ax). See also Kant, *What Real Progress Has Metaphysics Made in Germany*, 356 (XX:252–63).

108. Kant, *Critique of Pure Reason*, 704 (A855/B883).

109. Kant, *What Real Progress Has Metaphysics Made in Germany*, 356 (XX:263).

110. The academy agreed to the question in 1788, announced the question in 1790, and then extended the deadline for submissions from 1792 to 1795 due to a lack of submissions. Both of the runners-up in the competition (Karl Leonhard Reinhold and Johann Heinrich Abicht) were Kantians, but neither of them made the strong argument about the historical necessity of a critique of pure reason that Kant proposed in the drafts of his essay. Reinhold presents "Kantian criticism" (*Kantische Criticismus*) as the best solution to the problems that previous philosophers had faced, though he also acknowledges that it is merely a propaedeutic to a future system. See Karl Leonhard Reinhold, "Versuch einer Beantwortung der von der erlauchten Königl. Ak. Der Wissensch. zu Berlin aufgestellten Frage: Was hat die Metaphysik seit Wolff und Leibnitz gewonnen," in *Preisschriften über die Frage: Welche Fortschritte hat die Metaphysik seit Leibnitzens und Wolffs Zeiten in Deutschland gemacht?* ed. Prussian Royal Academy of Sciences (Berlin: Friedrich Maurer, 1796), 239–54.

111. Kant, *What Real Progress Has Metaphysics Made in Germany*, 357 (XX:264).

112. Kant, *What Real Progress Has Metaphysics Made in Germany*, 356, 364–71, 372–76 (XX:262, 273–80, 281–86).

113. Kant, *What Real Progress Has Metaphysics Made in Germany*, 356, 376–81 (XX:262–63, 286–92). Although he presents skepticism as a position preferable to dogmatism, Kant also says that skepticism "cannot properly be considered a serious view that has been current in any period of philosophy." See Kant, *What Real Progress Has Metaphysics Made in Germany*, 356–57 (XX:263).

114. Kant, *What Real Progress Has Metaphysics Made in Germany*, 364, 372, 381–84, 385–97 (XX:273, 281, 293–96, 296–311).

115. Kant, *What Real Progress Has Metaphysics Made in Germany*, 357 (XX:264).

116. Kant, *What Real Progress Has Metaphysics Made in Germany*, 357 (XX:264).

117. Kant, *What Real Progress Has Metaphysics Made in Germany*, 357 (XX:264).

118. Immanuel Kant, "On a Recently Prominent Tone of Superiority in Philosophy," trans. Henry Allison, in *Theoretical Philosophy after 1781*, ed. Henry Allison and Peter Heath (New York: Cambridge University Press, 2002), 439, 441–44 (VIII:398, 401–4). See also Immanuel Kant, *Proclamation of the Immanent Conclusion of a Treaty of Perpetual Peace in Philosophy*, trans. Peter Heath, in *Theoretical Philosophy after 1781*, ed. Henry Allison and Peter Heath (New York: Cambridge University Press, 2002), 456 (VIII:418).

119. Kant, *Proclamation of the Immanent Conclusion of a Treaty of Perpetual Peace in Philosophy*, 458 (VIII:420).

120. Kant, *Proclamation of the Immanent Conclusion of a Treaty of Perpetual Peace in Philosophy*, 457–58 (VIII:419).

121. Kant, *Proclamation of the Immanent Conclusion of a Treaty of Perpetual Peace in Philosophy*, 455–58 (VIII:415).

122. Kant, *Proclamation of the Immanent Conclusion of a Treaty of Perpetual Peace in Philosophy*, 458, 460 (VIII:422).

123. Karl Ameriks, "Reinhold on Systematicity, Popularity, and the Historical Turn," in *Kant and the Historical Turn: Philosophy as Critical Interpretation* (Oxford: Oxford University Press, 2006), 185. See also Karl Leonhard Reinhold, *Letters on the Kantian Philosophy*, ed. Karl Ameriks, trans. James Hebbeler (Cambridge: Cambridge University Press, 2005), 16.

124. "Royal road to me" is a phrase coined by Ivor Grattan-Guinness and used by Michael Kremer and Eric Schliesser to describe those histories that "confound the questions *How did we get here?* and *What happened in the past?*" See Ivor Grattan-Guiness, "Does History of Science Treat of the History of Science? The Case of Mathematics," *History of Science* 28 (1990): 157. See also Michael Kremer, "What Is the Good of Philosophical History?" in *The Historical Turn in Analytic Philosophy*, ed. Erich H. Reck (New York: Palgrave Macmillan, 2013), 311; and Eric Schliesser, "Philosophical Prophecy," in *Philosophy and Its History: Aims and Methods in the Study of Early Modern Philosophy*, ed. Mogens Laerke, Justin E. H. Smith, and Erich Schliesser (Oxford: Oxford University Press, 2013), 222.

## Conclusion

1. Kant, *Critique of Pure Reason*, 100–101 (Axi).

2. Dryden, "Author's Apology for Heroic Poetry and Poetic License," 106.

3. See, for example, Schönfeld, *The Philosophy of the Young Kant;* and Zammito, *Kant, Herder, and the Birth of Anthropology*.

4. Beiser, "Kant's Intellectual Development: 1746–1781," 42–43.

5. Beiser, "Kant's Intellectual Development: 1746–1781," 45.

6. Kant, *Correspondence* (Kant to Herz, June 7, 1771), 126 (X:122).

7. Kant, *Correspondence* (Kant to Herz, February 21, 1772), 133–34 (X:130–32).

8. Carl, *Der schweigende Kant,* 16–54.

9. Kant, *Correspondence* (Kant to Herz, February 21, 1772), 135 (X:132). There is no indication that Kant intended "eine Kritik der reinen Vernunft" ("a critique of pure reason") as the title of a forthcoming work in his 1772 letter to Herz. The earliest unequivocal reference to the title of the work Kant would publish in 1781 is found in a letter from Johann Caspar Lavater to Kant in 1774. See Kant, *Correspondence* (Lavater to Kant, April 8, 1774), 150 (X:165). Kant must have mentioned his work on the first *Critique* to Lavater in previous correspondence, which is unfortunately no longer extant.

10. Kant, *Critique of Pure Reason,* 101 (Axi–Axii).

11. Kant, *Critique of Pure Reason,* 101 (Axii).

12. Kant, *Critique of Pure Reason,* 113 (Bxxii).

13. Kant, *Critique of Pure Reason,* 132–33, 149–51 (A10/B24–A14/B28).

14. Kant, *Critique of Pure Reason,* 134, 151 (A14/B28).

15. Kant, *Critique of Pure Reason,* 110 (Bxv).

16. Kant, *Critique of Pure Reason,* 147–49 (B21–B24).

17. Kant, *Critique of Pure Reason,* 114 (Bxxiv).

18. Kant, *Critique of Pure Reason,* 114–20 (Bxxiv–Bxxxvi).

19. Kant, *Critique of Pure Reason,* 115 (Bxxxv).

20. Eberhard, "Das Gebiet des reinen Verstandes," 58–59 (III.2.289). See also Kant, *On a Discovery,* 283 (VIII:187).

21. Kant, *On a Discovery,* 332 (VIII:246).

22. Kant, *On a Discovery,* 333–36 (VIII:247–51).

23. Kant, *Critique of Pure Reason,* 704 (A855/B883).

24. Kant, *What Real Progress Has Metaphysics Made in Germany since the Time of Leibniz and Wolff,* 357 (XX:264).

25. Sassen, *Kant's Early Critics,* 57.

26. Sassen, *Kant's Early Critics,* 59.

27. Eberhard, "Über die Schranken der menschlichen Erkenntnis," 3 (I.2.10). See also Kant, *On a Discovery,* 284 (VIII:189).

28. Johann Schultz, *Exposition of Kant's "Critique of Pure Reason,"* trans. James C. Morrison (Ottawa: University of Ottawa Press, 1995), 3 (4). Schultz actually calls Kant's critique a *Lehrgebäude* ("edifice of doctrine") rather than a system in this passage, but he calls Kant's philosophy a *System* ("system") on pp. 5 (8) and 107 (188) and in many other passages.

29. Schultz, *Exposition of Kant's Critique of Pure Reason,* 9 (14).

30. Jacob Sigismund Beck, *Erläuternder Auszug aus den critischen Schriften des herrn Prof. Kant (Dritter Band, welcher den Standpunct darstellt, as welchem die critische Philosophie zu beurtheilen ist)* (Riga: Johann Friedrich Hartnoch, 1796), ix, 131.

31. Jacob Sigismund Beck, *The Principles of Critical Philosophy* (London: Johnson and Richardson, 1797), ix–x.

32. Reinhold, *Foundation of Philosophical Knowledge,* 64 (62).

33. Fichte, "Second Introduction to the *Wissenschaftslehre,*" 62–63 (229–31/477–78).

34. Kant, *Correspondence* ("Public Declaration concerning Fichte's *Wissenschaftslehre*"), 559 (XII:370).

35. Friedrich Wilhelm Joseph Schelling, *Philosophical Letters on Dogmatism and Criticism: The Unconditional in Human Knowledge: Early Essays by F.W.J. Schelling*, trans. Fritz Marti (Lewisburg, Pa.: Bucknell University Press, 1980), 163–64 (293–95).

36. Schelling, *Philosophical Letters on Dogmatism and Criticism*, 164–165 (294–296).

37. Schelling, *Philosophical Letters on Dogmatism and Criticism*, 163 (293–294).

38. Arthur Schopenhauer, *The World as Will and Representation*, vol. 1, ed. and trans. Judith Norman, Alistair Welchman, and Christopher Janaway (Cambridge: Cambridge University Press, 2010), 447 (498).

39. Schopenhauer, *The World as Will and Representation*, 1:453–54 (505–6).

40. Schopenhauer, *The World as Will and Representation*, 1:460 (513).

41. Friedrich Schlegel, *Athenaeum Fragments: Friedrich Schlegel's Lucinde and the Fragments*, ed. and trans. Peter Firchow (Minneapolis: University of Minnesota Press, 1971), 167 (§47).

42. Georg Wilhelm Friedrich Hegel, *Lectures on the History of Philosophy*, vol. 3, trans. E. S. Haldane and Frances H. Simson (New Jersey: Humanities, 1974), 428 (XX:333–34).

43. Hegel, *Lectures on the History of Philosophy*, 3:428 (XX:333–34).

44. Hegel, *Lectures on the History of Philosophy*, 3:429 (XX:333–34).

# Bibliography

## Works by Immanuel Kant

Kant, Immanuel. *Bemerkungen in den "Beobachtungen über das Gefühl des Schönen und Erhabenen."* Edited by Marie Rischmüller. Hamburg: Meiner Verlag, 1991.

———. *The Cambridge Edition of the Works of Immanuel Kant.* Edited by Paul Guyer and Allen W. Wood. New York: Cambridge University Press, 1992–.

*Immanuel Kant: Anthropology, History, and Education.* Edited by Robert B. Louden and Günter Zöller. Cambridge: Cambridge University Press, 2007.

*Observations on the Feeling of the Beautiful and Sublime.* Translated by Paul Guyer.

*Anthropology from a Pragmatic Point of View.* Translated by Robert B. Louden.

*Immanuel Kant: Correspondence.* Edited and translated by Arnulf Zweig. New York: Cambridge University Press, 1999.

*Immanuel Kant: Critique of Pure Reason.* Translated by Paul Guyer and Allen W. Wood. New York: Cambridge University Press, 1998.

*Immanuel Kant: Critique of the Power of Judgment.* Edited by Paul Guyer. Translated by Paul Guyer and Eric Matthews. New York: Cambridge University Press, 2000.

*Immanuel Kant: Lectures on Anthropology.* Edited by Allen W. Wood and Robert B. Louden. Cambridge: Cambridge University Press, 2012.

*Immanuel Kant: Lectures on Logic.* Edited and translated by J. Michael Young. New York: Cambridge University Press, 1992.

*Immanuel Kant: Lectures on Metaphysics.* Edited and translated by Karl Ameriks and Steve Naragon. New York: Cambridge University Press, 1997.

*Immanuel Kant: Notes and Fragments.* Edited by Paul Guyer. Translated by Curtis Bowman, Paul Guyer, and Frederick Rauscher. New York: Cambridge University Press, 2005.

*Immanuel Kant: Practical Philosophy.* Edited by Mary Gregor. New York: Cambridge University Press, 1996.

*An Answer to the Question: What Is Enlightenment?* Translated by Mary Gregor.

*Groundwork of the Metaphysics of Morals.* Translated by Mary Gregor.

*Toward Perpetual Peace.* Translated by Mary Gregor.

*The Metaphysics of Morals.* Translated by Mary Gregor.

*Immanuel Kant: Religion and Rational Theology*. Edited by Allen W. Wood and
George di Giovanni. New York: Cambridge University Press, 1996.
"What Does It Mean to Orient Oneself in Thinking?" Translated by Allen
W. Wood.
*Religion within the Boundaries of Mere Reason*. Translated by George Di
Giovanni.
*Immanuel Kant: Theoretical Philosophy after 1781*. Edited by Henry Allison and
Peter Heath. New York: Cambridge University Press, 2002.
*Prolegomena to Any Future Metaphysics That Will Be Able to Come Forward as a
Science*. Translated by Gary Hatfield.
*Metaphysical Foundations of Natural Science*. Translated by Michael Friedman.
*On a Discovery Whereby Any New Critique of Pure Reason Is to Be MadeSuperfluous
by an Older One*    . Translated by Henry Allison.
*What Real Progress Has Metaphysics Made in Germany since the Time of Leibniz
and Wolff?* Translated by Henry Allison.
"On a Recently Prominent Tone of Superiority in Philosophy." Translated
by Henry Allison.
*Proclamation of the Imminent Conclusion of a Treaty of Perpetual Peace in Philos-
ophy*. Translated by Peter Heath.
*Immanuel Kant: Notes and Fragments*. Edited by Paul Guyer. Translated by Curtis
Bowman, Paul Guyer, and Frederick Rauscher. New York: Cambridge
University Press, 2005.
*Immanuel Kant: Theoretical Philosophy, 1755–1770*. Edited by David Walford and
Ralf Meerbote. New York: Cambridge University Press, 1992.
*New Elucidation of the First Principles of Metaphysical Cognition*. Translated by
David Walford and Ralf Meerbote.
"The Only Possible Argument in Support of a Demonstration of the Exis-
tence of God." Translated by David Walford and Ralf Meerbote.
*Inquiry concerning the Distinctness of Natural Theology and Morality*. Translated
by David Walford and Ralf Meerbote.
"M. Immanuel Kant's Announcement of the Programme of His Lectures
for the Winter Semester 1765–1766." Translated by David Walford and
Ralf Meerbote.
*Dreams of a Spirit-Seer Elucidated by the Dreams of Metaphysics*. Translated by
David Walford and Ralf Meerbote.
*On the Form and Principles of the Sensible and the Intelligible World*. Translated
by G. D. Kerferd and D. E. Walford.
———. *Der Streit mit Johann August Eberhard*. Edited by Marion Lauschke and
Manfred Zahn. Hamburg: Meiner Verlag, 1998.
———. *Gesammelte Schriften, herausgegeben von der Preussischen Akademie der Wis-
senschaften*. Berlin: Walter de Gruyter, 1902–.
———. *Kant on Swedenborg: Dreams of a Spirit-Seer and Other Writings*. Translated
by Gregory R. Johnson. West Chester, Pa.: Swedenborg Foundation Pub-
lishers, 2003.
———. *Philosophical Correspondence, 1759–1799*. Edited and translated by Arnulf
Zweig. Chicago: University of Chicago Press, 1967.

## Other Works

Addison, Joseph. *Selections from "The Tatler" and "The Spectator."* Edited by Angus Ross. London: Penguin Classics, 1988.

Adlington, Richard. *Letters of Voltaire and Frederick the Great.* London: George Routledge and Sons, 1927.

Ahnert, Thomas. "Newtonianism in Early Enlightenment Germany, c. 1720 to 1750: Metaphysics and the Critique of Dogmatic Philosophy." *Studies in History and Philosophy of Science,* 35, no. 3 (2004): 471–91.

Allison, Henry E. *The Kant-Eberhard Controversy.* Baltimore: Johns Hopkins University Press, 1973.

Altmann, Alexander. *Moses Mendelssohn A Biographical Study.* London: Littman Library of Jewish Civilization, 1998.

Ameriks, Karl. *Interpreting Kant's Critiques.* Oxford: Oxford University Press, 2003.

———. *Kant and the Fate of Autonomy: Problems in the Appropriation of the Critical Philosophy.* Cambridge: Cambridge University Press, 2000.

———. *Kant and the Historical Turn: Philosophy as Critical Interpretation.* Oxford: Oxford University Press, 2006.

Antognazza, Maria Rosa. *Leibniz: An Intellectual Biography.* Cambridge: Cambridge University Press, 2011.

Ayer, Alfred J. *Language, Truth and Logic.* New York: Dover, 1952.

Bacon, Francis. *The New Organon.* Edited by Lisa Jardine and Michael Silverthorne. New York: Cambridge University Press, 2000.

———. *The Works of Francis Bacon.* Edited by James Spedding, Robert Leslie Ellis, and Douglas Denon Heath. New York: Garrett, 1870.

Baumgarten, Alexander. *Acroasis Logica.* Hildesheim: Georg Olms Verlag, 1983.

———. *Ästhetik.* Translated by Dagmar Mirbach. Hamburg: Meiner Verlag, 2007.

———. *Metaphysics.* Translated by Courtney D. Fugate and John Hymers. London: Bloomsbury, 2013.

———. *Sciagraphia encylopaedia philosophia.* Halle, 1768.

Bayle, Pierre. *Historical and Critical Dictionary: Selections.* Translated by Richard H. Popkin. Indianapolis, Ind.: Hackett, 1991.

Beck, Jacob Sigismund. *Erläuternder Auszug aus den critischen Schriften des herrn Prof. Kant.* Riga: Johann Friedrich Hartnoch, 1796.

———. *The Principles of Critical Philosophy.* London: Johnson and Richardson, 1797.

Beck, Lewis White. *Essays on Kant and Hume.* New Haven, Conn.: Yale University Press, 1963.

———. *Studies in the Philosophy of Kant.* Indianapolis, Ind.: Bobbs Merrill, 1965.

Beiser, Frederick C. *The Fate of Reason: German Philosophy from Kant to Fichte.* Cambridge, Mass.: Harvard University Press, 1993.

Bogolyubov, N. N., G. K. Mikhailov, and A. P. Yushkevich. *Euler and Modern Science.* Translated by Robert Burns. Washington, D.C.: Mathematical Associaiton of America, 2007.

Boileau, Nicolas. *The Works of Mons. Boileau Despreaux.* London: E. Sanger and E. Curll, 1711.

Burke, Edmund. *A Philosophical Enquiry into the Origins of the Sublime and Beauti-ful: And Other Pre-Revolutionary Writings*. London: Penguin Classics, 1999.

Caputo, John D. *Radical Hermeneutics: Repetition, Deconstruction, and the Hermeneu-tic Project*. Bloomington: Indiana University Press, 1988.

Carl, Wolfgang. *Der Schweigende Kant: Die Entwürfe Zu Einer Deduktion der Kat-egorien von 1781*. Göttingen: Vandenhoeck & Ruprecht, 1997.

Cassirer, Ernst. *Kant's Life and Thought*. Translated by James Haden. New Haven, Conn.: Yale University Press, 1981.

Clark, William, Jan Golinski, and Simon Schaffer. *The Sciences in Enlightened Europe*. Chicago: University of Chicago Press, 1999.

D'Amico, John F. *Theory and Practice in Renaissance Textual Criticism: Beatus Rhena-nus between Conjecture and History*. Berkeley: University of California Press, 1988.

Da Brescia, Fortunato. *Philosophia mentis (Tomus Primus: Logicam Continens)*. Brixia, 1749.

Descartes, René. *The Philosophical Writings of Descartes*. Translated by John Cotting-ham, Robert Stoothoff, and Dugald Murdoch. Cambridge: Cambridge University Press, 1985.

Di Giovanni, George, and H. S. Harris, eds. *Between Kant & Hegel: Texts in the Development of Post-Kantian Idealism*. Revised edition. Indianapolis, Ind.: Hackett, 2000.

Diogenes Laertius. *Lives of Eminent Philosophers*. Translated by R. D. Hicks. Cam-bridge, Mass.: Harvard University Press, 1925.

Dryden, John. *The Works of John Dryden*. Edited by Sir Walter Scott. Edinburgh: Constable, 1821.

Dryer, D. P. *Kant's Solution for Verification in Metaphysics*. Toronto: University of Toronto Press, 1966.

Erdmann, Benno. *Kant's Kriticismus in Der Ersten Und in Der Zweiten Auflage der "Kritik Der Reinen Vernunft."* Leipzig: Voss, 1878.

———. *Reflexionen Kants zur kritischen Philosophie, aus Kants Handschriftlichen Aufzeichnungen*. Leipzig: Feues Verlag, 1884.

Fichte, J. G. *Introductions to the Wissenschaftslehre and Other Writings*. Translated by Daniel Breazeale. Indianapolis, Ind.: Hackett, 1994.

Fischer, Kuno. *Geschichte der neueren Philosophie*. Heidelberg: Carl Winter, 1899.

Förster, Eckart. *Kant's Final Synthesis: An Essay on the "Opus Postumum."* Cambridge, Mass.: Harvard University Press, 2002.

———. "Kant's Notion of Philosophy." *The Monist* 72, no. 2 (1989): 285–304.

———. *Kant's Transcendental Deductions: The Three "Critiques" and the "Opus Postu-mum."* Stanford, Calif.: Stanford University Press, 1989.

———. *The Twenty-Five Years of Philosophy: A Systematic Reconstruction*. Cambridge, Mass.: Harvard University Press, 2012.

Forster, Michael N. *Kant and Skepticism*. Princeton, N.J.: Princeton University Press, 2008.

Foucault, Michel. *The Essential Foucault: Selections from the Essential Works of Fou-cault, 1954–1984*. Edited by Paul Rabinow. New York: New, 2003.

Genovisi, Antonio. *Elementorum Artis Logicocriticae*. Naples, 1753.

Gerhardt, Volker, Rolf-Peter Horstmann, and Ralph Schumacher, eds. *Kant und die Berliner Aufklärung: Akten Des IX Internationalen Kant-Kongresses.* Berlin: Walter de Gruyter, 2001.

Gilson, Etienne. *The Unity of Philosophical Experience.* San Francisco: Ignatius, 1999.

Gottsched, Johann Christian. *Ausgewählte Werke.* Berlin: Walter de Gruyter, 1973.

———. *Versuch einer critischen Dichtkunst für die Deutschen (Zweyte und verbesserte Auflage).* Leipzig: Bernhard Christoph Breitkopf, 1737.

———. *Versuch einer critischen Dichtkunst vor die Deutschen.* Leipzig: Bernhard Christoph Breitkopf, 1730.

Grafton, Anthony. *Defenders of the Text: The Traditions of Scholarship in an Age of Science, 1450–1800.* Cambridge, Mass.: Harvard University Press, 1994.

———. *Worlds Made by Words: Scholarship and Community in the Modern West.* Cambridge, Mass.: Harvard University Press, 2011.

Grattan-Guinness, Ivor. "Does the History of Science Treat of History of Science? The Case of Mathematics." *History of Science* 28, no. 80 (1990): 149–73.

Grier, Michelle. *Kant's Doctrine of Transcendental Illusion.* Cambridge: Cambridge University Press, 2007.

Grosholz, Emily R. *Representation and Productive Ambiguity in Mathematics and the Sciences.* Oxford: Oxford University Press, 2007.

Gründer, Karlfried. *Historisches Wörterbuch der Philosophie.* Basel: Schwabe, 1976.

Gründer, Karlfried, and Wilhelm Schmidt-Biggemann, eds. *Spinoza in der Frühzeit seiner religiösen Wirkung.* Heidelberg: Schneider, 1984.

Gumbrecht, Hans Ulrich. *The Powers of Philology: Dynamics of Textual Scholarship.* Urbana: University of Illinois Press, 2003.

Guyer, Paul, ed. *The Cambridge Companion to Kant.* Cambridge: Cambridge University Press, 1992.

———, ed. *The Cambridge Companion to Kant and Modern Philosophy.* Cambridge: Cambridge University Press, 2006.

———. *Kant and the Claims of Knowledge.* Cambridge: Cambridge University Press, 1987.

———. *Kant on Freedom, Law, and Happiness.* Cambridge: Cambridge University Press, 2000.

Hamann, Johann Georg. *Briefwechsel.* Edited by Walther Ziesemer and Arthur Henkel. Frankfurt am Main: Insel-Verlag, 1959–79.

Hankins, T. L. *Jean D'Alembert: Science and the Enlightenment.* New York: Gordon and Breach, 1990.

Hanson, Norwood Russell. "Copernicus' Role in Kant's Revolution." *Journal of the History of Ideas* 20, no. 2 (1959): 274.

Harnack, Adolf. *Geschichte der königlich Preußischen Akademie der Wissenschaften zu Berlin*, vol. 1. Berlin: Reichsdruckerei, 1900.

Hegel, Georg Wilhelm Friedrich. *Lectures on the History of Philosophy*, vol. 3: *Medieval and Modern Philosophy.* Translated by E. S. Haldane and Frances H. Simson. Lincoln: University of Nebraska Press, 1995.

Heidegger, Martin. *Being and Time.* Translated by John Maquarrie and Edward Robinson. New York: Harper Perennial Modern Classics, 2008.

————. *The End of Philosophy*. Translated by Joan Stambaugh. Chicago: University of Chicago Press, 2003.

Henrich, Dieter. "Über Kants Früheste Ethik." *Kant-Studien* 54 (1963): 404–31.

Herder, Johann Gottfried. *Johann Gottfried Herder: Selected Early Works, 1764–1767*. University Park: Pennsylvania State University Press, 1991.

Hobbes, Thomas. *Leviathan*. Edited by Richard Tuck. Cambridge: Cambridge University Press, 1996.

————. *On the Citizen*. Edited by Richard Tuck. Cambridge: Cambridge University Press, 1998.

Höffe, Otfried. *Kant's "Critique of Pure Reason": The Foundation of Modern Philosophy*. Dordrecht: Springer, 2009.

Home, Henry. *Elements of Criticism*. Honolulu: University Press of the Pacific, 2002.

Hume, David. *Essays: Moral, Political, and Literary*. Indianapolis, Ind.: Liberty Fund, 1987.

————. *A Treatise of Human Nature*. 2nd edition. Oxford University Press, 1979.

Hutcheson, Francis. *An Inquiry into the Original of Our Ideas of Beauty and Virtue*. Indianapolis, Ind.: Liberty Fund, 2008.

Hutchings, Kimberly. *Kant, Critique and Politics*. London: Routledge, 1995.

Johnson, Samuel. *A Dictionary of the English Language: An Anthology*. London: Penguin Classics, 2007.

————. *Selected Essays*. London: Penguin Classics, 2003.

Kitcher, Philip. "Kant and the Foundations of Mathematics." *Philosophical Review* 84, no. 1 (1975): 23–50.

Kraye, Jill, ed. *The Cambridge Companion to Renaissance Humanism*. Cambridge: Cambridge University Press, 1996.

Kuehn, Manfred. *Kant: A Biography*. Cambridge: Cambridge University Press, 2001.

Laerke, Mogens, Justin E. H. Smith, and Eric Schliesser, eds. *Philosophy and Its History: Aims and Methods in the Study of Early Modern Philosophy*. Oxford: Oxford University Press, 2013.

Lambert, Johann Heinrich. *Über die methode die Metaphysik, Theologie, und Moral richtiger zu beweisen*. Edited by K. Bopp. Berlin: Verlag von Reuther & Reichard, 1918.

Lavater, Johann Caspar. *Reisetagebücher*. Edited by Horst Weigelt. Göttingen: Vandenhoeck & Ruprecht, 1997.

Laywine, Alison. *Kant's Early Metaphysics & the Origins of the Critical Philosophy*. Atascadero, Calif.: Ridgeview, 1994.

————. "Kant in Reply to Lambert on the Ancestry of Metaphysical Concepts." *Kantian Review* 5, no. 1 (2001): 1–48.

————. "Kant on Sensibility and Understanding in the 1770s." *Canadian Journal of Philosophy* 33, no. 4 (2003): 443–82.

Leibniz, Gottfried Wilhelm. *Theodicy*. Edited by Austin M. Farrer. Translated by E. M. Huggard. New York: Cosimo Classics, 2010.

Lessing, Gotthold Ephraim. *Hamburg Dramaturgy*. New York: Dover, 1962.

————. *Sämtliche Schriften*. Edited by Karl Lachmann. Berlin: Walter de Gruyter, 1892.

Levine, Joseph M. *The Battle of the Books: History and Literature in the Augustan Age.* Ithaca, N.Y.: Cornell University Press, 1994.

Liddell, H. G., and Robert Scott. *Greek-English Lexicon.* Oxford: Oxford University Press, 1996.

Ligota, Christopher, and Jean-Louis Quantin. *History of Scholarship: A Selection of Papers from the Seminar on the History of Scholarship Held Annually at the Warburg Institute.* Oxford: Oxford University Press, 2006.

Longuenesse, Béatrice. *Kant and the Capacity to Judge: Sensibility and Discursivity in the Transcendental Analytic of the "Critique of Pure Reason."* Princeton, N.J.: Princeton University Press, 2001.

Malter, Rudolf. *Immanuel Kant in Rede und Gespräch.* Hamburg: Meiner Verlag, 1990.

Maupertuis, Pierre-Louis Moreau. *Oeuvres.* Edited by Giorgio Tonelli. Hildesheim: Georg Olms Verlag, 1974.

McQuillan, J. Colin. "A Merely Logical Distinction? Kant's Objection to Leibniz and Wolff." *Epoché* 20, no. 2 (2016): 387–405.

Meier, Georg Friedrich. *Anfangsgründe aller schönen Wissenschaften.* Hildesheim: Georg Olms Verlag, 1976.

———. *Beurtheilung der Gottschedischen Dichtkunst.* Hildesheim: Georg Olms Verlag, 1975.

Mendelssohn, Moses. *Gesammelte Schriften.* Edited by Eva J. Engel et al. Stuttgart-Bad Cannstatt: Frommann-Holzboog Verlag, 2004.

———. *Moses Mendelssohn: Philosophical Writings.* Translated by Daniel O. Dahlstrom. Cambridge: Cambridge University Press, 1997.

Mensch, Jennifer. "The Key to All Metaphysics: Kant's Letter to Herz, 1772." *Kantian Review* 12, no. 2 (2007): 109–27.

Miles, Murray. "Kant's 'Copernican Revolution': Toward Rehabilitation of a Concept and Provision of a Framework for the Interpretation of the *Critique of Pure Reason.*" *Kant-Studien* 97, no. 1 (2006): 1–32.

Mohr, Georg. *Kant's Theoretische Philosophie: Text und Kommentar.* Frankfurt am Main: Suhrkamp Verlag, 2004.

Mohr, Georg, and Marcus Willaschek, eds. *Immanuel Kant: "Kritik der reinen Vernunft."* Berlin: Akademie Verlag, 1998.

Moreri, Louis. *Le Grand Dictionnaire historique.* Lyon, 1671.

Munk, Reinier. *Moses Mendelssohn's Metaphysics and Aesthetics.* Dordrecht: Springer, 2011.

Nicolai, Friedrich. *Kritik ist überall, zumal in Deutschland, nötig: Satiren und Schriften zur Literatur.* Munich: C.H. Beck Verlag, 1991.

Osterrieder, Hermann. *Logica Critica.* Ratisbon: Joannis Michaelis Englerth, 1760.

Pope, Alexander. *The Major Works.* Edited by Pat Rogers. Oxford: Oxford University Press, 2006.

Popkin, Richard H. *The History of Scepticism: From Savonarola to Bayle.* Oxford: Oxford University Press, 2003.

Priest, Stephen, ed. *Hegel's Critique of Kant.* Oxford: Oxford University Press, 1987.

Reck, Erich H. *The Historical Turn in Analytic Philosophy.* Basingstoke, Eng.: Palgrave Macmillan, 2013.

Reinhold, Karl Leonhard. *Letters on the Kantian Philosophy.* Edited by Karl Ameriks. Translated by James Hebbeler. Cambridge: Cambridge University Press, 2006.

———. "Versuch einer Beantwortung der von der erlauchten Königl. Ak. Der Wissensch. zu Berlin aufgestellten Frage: Was hat die Metaphysik seit Wolff und Leibnitz gewonnen." In *Preisschriften über die Frage: Welche Fortschritte hat die Metaphysik seit Leibnitzens und Wolffs Zeiten in Deutschland gemacht?* Edited by the Prussian Royal Academy of Sciences. Berlin: Friedrich Maurer, 1796.

Röttgers, Kurt. *Kritik und Praxis: Zur Geschichte des Kritikbegriffs von Kant Bis Marx.* Berlin: Walter De Gruyter, 1975.

Sassen, Brigitte, ed. *Kant's Early Critics: The Empiricist Critique of the Theoretical Philosophy.* Cambridge: Cambridge University Press, 2000.

Schelling, Friedrich Wilhelm Joseph. *The Unconditional in Human Knowledge: Four Early Essays.* Translated by Fritz Marti. Lewisburg, Pa.: Bucknell University Press, 1980.

Schlegel, Friedrich. *Friedrich Schlegel's Lucinde and the Fragments.* Translated by Peter Firchow. Minneapolis: University of Minnesota Press, 1971.

Schleiermacher, Friedrich. *"Hermeneutics and Criticism" and Other Writings.* Translated by Andrew Bowie. New York: Cambridge University Press, 1998.

Schonfeld, Martin. *The Philosophy of the Young Kant: The Precritical Project.* New York: Oxford University Press, 2000.

Schopenhauer, Arthur. *The World as Will and Representation.* Volume 1. Translated by Judith Norman and Alistair Welchman. Cambridge: Cambridge University Press, 2010.

Schultz, Johann. *Exposition of Kant's "Critique of Pure Reason."* Ottawa: University of Ottawa Press, 1996.

Sedgwick, Sally, ed. *The Reception of Kant's Critical Philosophy: Fichte, Schelling, and Hegel.* Cambridge: Cambridge University Press, 2000.

Simon, Richard. *A Critical History of the Text of the New Testament.* London: R. Taylor, 1689.

Simonsuuri, Kirsti. *Homer's Original Genius: Eighteenth-Century Notions of the Early Greek Epic.* Cambridge: Cambridge University Press, 1979.

Smith, Norman Kemp. *A Commentary to Kant's "Critique of Pure Reason."* Basingstoke, Eng.: Palgrave Macmillan, 2003.

Spinoza, Baruch. *Ethics.* Translated by Samuel Shirley. Indianapolis, Ind.: Hackett, 1992.

Stark, Werner. *Nachforschungen zu Briefen und Handschriften Immanuel Kants.* Berlin: Akademie Verlag, 1993.

Strawson, Peter. *The Bounds of Sense: An Essay on Kant's Critique of Pure Reason.* London: Routledge, 2004.

Swift, Jonathan. *A Tale of a Tub: Written for the Universal Improvement of Mankind, To Which Is Added, An Account of a Battel between the Antient and Modern Books in St. James's Library.* London: J. Nutt, 1704.

Temple, William. *Miscellanea.* Edited by Jonathan Swift. London: B. Looke, 1701.

Tonelli, Giorgio. "'Critique' and Related Terms Prior to Kant: A Historical Survey." *Kant-Studien* 69 (1978): 119–148.

———. "Der Streit Über die Mathematische Methode in der Philosophie in der Ersten Hälfte Des 18. Jahrhunderts und die Entstehung von Kants Schrift Über Die 'Deutlichkeit.'" *Archiv Für Philosophie* 9 (1959): 51–84.

———. "Kant's *Critique of Pure Reason* within the Tradition of Modern Logic." In *Akten des 4. Internationalen Kant Kongresses*. Berlin: Walter de Gruyter, 1975.

———. *Kant's "Critique of Pure Reason" within the Tradition of Modern Logic*. Edited by David H. Chandler. Hildesheim: Georg Olms Verlag, 1994.

Vaihinger, Hans. *Commentar Zu Kants "Kritik Der Reinen Vernunft."* Stuttgart: Spemann Verlag, 1881.

Velkley, Richard L. *Freedom and the End of Reason: On the Moral Foundation of Kant's Critical Philosophy.* Chicago: University of Chicago Press, 1989.

Vleeschauwer, Herman-Jean. *The Development of Kantian Thought: The History of a Doctrine.* Translated by A. R. C. Duncan. London: Thomas Nelson and Sons, 1962.

Von Arnim, Hans. *Stoicorum Veterum Fragmenta.* Munich: K.G. Saur Verlag, 1978.

Walsh, W. H. *Kant's Criticism of Metaphysics.* Edinburgh: Edinburgh University Press, 1975.

Watkins, Eric. *Kant's "Critique of Pure Reason": Background Source Materials.* Cambridge: Cambridge University Press, 2009.

Wellek, Rene. *Concepts of Criticism.* Edited by Stephen G. Nicholas. New Haven, Conn.: Yale University Press, 1963.

Werkmeister, W. H. *Kant's Silent Decade: A Decade of Philosophical Development.* Tallahassee: University Presses of Florida, 1979.

Wilson-Okamura, David Scott. *Virgil in the Renaissance.* Cambridge: Cambridge University Press, 2010.

Wolff, Christian. *Discourse on Philosophy in General.* Translated by Richard J. Blackwell. Indianapolis, Ind.: Bobbs-Merrill, 1963.

———. *Gesammelte Werke.* Edited by Jean École et al. Hildesheim: Georg Olms Verlag, 1962–.

———. *Vollständiges Mathematisches Lexikon.* Leipzig, 1747.

Wolff, Friedrich August. *Darstellung der Altertums-Wissenschaft.* Berlin: Realschulbuchhandlung, 1807.

Wotton, William. *Reflections upon Ancient and Modern Learning.* London: J. Leake and P. Buck, 1694.

Zammito, John H. *Kant, Herder, and the Birth of Anthropology.* Chicago: University of Chicago Press, 2000.

# Index

Achenwall, Gottfried, 146n32, 148n55
Addison, Joseph, 8
Ameriks, Karl, 111, 130n114
Antognazza, Maria Rosa, 158n83
Aristophanes, 4
Aristotle, 7, 59, 79

Bacon, Francis, 5
Baumgarten, Alexander, 13–14, 16–17, 32, 50
Bayle, Pierre, 6, 126n28
Beck, Jacob Sigismund, 119
Beck, Lewis White, 43
Beiser, Frederick, 124n5, 131n3
Bentley, Richard, 7
Berkeley, George, 63, 89, 117
Boer, Karin de, 154n187
Boileau, Nicolas, 7
Bormann, Claus von, 123n1
Buck, Johann, 44
Burke, Edmund, 11–12

Carl, Wolfgang, 61
Christiani, Carl August, 44
Chrysippus, 4
Copernicus, Nicolaus, 81, 82
critique concept: in the eighteenth century, xi, 3–20, 113–14, 121; in Kant, ix, xi, 3, 6, 12, 16–17, 19–20, 60–62, 64, 70, 76, 86, 90, 109, 113–14, 115–16, 120–21, 128nn70–71
*Critique of Pure Reason*: as an apology for Leibniz, 108, 118; a priori cognition in, 72–77, 79, 82–83, 85–87, 89, 95, 98, 101, 116; composition, 30, 42–43, 52, 57, 59–61, 139n7; "Copernican revolution" in, 81–82; critical reception, xiii, 63, 89, 91, 96, 97, 102–4, 116–20; "divine under-standing" in, 57–57; editions (A and B), 35, 61, 63–64, 102, 151n137; faculty in, 63, 70–72, 74, 77, 82, 83, 86, 152n147; hypotheses in, 81–83, 151n137; judicial metaphors, 65, 68, 69, 70, 78, 80, 115–16, 150n112; metaphysics in, 35, 52, 64–70, 72, 75–76, 78–82, 84–86, 89, 91–92, 95, 98–99, 111, 116, 121, 123n2; originality of, 102–9, 111, 118; phenomenology absence from, 52; principles in, 77, 80–81, 86; *Prolegomena*'s relationship to, 91–94; purpose and utility of, ix, xi, xii–xiii, 64–65, 70–71, 76–78, 81, 87–88, 96–102, 109, 111, 117; reason in, 64–73, 76–77, 80, 84–86, 98, 116, 119, 149n70; religion in, 83, 98–99, 100, 156n59; republican spirit, 69–70; space and time in, ix, 45, 49, 58, 72, 82, 89, 90, 93, 94, 98, 102, 104, 117; structure, 61; title, 42–43, 60, 115, 129n84, 161n9; understanding in, 83–87, 89, 103, 108
sections: "Analytic of Concepts," 87; "Analytic of Principles," 64, 77; "Antinomy of Pure Reason," 84; "Architectonic of Pure Reason," 72; "Canon of Pure Reason," 156n53; "Deduction of the Pure Concepts of the Understanding," ix, x, 42, 63, 64; "Discipline of Pure Reason," 69, 70; "History of Pure Reason," xiii, 109, 118, 146n33; "Introduction," xii, 64, 66, 71, 72–73, 86–87, 97, 101, 115–16, 117, 120, 121; "Paralogisms of Pure Reason," 64; "Preface" (A), xii, 63, 64–72, 75, 78, 80, 81, 86, 87–88, 91, 95, 113, 115–16, 121,